The Power of Legitimacy

The Power of Legitimacy

ASSESSING THE ROLE OF NORMS IN CRISIS BARGAINING

Christopher Gelpi

For David,
Many thanks and best wishes
to a wonderful colleague!

PRINCETON UNIVERSITY PRESS

PRINCETON AND OXFORD

Published by Princeton University Press, 41 William Street, Princeton,
New Jersey 08540
In the United Kingdom: Princeton University Press, 3 Market Place,
Woodstock, Oxfordshire OX20 1SY

Library of Congress Cataloging-in-Publication Data

Gelpi, Christopher, 1966–
The power of legitimacy: assessing the role of norms in crisis bargaining /
Christopher Gelpi.
p. cm.
Includes bibliographical references and index.
ISBN 0-691-09248-6 (cloth : alk. paper)
1. Conflict management. 2. Security, International. 3. International relations—
Moral and ethical aspects. 4. International relations—Psychological aspects.
5. International relations—Decision making. I. Title.

JZ5595.5 .G45 2003
327.1'7—dc21   2002023129

British Library Cataloging-in-Publication Data is available

This book has been composed in Galliard

Printed on acid-free paper. ∞

www.pupress.princeton.edu

Printed in the United States of America

1 3 5 7 9 10 8 6 4 2

For Janet, Mitchell, and Grace

Contents

Illustrations

FIGURES

TABLES

Acknowledgments

So many friends and colleagues at Michigan, Harvard, Duke, and elsewhere have provided comments and support on this project over the past decade that I hesitate to try to mention all of them. To begin with, however, thanks must go to Paul Huth, for his unstinting support throughout my graduate career at the University of Michigan and in my years since leaving Ann Arbor. Paul has consistently been a supportive and valuable mentor and colleague. I greatly appreciate his efforts. I would also like to thank William Zimmerman and Chris Achen for their generous support and candid advice during my work on this manuscript at the University of Michigan. Their constructive criticism both improved the work and expedited its completion. Special thanks also go to Scott Bennett, Marc Busch, Peter Feaver, Scott Gartner, Hein Goemans, Joseph Grieco, Ted Hopf, Robert Keohane, Lisa Martin, Dan Reiter, Steve Rosen, Al Stam, Steve Van Evera, and Celeste Wallander for providing thoughtful and extensive written comments on various drafts of the manuscript. Thanks to Michael Griesdorf and Jeff Ritter for their excellent research assistance—especially regarding the case study chapters. And thanks to the many graduate students and faculty in the political science departments at the University of Michigan, Harvard University, and Duke University who have made those departments such stimulating and friendly environments for me over the past ten years.

During my years as a graduate student at Michigan, I enjoyed generous financial support. In particular, I would like to thank the MacArthur Foundation, the Regents of the University of Michigan, and the University of Michigan Department of Political Science for their financial support.

In addition to financial means, however, one also needs a great deal of emotional support to complete a manuscript like this one. I would like to thank my family and particularly my parents, Albert and Barbara Gelpi, for their encouragement throughout my academic career and throughout my life. I would also like to thank my wonderful children, Mitchell and Grace. Their playful presences may have delayed the completion of this work, but in the process they gave great joy and meaning to my life beyond measure. Finally, I owe the greatest debt of all to my beloved wife, Janet Newcity. She consistently presented me with challenging questions that have greatly improved this work, including particularly important insights concerning my data sources and research design. Moreover, she always knew just what to say when I wasn't sure I was ever going to finish. She tolerated me when the work on this manuscript made me intolerable, and she helped me to keep pressing forward. Without the help of her incisive mind and encouraging words, I don't know how I would have made it.

Abbreviations

CIA	Central Intelligence Agency
COW	Correlates of War
CTFT	contrite tit-for-tat
GATT	General Agreement on Tariffs and Trade
GNP	gross national product
IAEA	International Atomic Energy Agency
ICB	International Crisis Behavior [Project]
ICBMs	intercontinental ballistic missiles
ICJ	International Court of Justice
IDF	Israeli Defense Force
IMF	International Monetary Fund
IOs	international organizations
MID	Militarized International Disputes
NGOs	nongovernmental organizations
NPT	Nonproliferation Treaty
OAS	Organization of American States
PD	prisoner's dilemma
PRC	People's Republic of China
SAM	surface-to-air missile
SLBMs	submarine-launched ballistic missiles
TASS	Soviet news agency
TFT	tit-for-tat
UN	United Nations
UNEF	United Nations Emergency Force
UNTSO	United Nations Truce Supervision Organization
UPI	United Press International
US	United States (used as adj. only; sp. out as noun)
WSAG	Washington Special Actions Group
WTO	World Trade Organization

CHAPTER 1

Normative Structures in International Politics

O ver the past decade the structure of world politics has undergone a number of substantial changes. For the past half-century we have lived in an international system dominated by the bipolar rivalry between the United States and the Soviet Union. Although the Cold War system has dissolved as quickly as it emerged, it is still not clear what kind of international structure will take its place. For example, scholars have debated whether the world is moving toward multipolarity with the rise of Europe, Japan, and perhaps China, or whether American dominance is still sufficient to define the international system as unipolar.[1] But while these analysts have been charting trends in relative power to predict the emergence of new rivalries, others have begun to consider the construction of an entirely different kind of systemic structure. Departing from prevailing conceptions of the international system, these scholars have suggested that state leaders' understandings of their international environment may constitute an international structure that is as influential as the measures of relative power that are traditionally viewed as giving shape to world politics.

CAN OUR HISTORY EXPLAIN OUR THEORIES?

Perhaps it should not be surprising that changes in the structure of the international system have led us to reevaluate many of the theories we use to understand international relations. The bipolar system of the past half-century emerged from a long and bloody war that was almost immediately replaced by a tense military standoff between the victorious parties. Predictably, these events led scholars to argue that the international system is fundamentally shaped by the unbridled competition for power among the dominant states in the system. Since its inception in the 1950s, this "realist" vision of world politics has exploded into a whole family of theoretical approaches. This field has become so broad that some might question whether the label "realist" continues to have mean-

---

[1] John Mearsheimer (1990, 2001) typifies this kind of analysis in his discussion of the history of Great Power politics as well as international security following the end of the Cold War.

ing.[2] At its core, however, the "realist" approach to world politics asserts that two central realities permeate every aspect of world politics.[3] First, the constant environment in which all of international politics takes place is one of anarchy. That is, no power stands above that of the nation-state. Second, the only variable that can shape this environment significantly is the relative distribution of power among the states in the system. Specifically, the prevalence of conflict and the ease of achieving cooperation may vary depending on whether one, two, or three or more states dominate the system. This approach tends to see conflict as a pervasive aspect of world politics, and argues that the only possible constraint on the outbreak of violence is a countervailing threat of violence. Through the maintenance of this so-called balance of power, violence can often be avoided, but these intermissions between disputes are not what one would normally consider a "peace." Finally, realists assert that international agreement, institutions, and the like are of no consequence in reducing international conflict. What counts are the interests of states and their ability to achieve and maintain them by force.

The realist vision of the international system as rooted exclusively in power and national interests has had a profound influence on the development of theories of foreign policy behavior over the past several decades. Perhaps the single most prominent and popular theoretical approach to foreign policy to emerge during this period has been the rational theory of deterrence.[4] Although scholars have produced many specific variants of deterrence theory, all of these arguments share several presumptions. Once again, deterrence theorists view conflict as a pervasive aspect of international politics. In addition, they argue that the best way for a state to prevent its enemies from starting a conflict or seizing its valued assets is to threaten to inflict such damage on them that they prefer complying with their opponent's wishes to risking a conflict. Specifically, theories of deterrence present two necessary and sufficient conditions for preventing enemies from initiating a conflict: (1) demonstrate a capability to inflict severe damage on one's opponent; and (2) demonstrate a willingness to use this capability if its opponent does not comply.

---

[2] For a critique of the realist paradigm as either theoretically incoherent or manifestly false, see Legro and Moravcsik (1999).

[3] The list of major realist works is a very long one, but some of the most prominent and representative of this approach are Carr (1946) and Morgenthau (1985). Perhaps the central realist work in this regard is Waltz (1979). A more recent statement of the realist perspective on world politics can be found in Mearsheimer (2001).

[4] Again, the list of prominent realist works on deterrence is extremely long, but some of the more significant ones are Schelling (1960, 1966); Russett (1967); Mearsheimer (1983); and Huth (1988).

These two foreign policy prescriptions epitomize the realist-inspired vision of international politics.

But while the bipolar Cold War system was created and perpetuated through violence and the threat of violence, the system collapsed in a very different way. No great military conflict caused the disintegration of the USSR or its abandonment of its Eastern European empire. Rather than violence or a dramatic shift in power resources, the bipolar Cold War system ended because of changes in the foreign policy ideas held by important policy makers.[5] Gorbachev's rise to power in 1985, for example, eventually sparked Soviet "new thinking" about their security policy.[6] This new thinking included a reconceptualization both of legitimate Soviet security needs and of the most effective ways to meet those needs. Furthermore, the European velvet revolutions of 1989 were able to take place because of changes in leaders' beliefs—both in the USSR and in Eastern Europe—concerning the legitimacy of using force to impose pro-Soviet communist rule. There is no military or economic reason why the USSR and its Warsaw Pact allies could not have responded to the uprisings of 1989 just as they did to uprisings in Hungary in 1956 and Czechoslovakia in 1968. Similarly, there is no good military or economic reason that the USSR could not have remained unified and therefore remained a superpower. The best explanation of the change in Soviet behavior both at home and abroad is that Soviet elites changed their understanding of Soviet interests and how best to achieve them.

Perhaps it was the ideological collapse of the Cold War that has led theorists to explore conceptions of a new international structure that might be based on the influence of ideas as much as on the distribution of power. The most prominent previous example of such an attempt was made by President Woodrow Wilson following World War I. More recently, however, scholars have begun to look at reinvigorating the United Nations or some other international institution into a global security community which could give a new and more peaceful structure to world politics.[7] In the mid-1990s, Charles W. Kegley made a powerful call for

---

[5] For a discussion of the end of the Cold War as rooted in changes in the norms held by decision makers, see Evangelista (1995); Koslowski and Kratochwil (1994); Mendelson (1993); and Checkel (1993). For complementary discussions of the role of ideas in structural change and the end of the Cold War, see Stein (1994); Risse-Kapen (1994); and Lebow (1994).

[6] For discussions of Soviet "new thinking" as it began to diffuse the US-Soviet rivalry, see Gromyko and Hellman (1988); Meyer (1988); and Snyder (1987).

[7] A number of volumes were published in the wake of the Cold War concerning normative international structures in general as well as the role of specific institutions such as the United Nations (UN) in creating such a structure. See, for example, Rochester (1993); Weiss (1993); Ruggie (1993); and Falk, Johansen, and Kim (1993).

the reexamination of Wilsonian ideas concerning the rule of law and international security. Citing a wide range of events occurring during the early 1990s that he believed to be incompatible with traditional realism, Kegley suggests that "the time has arrived to revise and reconstruct classical realism, and build a refashioned paradigm inspired by Wilsonian idealism." (Kegley 1993, 143) Over the past several years, a number of scholars have begun to answer this challenge. In response to the ideological collapse of the Cold War, scholars such as Alex Wendt, Martha Finnemore, Kathryn Sikkink, and many other have begun to theorize about an international system in which ideas are as influential as material capabilities (Wendt 1992, 1999; Klotz 1995; Katzenstein 1996; Finnemore 1996; Keck and Sikkink 1998).

What Do You Mean, "Ideas Matter"?

We must be careful of what we mean, however, when we speak of "ideas" influencing systemic structures or foreign policy behavior. Even the most orthodox of realist approaches concedes the influence of ideas in the sense that national policy makers are human, and they have ideas about how they should behave and why they should behave that way. But there are at least two important differences between the role that realists allot to ideas in international relations and the role being considered by these new revisionists. First, realists argue that the ideas that influence policy are not complex. That is, they generally concern the link between means and ends, and they can be summed up in fairly brief "if . . . then" statements.

Second, and perhaps more important, realists insist that the ideas that policy makers hold are directly determined by other variables, such as relative power and national interests. Thus in the realist view, ideas do not have an independent causal effect on behavior, but are only cognitive intermediaries between environmental stimuli and policy makers' responses. A theoretical approach to international relations that includes the influence of norms and institutions, however, allows for a more complex vision of the role of ideas in foreign policy. First, making normative assessments as to whether behaviors are "legitimate" or not involves more complex ideas than can be accounted for by realist theory. Conceptions of "right" and "wrong" are more abstract and complex than simple "if . . . then" beliefs about the nature of the world.[8]

Moreover, according to this approach, normative standards are *not* exclusively determined by power and interests and may have an indepen-

---

[8] For a discussion of various ways in which ideas might "matter" in terms of explaining international behavior, see Goldstein and Keohane (1993).

dent causal impact of their own.[9] These revisionists note that a variety of different normative structures may operate within any given power structure.[10] Thus norms must develop in a manner that is in some ways independent of power and interests. If norms are not entirely determined by power and interests, then these ideas may have an independent influence on state behavior.

We must also recognize that the construction of a normative framework for world politics should not eliminate international conflict any more than the passage of a law should eliminate crime. Nor would such a framework imply that military power will become irrelevant to state behavior. Rather we should expect the development of commonly understood norms to help international policy makers take incremental steps toward reducing the incidence of violent conflict and stabilizing peaceful relationships. Conflicts should become less frequent as states' expectations about their relations converge, and the conflicts that do emerge should be more easily resolved in compliance with the accepted normative standards. Specifically, as I will discuss in chapter 3, we should expect the accession to behavioral norms to ease the enforcement of these standards for at least two reasons. First, norms define which acts are illegitimate and demand punishment by other states. Second, punishments should be more likely to result in compliance because the trespassers recognize the standards of behavior that they have violated as legitimate. In this manner, norms can help states to reestablish cooperative relations and minimize the long-term effects of disputes.

LEGITIMATE AGREEMENTS: THE BUILDING BLOCKS OF NORMATIVE STRUCTURE

Theories of an international structure based on ideas leads us inevitably to the consideration of theories of foreign policy behavior that incorporate the influence of norms. If norms and ideas are to have any impact at the systemic level, that influence must be exerted on individual decisions and actions by nation-states. Most of the evidence collected thus far concerning the influence of norms on foreign policy has been done in the

[9] For a discussion of the distinction between norms as independent causal variables and spurious correlates of cooperative interests, see Krasner, "Structural Causes and Regime Consequences," in Krasner (1983); and Krasner, "Regimes and the Limits of Realism: Regimes as Autonomous Variables," in Krasner (1983).

[10] Alexander Wendt's (1992, 1999) work is perhaps the central statement of this perspective. His contention is aptly summarized by the title of his 1992 article, "Anarchy Is What States Make of It." That is, Wendt argues that international anarchy and the material distribution of power do not—by themselves—predict anything about state behavior. Instead, Wendt argues that states must construct shared meanings for these material facts. These constructed understandings, in turn, influence behavior.

area of international political economy.[11] Work in this area is important and obviously represents a significant step toward establishing the independent role of ideas in international relations. But if norms are to become the foundation of more general approaches to international relations, then we must establish that these ideas can have an independent influence on military conflicts as well. One obvious reason for emphasizing the importance of military conflicts is that most structural changes in world politics have been a result of military conflict of one kind or another, and so militarized disputes would represent one of the most significant challenges to a normative international structure. Moreover, while realism represents a general approach to the study of world politics, its proponents have always held that its explanatory power is greatest when it comes to understanding security-related disputes. Consequently, if a normative approach to international relations is to subsume or supplant realism, it must be able to demonstrate the impact of norms on military conflicts.

The central aim of this work is to test the proposition that the construction of normative standards of behavior can influence state actions in security-related disputes. I hope to demonstrate that international security norms can and have helped to stabilize peace and cooperation even between states that represent substantial security risks to one another. Looking at the historical record, we find relatively few examples of formal regional—much less global—security organizations. There have been many fewer international security organizations, for example, than organizations that have existed to facilitate international trade. Nonetheless, the fact that security norms have not been as formalized as their economic counterparts does not imply that they cannot or have not affected behavior. I will examine the construction of security norms of a more decentralized nature. Specifically, I will examine the bilateral establishment of norms as settlements for security-related disputes and the way in which such bilateral settlements affect subsequent interactions over the same disputed issue. The finding that such bilateral norms affect security behavior would have several significant implications. First, such a finding would be important information for current national policy makers because it would provide them with another foreign policy tool. If security norms can stabilize cooperation, then leaders can move beyond deterrence toward a more constructive strategy for maintaining their security.

---

[11] The most prominent works in this area concern the construction of what are known as international regimes. See, for example, Krasner (1983) and Keohane (1984). I will elaborate further on my discussion of international regimes in chapter 2. Other more recent work has focused more explicitly on the development of international norms. See, for example, Keck and Sikkink (1998) and Klotz (1995). In general this work also has not focused on security affairs. Some exceptions are Price and Tannenwald (1996); Price (1995); Legro (1995); and Tannenwald (1999). A partial exception is Finnemore (1996).

Second, empirical support for the role of security norms would remind international relations theorists that we must not restrict our attention to conventional realist hypotheses concerning power, interests, and resources. Moreover, it would specifically suggest that we must give more careful consideration to the independent role that ideas may play in the conduct of world politics. Finally, the finding that norms can affect the resolution of security conflict would provide some encouragement for those who hope to build more elaborate security structures based on common normative standards of behavior.

I will test the proposition that norms affect the resolution of security-related disputes against the central competing realist paradigm for understanding military conflict: rational coercion theory.[12] This is perhaps the most appropriate competing explanation to consider in my analysis because of its powerful influence as a vision of foreign policy making throughout the Cold War. Moreover, it exemplifies the realist, power-based notions of international relations that deny any independent role for ideas in shaping foreign policy. Briefly, my findings indicate that these settlements *do* shape state leaders' responses to crisis-bargaining behavior in ways that cannot be explained by a purely realist framework. These results indicate that international security norms can and have helped to stabilize peace and cooperation, even between states that represent substantial security risks to one another. At the same time, however, traditionally realist variables—such as coercion and reputation for toughness—are central to my explanation of crisis outcomes. Thus my argument represents an important step toward integrating normative approaches with the prevailing—yet incomplete—realist approach to crisis bargaining.

My analysis proceeds as follows. In chapter 2 I will review the normative and realist literatures that relate most directly to my investigation of norms in security conflicts. In doing so, I hope to place my research in its proper perspective and define more precisely its contribution to our understanding of security policy. I will also outline some of the various theoretical and methodological pitfalls involved in the study of norms that I hope to circumvent in this work. In chapter 3 I will carefully outline normative and realist theoretical frameworks. Following the discussion of each theoretical model, I will develop specific testable hypotheses from each approach concerning militarized conflict behavior. In chapter 4 I will turn my attention to constructing a research design for testing

---

[12] As I will discuss and demonstrate in chapter 3, rational theories of deterrence and coercion are, in fact, identical in every significant respect. Their only difference is in the specific task to which deterrent and coercive threats are put. Deterrence concerns the prevention of an action before it begins, while coercion concerns the reversal of an action that has already been taken. I choose to phrase my discussion in terms of a theory of coercion because it is more appropriate to the bargaining behavior that I will examine.

these hypotheses. Specifically, I will identify the proper population of cases for my analysis, discuss the data set that I have created, and present the operational measures for the conceptual variables that I have outlined in chapter 3.

In chapter 5 I begin presenting my empirical analyses. These analyses sequentially address three related but distinct questions about international norms. I begin by asking *whether* norms influence behavior in security-related crises. Second, I investigate *how* they exert this influence. And finally I turn to the question of *when* such international norms will be effective. In chapter 5 I will present the results of my statistical tests of the realist and institutionalist models of crisis bargaining. As I described earlier, I find strong support for the hypothesis that states *can and do* construct normative standards that guide their behavior in militarized disputes.

In chapter 6 I shift my attention from an aggregate statistical analysis of dispute behavior to the execution of more detailed case studies from my data set. While the aggregate analysis in chapter 5 addresses the question of *whether* international norms matter, these case studies are better suited to illustrating *how* normative standards of behavior influence international conflict. Specifically, I examine two crises that illustrate the statistical findings in chapter 5, and demonstrate that the causal arguments presented in chapter 3 continue to make sense when we examine individual crises in detail.

In chapter 7 I turn my attention to the question of when international norms will shape security crises. While the analysis in chapter 5 demonstrates that norms do have an impact on military conflict, it also indicates that norms are not *always* effective. In this chapter I show that my theory about the impact of norms can also help us understand *when* norms will be influential. Finally, in chapter 8 I conclude by discussing the implications of my research for broader theorizing about international relations. In addition, I will draw attention to issues and topics that require further research and to the policy-making implications of my work.

I am keenly aware that this work will not represent the final word in our understanding of international norms. I begin my analysis with a broad discussion of the conceptualization of international norms, and proceed to examine these broad concepts though the lens of several extremely specific—and in some sense narrow—empirical tests. However, I am convinced that we can best advance our understanding of broad theoretical concepts through testing them in carefully crafted and concrete circumstances. Taken in this spirit, I believe that my results advance our understanding of the impact of international norms. At the same time, however, I recognize that the findings of my work may raise more new research questions than they answer.

Chapter 2

Power and Legitimacy in the Study of International Relations

T his chapter places my research in its proper context within the literature on international relations and international conflict. First, I will discuss the contrasting views of international politics that lie at the core of the dispute over the influence of international norms. Second, I will define two of the concepts that are most central to my analysis: power and legitimacy. Finally, I will review some of the more recent debates between realists and institutionalists concerning the relative importance of power and legitimacy in determining foreign policy behavior. In doing so, I hope to outline some of the significant problems and questions that my research must address.

Contrasting Visions of International Politics

As I discussed in the introductory chapter, the failure of realist theory to predict or explain the collapse of the Cold War seems to have led scholars to investigate the role of ideas in foreign policy and the possibility of building a new kind of structure for international relations based on the influence of ideas. A number of scholars, for example, have suggested the possibility of creating such a structure by reinvigorating various international security organizations and the norms that these institutions propagate. If such a change were to materialize, it would represent a powerful challenge to the traditional realist approach to world politics which has dominated the field of security studies for more than four decades.

The debate between realists and those who emphasize the role of international organizations, norms, and rules is not a new one, however. In fact, this debate dates back at least as far as the seventeenth-century works of Hobbes and Grotius. Hobbes's vision of the state of nature served in many ways as the intellectual basis for the realist view of the international system. In recounting this Hobbesian view, Hedley Bull writes that

> [I]nternational relations, in the Hobbesian view, represent pure conflict between states and resemble a game that is wholly distributive or zero-sum. . . . The Hobbesian prescription for international con-

duct is that the state is free to pursue its goals in relation to other states without moral or legal restrictions of any kind. Ideas of morality and law, on this view, are valid only in the context of a society, but international life is beyond the bounds of any society. (Bull 1977, 24–25)

The Grotian view, on the other hand, contrasts sharply with this stark depiction of international politics. The Grotians see a more nuanced global system in which cooperative and competitive incentives are mixed. Moreover, they question Hobbes's sharp division between the worlds of domestic and international politics by asserting that consensual understandings of moral and legal behavioral standards can be established on an international as well as a domestic level. Once again, Bull:

> The Grotian tradition describes international politics in terms of a society of states or an international society. As against the Hobbesian tradition, the Grotians contend that states are not engaged in a simple struggle, like gladiators in an arena, but are limited in their conflicts with one another by common rules and institutions. . . . The Grotian prescription for international conduct is that states, in their dealings with one another, are bound by the rules and institutions of the society they form. (Bull 1977, 26–27)

During the Cold War, the Hobbesians largely held the upper hand in the intellectual struggle over the study of military affairs. The onset of World War II, for example, brought academic scorn down on the ideas of Woodrow Wilson concerning international institutions and their role in maintaining the peace.

The end of the Cold War, however, has led to a revival of Grotian perspectives, which had—perhaps derisively—been labeled "idealism." The word "idealism" may still call up images of a world government that remains well beyond our grasp. Despite the continuing increase in global interdependence driven by an ever-accelerating spiral of technological innovation, states remain powerful actors and cling tightly to their autonomy and sovereignty. "Idealism," however, does not refer solely to utopian plans for everlasting peace. In fact, Wilsonian ideas about the role of law in shaping international security may have important effects even in a world of sovereign states. Increasingly, scholars have paid attention to the possibility of international governance (i.e., the maintenance of order according to some system of rules) without international government (i.e., a global legislature and executive power).

This recent work evolving from the Grotian tradition is itself divided into two rather distinct perspectives. At one end of the spectrum are the social constructivists.[1] These scholars contend that the influence of ideas is pervasive in international politics. In particular, constructivists argue that ideas constitute the identities of actors in the international system and shape actors' understandings of their own preferences and interests.

Alexander Wendt, for example, does not quite claim that material facts are irrelevant to international politics, but he comes close to this position. Specifically, Wendt argues that core realist variables such as "power" and "anarchy" are not "facts" of international politics and do not have any objective meaning. Instead, he claims that these material "facts" only take on meaning through the subjective and mutable ideas that we use to interpret them. For example, Wendt (1999, 35) writes that "the meaning of the distribution of power in international politics is constituted in important part by the distribution of interests, and that the content of interests are in turn constituted in important part by ideas."

Institutionalists represent a second branch of the Grotian tradition that stands in between constructivism and realism.[2] That is, institutionalists concede to realists the notion that the identities of actors as well as their power and interests are causally prior to the impact of ideas. Moreover, institutionalists concede that international norms and institutions may reflect the interests of powerful actors. Nonetheless, they claim that ideas— as embodied in mutually recognized norms, rules, and procedures—can have an independent impact on state behavior through the information that they provide to state leaders.

Early work in the institutionalist tradition focused on international economic organizations like the General Agreement on Tariffs and Trade (GATT) and the International Monetary Fund (IMF). Some scholars (Jervis 1983) even suggested that these types of arguments might not travel well to the realm of security affairs. More recently, however, institutionalists have extended their interest to military behavior (Wallander 1999; Haftendorn, Keohane, and Wallander 1999). Haftendorn, Keohane, and Wallander (1999), for example, present several analyses of the causes and consequences of security institutions across time and space. This volume reflects the renewed interest in the impact of institutions on security affairs. At the same time, its contents testify to the highly nuanced and varied effects of international institutions. Institutionalists will

---

[1] This list of constructivist work on norms is too long to list here and continues to grow rapidly. Some of the most significant works, however, are Wendt (1992, 1999); Legro (1995); Klotz (1995); Katzenstein (1996); Finnemore (1996); and Keck and Sikkink (1998).

[2] Once again, the institutionalist literature is too extensive to recite here. Some of the most influential early works in this tradition have been Krasner (1983); Keohane (1984); and Oye (1986).

be encouraged to find that—despite the varied substantive, geographic, and temporal focus of the chapters—each author in the volume discovers some evidence that international institutions have an independent influence on security behavior. At the same time, however, each chapter's findings arc couched cautiously and give great weight to the impact of material capabilities and the threat of force.

Thus interest in the impact of ideas and institutions on international security affairs has blossomed in the wake of the Cold War. In some cases the modern constructivist and institutionalist scholars have retained the sweeping perspective of their "idealist" counterparts. Wendt's (1999) *Social Theory of International Politics*, for example, presents itself as a constructivist reinterpretation of Waltz's (1979) central statement of structural realism. These abstract theoretical works serve as important guideposts for the study and interpretation of international affairs.

More commonly, however, both constructivist and institutionalist critics of realism have sought to ground their claims in specific empirical evidence. This approach has led the field into a potentially very fruitful debate over the conditions under which constructivist, institutionalist, or realist perspectives will be most useful in explaining security-related behavior. For example, Legro (1995) and Finnemore (1996) carefully examine the evolution of specific normative doctrines about the conduct of war and document the impact of these norms on military actions. Similarly, Duffield (1992) and Wallander (1999) examine the impact of international specific security institutions on European security policies and strategies. Rather than seeking global government, these works seek to understand whether international institutions can construct a highly varied and complex patchwork of commitments and understanding that transform international security relations. It is within this latter approach that this work seeks to make a contribution through the specific documentation of the concrete empirical effects of security norms.

CONCEPTUALIZING POWER AND LEGITIMACY

In one sense, the dispute between constructivists and institutionalists, on the one hand, and realists, on the other, concerns the relative importance of power and legitimacy in shaping international affairs. The realists assert that legitimacy has no place in the study of world politics, whereas the constructivists and institutionalists, while not disputing that power plays a role in shaping international behavior, contend that a mutual recognition of standards of legitimacy has important effects as well.

Concepts such as power and legitimacy can become both slippery and obscure if not treated carefully. Power, for example, is often defined as the ability to get others to do something that they would not do otherwise. While this simple sentence seems to capture what we intuitively mean by "power," it is often not the precise manner in which the term is used. Scholars will sometimes frame their research as investigating whether a state's power caused another state to behave in a certain manner. For example, one might speak of investigating whether American power prevented a Soviet invasion of Western Europe during the Cold War. If the United States influenced Soviet behavior in any way, however, then by definition it was American *power* that wielded that influence.

The problem here is the somewhat careless usage of the word "power." Rather than actually investigating whether power brings influence— which amounts to a tautology—researchers are generally truly interested in discovering which particular attributes will make an actor powerful. Framed in this manner, "power" refers to resources that an actor may use to create contingent rewards or punishments that may alter others' behavior.

Thus despite their loose rhetoric to the contrary, realists are not distinguished by their claim that power dominates international politics, but by their assertion that a particular set of resources is the primary source of power in world politics. In particular, realists tend to see power as deriving from resources that allow states to inflict material damage on other international actors. Realists may focus on international economics, military affairs, or any other international issue, and so the specific resources that realists point to as sources of power may vary from one issue area to another.[3] For example, with regard to the study of the oil trade, a realist might argue that power is rooted in a state's share of the global production of crude oil. If the issue at hand was nuclear arms control, however, a realist might say that power will be found in states' relative stockpiles of deliverable nuclear warheads.

In this study I will focus on militarized crisis bargaining. Thus the realist sources of power that I will identify focus on various aspects of military capabilities. Institutionalists should have no quarrel with the statement that power determines international behavior, but they would contend that power may be found in a much wider array of resources. In particular, institutionalists argue that power may be found in the ability to construct mutual standards of behavior and so on. To recognize this distinction, I shall generally refer to realist arguments as based on specific "capabilities" or "power resources." On occasion, however, I may use the term "power" in its more colloquial sense to simplify my syntax. Unless I state otherwise, I use the term to refer to power resources rather than the actual ability to manipulate behavior.

Legitimacy is perhaps an even more difficult concept to specify than is

[3] For a discussion of issue-specific concepts of power, see Keohane and Nye (1989).

power. In fact, many dictionaries fail to provide a definition that covers the use of this term in politics. Within the study of politics, however, scholars have largely conceived of legitimacy in one of two ways. The first view—rooted in international law—contends that a rule or a norm is legitimate if it is created by legitimate institutions (Hart 1961). This understanding of legitimacy has led to the importance of "right process" as a standard for assessing international law and legal rulings. For example, international legal scholars might view a particular judicial ruling as "legitimate" if it was reached properly through established procedures and represented a reasonable interpretation of existing law. Franck (1995, 26) writes that "legitimacy is that attribute of a norm which conduces the belief that it is fair because it was made and applied in accordance with right process." This understanding leads Franck to the conclusion that "once a state joins the community of states (today an inescapable incidence of statehood) the basic rules of community and of its legitimate exercise of community authority apply to the individual state regardless of whether consent has been specifically addressed." This view suggests that the legitimacy of particular norms or rules can be judged from the perspective of the "international community" as a whole.

A second view, however, contends that legitimacy exists primarily as the level of the individual actor rather than the community. That is, a particular rule or norm is legitimate if it enjoys support from the relevant set of actors. Hurd (1999, 380), for example, states that "legitimacy, as I use it here, refers to the normative belief by an actor that a rule or institution ought to be obeyed. It is a subjective quality, relational between actor and institution, and defined by the actor's perception of the institution." Similarly, Wendt (1999, 272) writes that "to say a norm is legitimate is to say that an actor fully accepts its claim on himself."

While both understandings of legitimacy may be useful for differing purposes, I rely on the latter understanding of legitimacy as rooted in the consent of individual actors. This focus on the consent of actors is most appropriate for my research because most of the "legitimate agreements" that I examine were not created by formal institutions, but emerged instead from ad hoc bilateral or multilateral negotiations. Moreover, the former understanding of legitimacy as rooted in community standards or practices rather than individual consent presumes the existence of a strong community. Most of the agreements that I examine, however, exist between states that are not viewed by rival states as sharing strong communal bonds.

But if individual consent is critical to my understanding of legitimacy, then what is "consent"? More specifically, who has consented, and how can we know that they have consented? The concept of consent has been debated by political philosophers for centuries, and is much too extensive to review here. This work, however, relies upon a theory of consent developed by Herzog (1989) that relates closely to the understanding of legitimacy that I discussed earlier. Herzog's central problem is to understand when individuals may be understood to have "consented" to rule by a government. In particular, Herzog is concerned with developing observable indicators of consent by citizens. He concludes that the state's responsiveness to the wishes of its citizens most fundamentally serves as its basis for asserting the consent of the governed and therefore its own legitimacy. "If we draw up a list of regimes that we intuitively want to say rest on the consent of the governed," he writes, "another list of those that don't, the states on the first list turn out to be the responsive ones. Consent here is just the opposite of repression, of policies being imposed with no regard for people's wishes" (Herzog 1989, 207).

Transporting this concept to my work on international agreements, I contend that international norms, institutions, and agreements are legitimate to the extent that they are *responsive* to the wishes of the contracting parties. A state's accession to an international agreement is embodied in the signature of its official representative. But accession alone clearly cannot constitute sufficient basis for imputing consent. Many states have acceded to international agreements in the face of coercive pressure, but cannot be said to have consented to their rules or norms. Perhaps the most obvious examples of such agreements have come in the wake of military defeat. For example, the Kaiser's Germany and Saddam Hussein's Iraq acceded to the terms imposed on them following World War I and the Gulf War. Neither defeated state, however, appeared to consent to the terms of those settlements.

Following from Herzog's definition, a state may meaningfully be said to have consented to the rules of an international agreement if the agreement is for the most part "responsive" to the wishes of the state. But this raises another question: how can an agreement be "responsive"? Institutions can be "responsive" because they interact with their members repeatedly over time. Agreements, however, do not act at all. Consequently, I measure the responsiveness of a norm or agreement through the process of its formation. That is, in practice I argue that an agreement is responsive to a state's wishes if that state has played a role in shaping the stipulations of the agreement.[4] That is, consent to an interna-

---

[4] As noted earlier, this definition of "consent" excludes coerced or imposed agreements—such as the imposition of unconditional surrender following a war. Some difficult problems arise, however, in determining what constitutes a "coerced" agreement. Any agreement is negotiated within a context that limits the choices of the contracting parties. Some limitations we would clearly allow while still describing the states as consenting to the agreement. At some point, however, the limitations become so severe as to constitute an imposed settlement. Exactly what that point might be (or if there is any single turning

tional agreement can be observed during the formation of the agreement through the responsiveness of each of the contracting parties to the wishes of the other parties. Empirically, this definition means that I look for evidence that each party to the agreement was willing to alter the terms of the agreement in some way to accommodate the wishes of the other party or parties. In the case of the Kennedy-Khrushchev understanding that resolved the Cuban missile crisis, for example, the USSR was clearly "responsive" to American wishes by pledging to remove its missiles from Cuba. The United States, however, was also "responsive" to Soviet requests for an explicit pledge not to invade Cuba. Perhaps more significantly, as I discuss in chapter 6, American responsiveness can be observed in its willingness to provide tacit assurances about the removal of missiles in Turkey as well as its flexibility regarding the monitoring of the withdrawal of Soviet missiles following Castro's attempts to scuttle the agreement.

It is also possible, of course, for a state to consent to an agreement that it had no role in constructing if that agreement nonetheless conforms with the state's wishes. Identifying behavioral signs that distinguish this kind of consent from an imposed settlement would be more difficult to discern, however. In such cases a researcher must attempt to reconstruct policy makers' preferences at the time they acceded to the agreement and attempt to determine the level of constraint under which they felt they were acting. Fortunately, my empirical research will be focusing on bilaterally and multilaterally constructed dispute settlements. Thus the question of a state consenting to an agreement that it did not construct is not an issue for my analysis.[5]

Legitimate Agreements and International Norms

If an international agreement or organization is legitimate, then I label the standards of behavior that it defines "norms." Unfortunately, the word "norm" is nearly as fraught with various meanings as "power" and "legitimacy." First, the word "norm" may be used simply as a descriptive term. That is, it may describe typical or "normal" behavior. Often this use of the term refers to a pattern of behavior that has developed over an extended period of time.

---

point) may be up for debate. The specific rules that I used to separate legitimate from imposed agreements are discussed in chapter 4 along with the rest of the research design.

[5] One assumption I do make, however, is that governments continue to consent to agreements that they have inherited from previous regimes. This procedure has been standard practice in international relations for some time and is critical for maintaining stable international relationships. I address this assumption and its impact on the effectiveness of international norms in greater detail in chapter 7.

A second conception of norms extends this descriptive focus on "typical" behavior to encompass expectations about future behavior. Much of the game theoretic work on norms, for example, views norms essentially as game equilibria. For example, Morrow (1994, 408–9) writes that

> equilibria also produce norms of behavior. . . . The expectations about one another's behavior are analogous to norms within a regime. . . . Like norms, players' cognizance of one another's equilibrium strategies allows them to determine when another player has deviated from suggested behavior. Norms then are generated by an equilibrium in the model. . . . Different regimes produce norms of differing strength just as the equilibria in the model do.

Notably this typical game theoretic view of norms focuses on the informational content of norms, but it excludes notions of obligation. Actors follow norms purely because it is in their interest to do so in the narrow sense of following their equilibrium strategies.

A third understanding of norms adds a sense of obligation to the game theoretic notions of expectations about behavior. Katzenstein (1996, 5), for example, defines norms as "collective expectations about the proper behavior of actors with a given identity." The critical word in this definition is "proper," which indicates that norms for Katzenstein are not expectations about how states will behave, but about how they ought to behave. This is the typical use of the term "norm" in the constructivist literature.

As I shall discuss later in this chapter as well as in chapter 3, my approach to the study of norms is essentially institutionalist rather than constructivist. Nonetheless, my understanding of the term "norm" is consistent with its use in the constructivist literature as well. As my discussion of legitimacy indicated, my argument about norms depends critically on the notion of obligation that states accept when they consent to an international norm. This sense of obligation, I argue, is central to the impact of norms as a signal of intentions during bargaining, and it is also central to their role in the development of a reputation for "trustworthy" behavior. "Trustworthiness" implies a level of obligation that reaches beyond game theoretic notions of equilibrium behavior. Moreover, the game theoretic understanding of norms is not as applicable to my work because I focus on responses to the violations of norms. If norms are game equilibria, however, then states do not have incentives to violate them. My understanding of norms does not imply that states generally comply with their prescriptions. In fact, that is—in part—what I am attempting to determine. Instead, when I say that a state has violated a norm, I mean that it has behaved in a way that it had previously recognized as illegitimate.

Since consenting actors accept the obligation to abide by them, norms construct common behavioral expectations within the group where they operate. For example, the signatories of the Nonproliferation Treaty (NPT) may reasonably be thought of as consenting to the norm of nuclear nonproliferation. As a result, non-nuclear member states have all subscribed to the norm that they ought not to develop nuclear weapons. These non-nuclear member states have also consented to the norm that they ought to submit to international inspection of their nuclear programs by the International Atomic Energy Agency (IAEA). The nuclear member states of the NPT, on the other hand, have consented to the norm that they ought to limit and eventually eliminate their nuclear weapons stockpile. All members of the NPT share the common understanding that each party ought to comply with its obligations under the agreement.

Norms alone, however, are often not enough to create a successful agreement. Because the specific behavioral implications of general norms are likely to be vague in many circumstances, more concrete rules are also an essential part of a successful agreement. Without the specific instruction of rules, disputes would inevitably develop regarding whether a norm had been violated, and such disputes, in turn, undermine the legitimacy of the agreement. Returning to the NPT, the behavior of the nuclear powers suggests that simply sharing a normative expectation of lowering stockpiles has a limited impact on behavior in the absence of rules for implementing this obligation. Since its inception, the non-nuclear members have almost continually complained that the nuclear states are not living up to their obligations to disarm under the NPT. The more specific rules about inspection of nuclear power programs in the non-nuclear states, on the other hand, have led to much greater compliance and clarity regarding which states are or are not in violation of their obligations.

Although my definition of a norm is drawn largely from the constructivist literature, my use of the term also parallels the use of this term in much of the institutionalist literature. In fact, as I shall discuss later in this chapter and in chapter 3, the significant distinctions between the constructivist and institutionalist approaches lie not as much in their understanding of norms as in the causal pathways by which norms are thought to influence behavior. Thus my description of legitimate international agreements as international norms is also consistent what institutional scholars have referred to as international "regimes." Stephen Krasner (1983, 2), for example, defined regimes as

> sets of implicit or explicit principles, norms, rules, and decision-making procedures around which actors' expectations converge in a

given area of international relations. Principles are beliefs of fact, causation and rectitude. Norms are standards of behavior defined in terms of rights and obligations. Rules are specific prescriptions and proscriptions for action. Decision-making procedures are prevailing practices for making and implementing collective choice.

Like my own use of the term "norm," Krasner's definition of a regime emphasizes obligations to observe prescribed or proscribed behavior. Because he is referring to more elaborately institutionalized norms than the "legitimate dispute settlements" that I focus on, Krasner's definition is somewhat broader than my use of the word "norms." As a result of this breadth, however, Krasner's remains rather vague in certain respects. For example, must a regime have all of the characteristics he lists? Which aspects—if any—are secondary? If an institution upholds certain norms and rules, but lacks any explicit statement concerning "beliefs of causation," is it still a regime?

Once again, however, my focus on specific and narrowly constructed legitimate dispute settlements helps to avoid these problems. My discussion of legitimate dispute settlements focuses on three necessary characteristics: norms, rules, and consent. If a dispute settlement is consensual, it places obligations on the consenting parties, and if it specifies rules for implementing those obligations, then I define the agreement as a "legitimate dispute settlement."

THE ORIGINS AND INFLUENCE OF INTERNATIONAL NORMS

Given this understanding of legitimacy, international norms, and legitimate agreements, where do I expect international norms to come from, and whose behavior should they influence? Perhaps the most common answer given by constructivist scholars is that norms emerge as an aspect of the structure of the international system. According to this view, norms may be inserted into international discourse by states (Krasner 1995; Tannenwald 1999), by international organizations (IOs), nongovernmental organizations (NGOs), or transnational actors (Klotz 1995; Finnemore 1996; Keck and Sikkink 1998). Whatever their initial source, however, this perspective on norms implies that the adoption of norms by the international community transforms them into "social facts" that cannot be altered by individual actors (Wendt 1999). This view is also consistent with legal understandings of international norms and legitimacy such as those discussed by Franck (1990, 1995) and Hart (1961). According to this view, states learn—or are taught—international norms by their external environment.

A second view of international norms contends that they emerge from the domestic politics of individual states. For example, Legro (1995) argues that adherence to norms about the laws of war during World War II emerged from the culture of military organizations within Britain, Germany, and the other combatants. Similarly, Johnston (1995) argues that Chinese norms regarding the use of force emerge from the culture of Chinese military institutions.

Once again, these understandings of the origins of international norms may be very appropriate for certain kinds of inquiries. Given my focus on legitimate dispute settlements, however, neither of them is entirely appropriate here. As I discussed earlier, the disputants that I examine do not appear to have a sufficient sense of obligation to a common community—at least with regard to the issues in dispute between them—that they would feel constrained by common systemic norms regarding those issues. That is, the issues in dispute here are of sufficient importance that states are unlikely to feel constrained by norms to which they have not given individual consent.[6] At the same time, my rationalist perspective on crisis bargaining views states as unitary actors. Thus my perspective on bargaining does not leave room for the norms to emerge as a consequence of domestic politics.

Instead, I argue that norms emerge out of the interactions of the bargaining states themselves. This understanding of norms as bilaterally or multilaterally negotiated contracts follows both from my understanding of legitimacy as rooted in the specific consent of states and from my empirical focus on bargaining between hostile states.

In their analysis of alliance norms, Kegley and Raymond (1990) articulate a three-dimensional typology of norms. First, they distinguish universal norms from those that make claims only on specific partners to the norm. Second, they distinguish between norms that are substantive and those that are procedural. "The former are rules about permissible and impermissible conduct that imply obligation"; Kegely and Raymond (1990, 22) write that "the latter specify how these rules are to be ascertained or applied." Finally, they distinguish between formal (or explicit) and informal (or tacit) norms.

Viewed in this framework, the norms I examine are partner-specific agreements. They are generally about substantive rather than procedural issues, but some of the norms do involve issues of process—especially regarding the verification of compliance. The core of the Kennedy-Khruschev understanding, for example, was a substantive agreement over the status of Cuba. However, as I will discuss in chapter 6, the agreement also included some procedural discussions about the verification of Soviet

---

[6] As I will discuss in chapter 6, Kennedy's behavior during the Cuban missile crisis illustrates this point.

withdrawal. Finally, most of the norms I examine are formal at least in the sense that they are explicitly written down. A decided minority of the legitimate dispute settlements, however, are informal or tacit.

METHODOLOGICAL PROBLEMS IN ASSESSING THE IMPACT OF NORMS

Institutionalism and constructivism have been largely concerned with the way in which norms and rules may overcome barriers to international cooperation. Unfortunately, analysts in this area have encountered great difficulty in disentangling the nexus between international norms, state interests, and state behavior. For example, as I discussed earlier, constructivist scholars contend that norms are a cause of state interests (Finnemore 1996). This is the impact of norms on preferences that I discussed earlier in this chapter. At the same time, constructivists, institutionalists, and realists would all agree that state interests both shape the construction of international norms and influence cooperative state behavior. Arthur Stein, for instance, writes, "The existence or non-existence of regimes to deal with given issues, indeed the very need to distinguish them by issue, can be attributed to different constellations of interests in different contexts." (Stein in Krasner 1983) Finally, institutionalists contend that norms have a direct and independent impact on state behavior despite the fact that norms may be caused by state interests (Gelpi 1997; Simmons 1999; Tannewald 1999).[7] As I discuss in chapter 3, norms may have this effect through the information that they convey to state decision makers about how to interpret the behavior of other states and through their utility in developing a reputation for trustworthy behavior.

This causal nexus between international norms, state interests, and state behavior is illustrated in figure 2A. The figure clearly illustrates the substantial methodological problems that exist in identifying and measuring the causal effects of norms. First, with regard to constructivist arguments, their claim that norms cause state interests is always subject to the criticism that the causal arrow moves in the other direction. For example, historian W. N. Mendicott, who is skeptical about the role of norms in maintaining the peace during the Concert of Europe during the early nineteenth century, writes that "[a]s long as Europe remembered the

---

[7] Constructivists would not disagree with the assertion that norms have a causal impact on behavior independent of their impact on state interests. For example, Tannenwald (1999) refers to this causal pathway as the "regulative" or "constraining" effect of norms. She acknowledges, however, that these effects are consistent with rationalist approaches such as institutionalism. The primary feature that distinguishes institutionalist and constructivist perspectives on norms is the constructivist emphasis on norms as a cause of state interests.

horrors of the Napoleonic wars it remained, for the most part, at peace, and therefore, in concert; but it was the peace that maintained the Concert and not the Concert that maintained the peace."[8]

Thus to demonstrate that a norm promoted cooperation by altering a state's interests, we must show that cooperation occurred because of an interest that did not exist before the regime was created, *and* we must show that the interest was clearly created by the regime and would not otherwise have existed. The extreme difficulty of this task should be quite clear. First, we would need a measure of interests in cooperation that is operationally separate from cooperative acts and which can differentiate between new and old interests. Second, and even more difficult, we would need to develop a causal model of *interests* in cooperative behavior that could be differentiated from a model of cooperative behavior itself. Such a model would have to identify variables that create interests in cooperative behavior but which are not also direct causes of cooperative behavior.[9] In sum, at this time we lack a causal model of state interests that is sophisticated enough to allow us to separate out the interaction between cooperative interests and behavior as well as the effects of norms and other factors in shaping these interests and behaviors.

Even the more limited institutionalist claims about the impact of international norms are plagued by methodological problems. As figure 2A indicates, institutionalists concede that international norms are a consequence of state interests and not their cause. Despite this concession, institutionalists claim that international norms continue to have an impact on state behavior that is independent of state interests. While this perspective avoids the difficult problems of simultaneous causation discussed earlier, it does not avoid the potential for a purely spurious correlation between norms and behavior. That is, Friedrich Kratochwil writes, "If it is 'interests' that we are to consult, then 'interests' alone should explain the emergence of cooperation. Norms and regimes are in that case, at best, epiphenomena" (Kratochwil 1989, 48). A realist critic of international norms and regimes presents this critique more bluntly stating, "All those international arrangements dignified by the label regime are only too easily upset when either the balance of bargaining power or the perception of national interest (or both together) change among states who negotiate them" (Strange in Krasner 1983).

[8] Quoted in Holsti, "Governance without Government: Polyarchy in Nineteenth-Century European International Politics," in Rosenau (1992, 47).

[9] Statistically, the problem here is one of simultaneity bias. In principle, this problem can be corrected through the use of structural equations, but as I discuss in the text, this particular question does not seem easily amenable to such an analysis. For a more complete discussion of the problem of simultaneity bias, as well as the logic behind and requirements for a structural equations analysis, see Hanushek and Jackson (1977).

State Interests, International Norms, and Cooperative Behavior

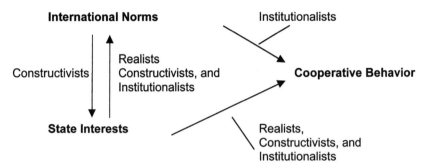

Figure 2A Theoretical Perspectives on the Causal Relationships among International Norms, State Interests, and Cooperative Behavior

Resolving this claim of a spurious correlation does not require the construction of a model of state interests—as does the simultaneity problem discussed earlier. However, it would require an accurate measurement of state "interests" in each of the cases we examine to distinguish the impact of these interests from the impact of a norm. While this might represent an easier task than resolving the simultaneity problem, the wide range of issues involved in international crises makes the development of a single accurate measure—or even a series of accurate measures—of state interests to be a daunting problem. One could, of course, pick out certain sets of issues—like territory, access to resources, and so on—that states have an "interest" in obtaining or retaining. Developing these rudimentary bases of interests into comprehensive measures that can plausibly serve as control variables in accounting for the impact of "state interests," however, is a daunting task.

As a result of these problems of simultaneity and spuriousness, we cannot assess the impact of international norms by comparing levels of cooperation between those who share norms and those who do not. Kratochwil raises a second reason to object to the analysis of levels of cooperation in assessing the importance of norms and legitimate agreements. The author writes, "Although a look at behavior is certainly necessary when we want to decide on the effectiveness of rule-guidance provided by the regime, the converse inference that a regime must be weak when we observe inconsistent behavior does not necessarily follow." (Kratochwil 1989, 63) To point to a familiar domestic example that demonstrates this point, the fact that some grocery shoppers with more than the maximum of fifteen items use the express lane when checking out should not lead us to infer that the widely recognized norm against such actions does not affect shoppers' behavior.

If the legitimate international norms are to have an effect in international relations, we must determine whether the punishments of violations can be effective in bringing compliance, and whether they can help to reestablish cooperative relations. If punishments cannot bring transgressing states back into compliance with legitimate international agreements, then these agreements are almost certain to erode and collapse over time. After all, a state that will not comply in the face of punishment is likely to retaliate, which will invite still further punishment. In addition to threatening the peace between the disputing parties, these continuing spirals of conflict may undermine support for the agreement in general as they erode confidence in its effectiveness.

For all of these reasons, I contend that a simple research design comparing levels of cooperation within and outside legitimate agreements is insufficient for understanding the effectiveness of these institutions. Instead, I believe a more informative approach is to study *responses to the violations* of legitimate agreements. Specifically, as I discuss in greater detail in chapter 4, I select cases of *reinitiated* international crises. That is, I select crises that have emerged at least once before. I then compare responses to coercive bargaining tactics in crises in which a previous legitimate dispute settlement has been violated to responses to the same types of behavior in crises in which no agreement has been violated.

Using this approach, I am able to resolve some of the long-standing empirical problems in assessing the impact of norms. In particular, my approach has the virtue of selecting cases in which we can observe a *conflict of interests*. That is, while states may initially have constructed agreements that were in their interests, the fact that they have *violated* the agreement and have initiated a new international crisis over the issue indicates that state "interests" in cooperative behavior can no longer explain the impact of norms. Returning to figure 2A, this procedure essentially seeks to hold interests constant at a level where actors do not share many common interests in a cooperative outcome.

This approach allows me to distinguish the impact of international norms from the impact of state interests on crisis-bargaining behavior. However, by selecting my cases so as to hold interests constant at a level where states are engaging in military conflict, I am obviously unable to assess arguments about the relationship between international norms and state interests.

Consequently, as I discuss in greater detail in chapter 3, my argument pursues an institutionalist rather than a constructivist perspective on international norms. Thus I frame my argument in terms of the way in which norms shape the *information* that decision makers have about the *intentions* of other actors. Throughout my derivation of hypotheses, each state's interests in cooperative outcomes remain constant. Second, rather than attempting to compare levels of cooperative behavior, I shall show that the effects of legitimate agreements may be seen more clearly in the way that they can help states to reestablish cooperative relations following the violation of an agreement. Specifically, I shall develop hypotheses concerning the way that the informational effects of norms should alter states' responses to the punishment of or accession to the violation of an agreement. With this institutionalist perspective in mind, I now turn my attention to a brief review of some of the existing evidence regarding the informational and reputational effects of norms.

EXPANDING THE CANVAS: INSTITUTIONALIST EVIDENCE ON THE IMPACT OF NORMS

While the renewed interest in norms as they relate to international security is relatively young, students of the international political economy have been speaking in these terms for quite some time. Most prominently, as I mentioned earlier, a very substantial body of work on international regimes has developed in the international political economy literature over the past twenty years.[10] International regimes may increase cooperation in a variety of ways—not all of which relate to the concepts of norms or legitimacy. By bundling issues together, for example, regimes lower the marginal cost of negotiating new international agreements. Thus once one has set up a set of rules and procedures providing for the international exchange of mail, it becomes easier to agree on a system for delivering overnight packages, since the postal regime may be used as a model and as an infrastructure for implementing the agreement. Similarly, the organizations that support international regimes often collect extensive information about the behavior of member states, making it easier to identify cheaters.

However, most of the arguments about the effects of international regimes are related to the legitimacy of the agreements that constitute them. For example, Robert Keohane has noted that because of unequal information about other states' preferences and intentions, states may be unable to determine whether others have hostile or benign intentions. But by defining explicit standards of behavior that member states are obligated to uphold, he argues, regimes facilitate the construction of reputations both for cooperating with states that comply with international

---

[10] The literature on international regimes is much too extensive to be represented here in its entirety. A few of the most prominent works in this area are Keohane and Nye (1989); Krasner (1983); Keohane (1984); Oye (1986); and Keohane (1986).

norms and for punishing those which do not. These reputations, then, can help cooperative states to identify one another. Specifically, Keohane writes that

> a government's reputation therefore becomes an important asset in persuading others to enter into an agreement with it. International regimes help governments to assess others' reputations by providing standards of behavior against which performance can be measured, by linking these standards to specific issues, and by providing forums, often through international organizations, in which these evaluations can be made. (Keohane 1984, 94)

More recently, scholars such as Simmons (1999) have extended this line of analysis to an empirical analysis of legal commitments to the IMF.

Although much of the institutionalist work concerning the role of norms in international relations has been in the area of political economy, some interest in this topic could be found in security studies before the recent renaissance. For example, the nineteenth-century Concert of Europe has often been studied as an example of the most prominent "security regime."[11] The Concert clearly established a norm regarding the maintenance of the existing balance of power in Europe. Toward that end, it also established rules for altering the status quo, and it even went to the lengths of calculating out units of national power in terms of troops, population, and control of strategic territories. Moreover, the Concert established decision-making procedures such as the Congress system, and enshrined consensus-seeking compromise as the accepted mechanism for shaping policy. Finally, the leaders of nineteenth-century Europe also provided for sanctions to enforce the rules of the regime.

As I mentioned earlier, methodological problems have led some to question the Concert's effectiveness in limiting international conflict, but nearly all scholars agree that it represents the most comprehensive attempt to establish legitimate norms and rules to guide security relations in modern history. Institutional theorists, moreover, point to it as the quintessential example of norm-guided security behavior. In assessing more recent eras of international politics, however, institutionalists have tended to look for more limited examples of norm-guided behavior. A number of the chapters in Haftendorn, Keohane, and Wallander (1999) focus on more recent examples of the informational effects of what I would term international norms.

---

[11] For a good discussion of the structure and effectiveness of the Concert of Europe, see Holsti in Rosenau (1992) and Richardson in Haftendorn, Keohane, and Wallander (1999). The empirical work on other norms in the security area from an institutionalist perspective remains fairly limited, but attention to this area is increasing. See, for example, Wallander (2000).

Finally, some work using computer simulations of international interaction is also relevant to the institutionalist perpective on international norms. For example, Robert Axelrod's work concerning the evolution of cooperation is at least implicitly concerned with the development of norms (Axelrod 1984, 1986). Axelrod's most successful strategies, such as tit-for-tat (TFT), are those that tacitly communicate with the other player to construct what might be considered a norm of reciprocity. I should note, however, that this use of the word "norm" is limited to the game theoretic interpretation that I discussed earlier.

Subsequent research has revealed several strategies that outperform tit-for-tat in a variety of circumstances. One such strategy has become known as "Pavlov," and it is based on the simple principle of: "win-stay, lose-shift" (Nowak and Sigmund 1992, 1993).[12] That is, a player will use the same strategy it did in the previous round if it successfully cheated the opponent or if the two players cooperated, but it will change to the opposite strategy if it was exploited by its opponent or if both players defected.

A second strategy that appears to be superior to TFT in a wide variety of circumstances is known as "contrite tit-for-tat" (CTFT). This strategy has proven particularly successful in prisoner's dilemma games that allow for the possibility of "noise" in the interaction—such as misperceiving a cooperative act as a defection or an unintentional or involuntary defection (Signorino 1996). CTFT behaves like TFT with the exception that if during a particular round of the game a player defects while its opponent cooperates, CTFT requires the defecting player to cooperate during the subsequent round. Moreover, CTFT will then wipe the slate clean after this apology and act as if the game were beginning again. In this way, CTFT causes players to apologize, accept punishment for their transgression, and restore the cooperative relationship without the risk of echoing defections that can result from strictly "tit-for-tat" behavior.

Interestingly, the behavioral prescriptions of both Pavlov and CTFT are similar to those described by my normative bargaining model. Thus perhaps one way of thinking about the adoption of norms and dispute settlements is that they are costly signals that allow states to weed out aggressive states so that they may adopt a Pavlov or CTFT strategy rather than the less productive and forgiving tit-for-tat.[13]

---

[12] I would like to thank Stephen Rosen for bringing this literature to my attention.

[13] Unfortunately, empirical tests of the reciprocity norm implied by Axelrod and others have generally correlated states' levels of hostility toward one another, and have taken evidence of a positive correlation as supportive of a link between reciprocity and cooperation (Goldstein and Freeman 1990; Goldstein 1991; Ward 1992). In fact, these studies simply document the use of reciprocal strategies by nation-states. They do not address the crucial link between punishing violations of the norm of reciprocity (i.e., unprovoked defection) and the restoration of cooperative relationships.

Contesting Legitimacy as an Explanatory Concept

These institutionalist perspectives developed as a critique of the traditional realist approach to international politics.[14] Realists, of course, have been quick to respond to this attack. In general, as indicated in figure 2A, this debate has centered on the manner in which states identify their interests and the relationship between international institutions, legitimacy, and national power. For example, some authors have suggested that while Axelrod's results are interesting on a theoretical level, the restrictive assumptions that are necessary to generate the results make their practical utility for the empirical analysis of world politics somewhat dubious (Grieco 1988, 1990). Drawing on this traditional approach, Joseph Grieco has argued that

> the major goal of states in any relationship is not to attain the highest possible individual gain or payoff. Instead, *the fundamental goal of states in any relationship is to prevent others from achieving advances in their relative capabilities. . . .* Indeed, states may even forego increases in their absolute capabilities if doing so prevents others from achieving even greater gains [emphasis original]. (Grieco 1988, 498)

This set of assumptions about state interests has become known as "defensive positionalism" or more generally "defensive realism." Other realists, such as Mearsheimer (2001), press even further than Grieco toward what has become known as "offensive realism." This view contends that states are driven to aggressive behavior because of the need to seize as much power as is materially possible. If either Grieco or Mearsheimer are accurate in their description of the international system, then institutionalist analyses—based as they are on the assumptions of egoistic rather

[14] As I discussed earlier, "realists" are actually a loose conglomeration of theorists who share a few very basic assumptions about international politics. Keohane argues that the realist approach boils down to three assumptions: (1) states are the central actors in world politics, (2) states behave as if they were unitary and rational, and (3) states seek to maximize their power (Keohane 1986). Clearly, there remains room for fairly sharp differences underneath this broad canopy. In addition to focusing on different substantive areas of international relations, realists also emphasize different causal paths between power resources and foreign policy behavior. "Structural" realists, for example, focus their attention on the structure of the international system. Rational deterrence theorists, on the other hand, are just as "realist" in terms of their basic assumptions, but they focus on dyadic variables such as the relative capabilities and levels of resolve in analyzing international conflict. I believe that the challenges to regime theory do not relate directly to "structural" arguments about the polarity of the system. As mentioned earlier, the debate centers on the nature of state preferences and the relative importance of military power resources and norms. Thus when I discuss "realists," I am referring to this latter group, and not those concerned with polarity and the incidence of war.

than positional actors and variable rather than zero-sum games—miss the mark.[15]

Snidal (Snidal 1991a, 1991b) responded to Grieco's attacks by demonstrating that the analysis of "absolute gains" in prisoner's dilemmas is only inappropriate when states are solely concerned with relative gains *and* only two states are interacting.[16] Snidal's conclusion suggests that it is *Grieco's* approach—not to mention Mearsheimer's—that is guilty of making restrictive assumptions, but ultimately the applicability of these two models may be an empirical rather than a theoretical question.

In addressing this empirical question, a number of scholars have speculated that international institutions may be limited in their ability to shape security affairs.[17] Although these scholars may be correct in pointing out that the conflicts facing states are more severe in the security area, this difference is, at most, a matter of degree. There is little *a priori* reason to believe that relations concerning security and political economy should be qualitatively different. Kratochwil, for example, notes that such arguments seem "rather persuasive in pinpointing the reasons why 'regimes' should be 'weak' in these circumstances. Nevertheless, it would seem necessary to separate the question of strength, or effectiveness, of rules and norms from the question of their existence and function; otherwise we are likely to end up with a circular argument or some type of *ad hocery*." (Kratochwil 1989, 46)

Alternatively, the skeptics may be correct if we take their critique to mean that a comprehensive multilateral security institution along the lines of the Concert of Europe has been out of our reach for some time. Successful international economic institutions, however, have tended to be narrowly defined and issue oriented rather than sweeping and comprehensive. Even the largest economic organizations such as the World Trade Organization (WTO), for example, do not attempt to regulate all economic interaction, but limit themselves to a single set of issues. Should we not expect a similar patchwork pattern in the security area?

For example, numerous scholars have argued that certain aspects of even the bitterly hostile relations between the United States and the So-

---

[15] For some similar critiques see Jervis (1988) or Goldstein and Freeman (1990).

[16] For another critique of Grieco's approach, see Powell (1991).

[17] Perhaps the most influential of these statements was made by Jervis (1983). He argued that institutions were unlikely to be effective in security affairs because the costs of being exploited were too high and because security affairs often involved "zero-sum" issues. However, realists argue that security relations are nearly zero-sum because the only reliable way for a state to ensure its security is to maximize its power relative to that of other states. If institutionalists are correct in arguing that security can be gained through other means—such as the construction of norms—then security relations would not be zero-sum. In a sense, this realist assertion that security can only be maintained through superior power resources is the central presumption that I am attempting to challenge in this work.

viet Union during the Cold War were moderated by limited and some-times tacit security agreements. In discussing the operation of "primitive rules of prudence" in US-Soviet relations, Graham Allison writes, "What preserved the peace, therefore, was a *web of mutual understandings* of what each superpower could and could not do [emphasis original]." (Allison and Ury 1989, 10) One prominent example of such a "primitive rule" which Allison points to is the superpowers' tacit agreement not to interfere in the other's areas of "dominant security concern."

Jervis (1983, 188) argued that such understandings cannot be counted as "security regimes" because they "derive from the ability of each state to punish the other if it steps too far out of bounds and from each one's ability to see that the other's restraint depends on its own moderation." This criticism misses the point, however. Of course these agreements depend upon the threat of enforcement for their effectiveness. How could it be otherwise? Keohane argues that regimes are effective because of their ability to identify "defectors," but this information should have little effect on state behavior—at least from an institutionalist perspective—if there is no possibility that the defectors will be punished. In the absence of supranational institutions capable of enforcing the agreement's injunctions, this task will inevitably be left to the contracting parties that constructed the norms and rules. The fact that the states themselves carry out this enforcement should not lead us to conclude that the norms are of no consequence. On the contrary, it is the presence of a norm that redefines coercive behavior as a "punishment" or as "enforcement." By reframing coercive behavior in this manner, norms can help to facilitate compliance and a reestablishment of cooperation.

To date, the institutionalists and their skeptics have each mustered a scattering of case studies to support their own positions (Oye 1986; Grieco 1990; Mearsheimer 1994/1995, 2001; Haftendorn, Keohane, and Wallander 1999; Wallander 1999). Unfortunately, no study has yet moved beyond debating illustrative cases of potentially norm-guided behavior toward a more systematic demonstration of when and where these patterns of behavior are likely to appear.

Nonetheless, even institutionalists concede that their empirical evidence for the independent impact of international norms and institutions is thin (Keohane and Martin 1995). The evidence regarding the independent impact of norms and institutions on security-related behavior is especially so. I hope that this work represents a more complete comparative test of realist and institutionalist frameworks as they relate to international crisis bargaining. As such, I hope that my findings will press the empirical debate over the impact of norms to the center of security affairs.

Doing so, however, requires me to derive specific hypotheses that can distinguish between the realist and institutionalist approaches to crisis bargaining. It is to this next task that I turn my attention in chapter 3.

Norms, Dispute Settlements and Hypotheses on Crisis-Bargaining Behavior

The central argument of this work concerns international agreements—dispute settlements in particular—and the information that these agreements give decision makers about the intentions of other actors. Perhaps the defining characteristic of international politics is that it lacks a recognized authority to arbitrate disputes. This anarchic environment creates a great deal of conflict between states as they each seek their own individual security. It has also caused many theorists to abandon the concept of legitimacy in favor of military capabilities when seeking to understand international security. While I do not wish to deny the importance of traditional power resources in shaping international relations, I do wish to reexamine the role that legitimacy can play in explaining cooperation in security affairs. I will argue that international agreements such as dispute settlements allow states to construct standards of behavior that they construe as legitimate. States, in turn, can legitimate their behavior in terms of these standards. The construction of these legitimate points of reference solidifies cooperation between states by helping them to *reestablish* cooperative relations should the agreement be violated.

In making this argument regarding legitimacy and international agreements, I employ a rational choice approach to modeling state behavior. In addition, since I conceive of states as unitary actors, I consistently assume the existence of a single dominant foreign policy decision maker within each state. No one seriously argues that rational choice is a perfect descriptive representation of human decision processes. However, the oversimplifications of a rational approach can be useful inasmuch as they simplify reality by capturing the *essential* characteristics of a process while abstracting away from many of the details. Although rational choice theory is not always perfectly descriptive of the decision process, I believe there is solid evidence that it does a good job of summarizing the essential processes that people go through in making decisions—especially decisions that have important implications for them. Moreover, the empirical success that many scholars have had in using rational choice models suggests that my use of this approach may be fruitful.[1]

---

[1] The list of prominent empirical studies taking a rational choice approach to modeling foreign policy decisions is far too long to recite here. Three examples of explicit tests of the

I will present my argument in four steps. I will begin by describing the theoretical context for my argument concerning international norms. This argument is rooted in the literature on signaling games and the role of information in shaping behavior. In particular, I will discuss why I believe that international norms can provide information to state leaders that alter their interpretations of bargaining signals. Second, I will present the conventional wisdom regarding bargaining strategies in international crises, the signals they send, and their hypothesized effects on crisis outcomes. This conventional argument is rooted in rationalist theories of deterrence and coercion. These theories have generally been regarded as "realist" approaches to crisis bargaining. Third, I will derive hypotheses from my own argument about international norms. I frame these hypotheses in terms of the way that norms alter the interpretation of bargaining signals so as to generate deviations from the conventional realist approach to crisis bargaining. Finally, I will return to the realist model of crisis bargaining to derive alternative hypotheses about the impact of military capabilities and other factors on crisis outcomes.

How Norms Influence Crisis Bargaining

Within the rationalist paradigm that I adopt, there remain several different ways in which norms could influence international conflict. First, norms could determine who is an "actor" in international politics. Constructivists often refer to this influence as the *constitutive* impact of norms, or they refer to norms as shaping actors' *identities* (Katzenstein 1996; Tannenwald 1999). The norm of state sovereignty, for example, has had a constitutive effect by privileging states as legitimate actors in international politics (Krasner 1995; Hurd 1999).[2]

Second, international norms could shape the *preferences* of actors in the international system. This is also a causal pathway that is frequently emphasized by constructivists. Rather than assuming a particular set of preferences, this approach problematizes state interests and argues that states (and other international actors) look to international norms to construct

---

rational models of crisis bargaining are Huth (1988); Huth and Russett (1993); and Pape (1996).

[2] Ironically, although Krasner views his work as a critique of the normative impact of sovereignty, he also discovers evidence that may lead to a very different conclusion. Krasner's central argument is that sovereignty was constructed and articulated as a norm to privilege and protect the positions of the Great Powers in the international system. However, Krasner also notes that their endorsement of the norm led the Great Powers to respect the borders of small, weak states that emerged in the wake of the collapse of the Holy Roman Empire. The reticence to conquer such weak states would appear to be significant evidence of sovereignty's powerful constitutive impact.

their own utility functions—to use the rationalist term. Finnemore (1996), for example, argues that states often learn—or are taught—what is in their interest through the spread of norms through international society. Similarly, Goertz and Diehl (1992) argue that normative beliefs about colonialism shaped whether states viewed the continuation of colonial empires to be "in their interest."

While these are important and potentially powerful causal pathways for the impact of norms, I do not rely on them in constructing my argument. First, as I discussed in chapter 2, disentangling the impact of norms and interests on one another is fraught with difficult problems of simultaneity bias. We lack both a sufficiently specific theoretical model of state interests as well as sufficiently nuanced data to build a general system of equations that could address this issue for a wide range of international military crises. As I also discussed in chapter 2, my solution to this methodological problem is to examine the impact of norms when state interests clearly conflict. Thus rather than focusing directly on norms as a source of cooperation, I demonstrate that the effect of norms can be observed without the persistent concerns about spuriousness and simultaneity by studying responses to the *violations* of norms. This procedure effectively differentiates between the impact of norms and interests on cooperative behavior. It is clearly not suited, however, to investigating the relationship between norms and interests.

Moreover, while these kinds of effects may be important in a variety of contexts, they do not appear to be relevant to most of the types of crises I examine. The dispute settlements I examine do not generally redefine the identities of actors in the dispute nor do they generally alter state preferences. As I discussed in chapter 1, the collapse of the Cold War in the wake of the Soviet "new thinking" may be an example of norms and ideas reshaping interests. However, such situations would seem to be relatively rare in the study of militarized crisis bargaining.

Consequently, my argument does not assume that norms alter actors' identities or preferences. In other words, I adopt institutionalist premises about the impact of international norms. Like most of the recent institutionalist scholarship, I assume that realists are correct in their assumptions about the egoistic preferences of state leaders (Keohane 1984; Keohane and Martin 1995). This approach has the virtue of simplifying the empirical problem of identifying the impact of norms. Moreover, by addressing realist arguments about crisis bargaining on their own terms, institutionalist arguments have the potential to show that realist conclusions about the role of norms in international security affairs do not derive from realist premises.

So how can norms affect crisis bargaining within an institutionalist framework? As I discussed in chapter 2, game theorists often view norms

as game equilibria. This conception is not useful for my argument, however. As I noted earlier, to disentangle the impact of norms from the
impact of state interests on cooperative behavior, I specifically select cases
in which state interests conflict (i.e., military crises). One of my key explanatory variables is whether or not a norm has been violated in this
context. But if norms are game equilibria, then no state has an incentive
to violate a norm once it has been established. This static conception of
norms is not well suited to examining the dynamic issue of how norms
can be reestablished after a violation.

Finally, norms can be viewed as influencing the beliefs and ideas of
state leaders. This is becoming perhaps the most prevalent causal pathway
emphasized by institutionalist scholars (Keohane and Goldstein 1993;
Gelpi 1997; Simmons 1999).[3] Specifically, I argue that norms affect
crisis-bargaining behavior because of their impact as signals of intent that
shape the interpretation and meaning attached to bargaining behavior
and because of the way that they engage states' reputations for being
trustworthy in the sense of adhering to their commitments.

As I discussed in chapter 2, institutionalist arguments about reputation
for trustworthiness originated with arguments about international economics and monetary affairs. Such concerns might not initially seem central to militarized crises. Much of the research on crisis bargaining, however, suggests that successful bargaining is a function of both a reputation
for toughness *and* a reputation for trustworthiness (Axelrod 1984; Huth
1988; Leng 1993). Recent literature on war termination (Goemans 2000)
also indicates that leaders need to show concern for their reputation for
trustworthiness *even* in the midst of a full-scale war. Without such a reputation it becomes nearly impossible to implement a settlement that will end
the war, short of utter destruction for one of the combatants. The fact that
most wars do not end in the utter destruction of one of the combatants
indicates that leaders *do* cultivate a reputation for keeping promises even in
the most confrontational circumstances. What most theories of crisis bargaining and war termination have not recognized, however, is the importance of norms in creating these reputations for trustworthiness.

[3] Another causal pathway that has recently been explored by institutionalist scholars is the
impact of "legalization" of norms (Abbott et al. 2000; Goldstein et al. 2000; Keohane,
Moravcsik, and Slaughter 2000). This avenue of inquiry seeks to bridge the gap between
the study of international relations and international law. Keohane, Moravcsik, and Slaughter (2000), for example, investigate the growth of "legalized" dispute resolution. Their
analysis depends heavily, however, on the *delegation* of authority to neutral third parties
such as courts and dispute resolution panels. This argument may be useful in a variety of
contexts, but it does not apply well to the crises that I examine. The negotiation, application, and enforcement of the dispute settlements I examine are generally quite bilateral. For
a review of the emerging nexus between international relations and international legal
scholarship, see Slaughter, Tumello, and Wood (1998) and Slaughter-Burley (1993).

An examination of the cases in my data set also indicates that even very bitter rivals care whether their enemies believe that they will keep their promises. As the discussion in chapter 6 indicates, the USSR was quite sensitive to the claim that they had violated their promise not to base offensive missiles in Cuba in the wake of the Cuban missile crisis. Soviet leaders went to great pains to avoid stating directly that they had violated their agreement and clearly wanted American leaders to recognize that they had resumed compliance after being caught. In particular, private Soviet statements to Castro during the construction of the Kennedy-Khrushchev understanding indicate that the Soviet leaders cared about their own reputation with the United States, and also believed that American concerns about maintaining a reputation for trustworthiness represented an important mechanism for constraining the United States.

Since I will examine the violations of security norms as embodied in legitimate dispute settlements, my analysis will focus on behavior in reinitiated international crises. Thus in each case I analyze a state that has previously initiated a dispute. This previous dispute was then resolved either with or without the conclusion of a legitimate dispute settlement. Then, in each case, one of the states reinitiated the dispute over the same issue. I identify the state that is first to threaten or take militarized action to alter the outcome of the previous dispute as the challenger in the reinitiated dispute. The defender, on the other hand, is the state against which the challenger's militarized threat or act is directed. In each case, the defender was forced to respond to the challenger by using some kind of bargaining strategy in an attempt to persuade the challenger to yield. Finally, each reinitiated dispute is resolved in one of three ways: (1) the challenger remains intransigent and forces concessions on the defender, (2) the challenger accepts a compromise, or (3) the challenger abandons its bid to overturn the status quo. I will focus my attention on explaining the challenger's response to the defender's bargaining strategy. That is, I hope to predict whether or not the defender will be able to persuade the challenger to abandon its revision of the status quo.

International Politics and Signaling Games

The informational and reputational effects of international norms are perhaps most clearly understood through an analogy to rational choice games of signaling and adverse selection.[4] The problems of signaling and communication are fundamental to the study of international relations.

[4] It is important to emphasize that signaling games are used here as an analogy to guide thinking. While analogies may not fit in all of their details, the logic behind this line of argument is useful for illuminating the institutionalist view of norms.

In a loosely structured bargaining environment like the international system, determining the intentions and preferences of one's potential partners and adversaries is of crucial importance, yet this information is inherently private and difficult to assess. As a result, states are forced to rely on signals to communicate their intentions to others. As I argued previously, I do not believe that this decentralized environment implies that all notions of order and legitimacy must be set aside. It does imply, however, that the construction of legitimate standards is likely to be a decentralized process—beginning with dyads of actors and then possibly spreading to their neighbors and allies. Individual states must take the initiative to signal one another in an effort to construct mutually recognized standards of legitimate behavior. These standards will support cooperative behavior so that a single attempt to "cheat" on one's partners need not sour a generally cooperative relationship.

This situation is similar to what in the economics and game theory literature is referred to as a game of "signaling."[5] Signaling is a game that is played between two players—often labeled the principal and the agent. To begin the game, the agent's "type" is selected at random without the knowledge of the principal. The agent must then make some signal of its type to the principal. Finally, the principal and agent must decide whether or not to cooperate on the basis of the signal. The central problem in this game is for the principal to sort out the differing types of agents so that it can cooperate with the appropriate agents without getting exploited by the others.

In general there are two types of equilibria in signaling games: pooling and separating equilibria. In the pooling equilibria, the principal is unable to distinguish between the differing types because the agents' signals are unpersuasive. As a result, the principal treats all agents in a similar manner. In the separating equilibria, on the other hand, the agents find a way to send persuasive signals, allowing the principal to distinguish between the differing types and to treat each accordingly. Clearly, this outcome is more efficient for the principal since it may engage in cooperation with willing agents without suffering from the exploitative attempts of uncooperative ones.

The key to sending *persuasive* signals and achieving the separating equilibria is that the act of sending the signal must have *differential* costs for the two types of agents. For example, if agents may be one of two types (I and II), then for an agent's signal that it is type II to be persuasive, the signal must be more costly to send for type I than it is for type II. For a signal to be persuasive, the current costs of sending the signal

[5] My discussion of signaling follows closely from Rasmussen (1989); chapters 8 and 9.

combined with the potential costs of being exposed as a liar must out-weigh any expected future benefits of deception.[6]

Dispute Settlements as Persuasive Signals

At first glance, one might not think that dispute settlement agreements would have much persuasive force as signals of intent given the nature of the issues at stake in many militarized disputes. Since these settlements often relate to core security concerns, substantial gains can sometimes be made by deceiving one's opponent. Conversely, of course, a state risks some rather severe costs of being exploited when cooperating on such issues. Moreover, one might argue that there are few costs involved in signing an agreement—which after all is only a piece of paper—and even fewer in concluding a tacit settlement. Despite these obstacles, however, some research findings suggest that the legitimacy that dispute settle-ments grant to certain activities may have an effect on future dispute outcomes. In summarizing the empirical findings from their sweeping work on crisis bargaining, for example, Snyder and Diesing write:

> Perceptions of legitimacy are potent in determining bargaining power and outcomes. That is, the party that believes it is in the right and communicates this belief to an opponent who has some doubts about the legitimacy of his own position, nearly always wins. . . . These examples do not conclusively prove that legitimacy superiority always wins in the absence of gross military inequality but they do show that "being in the right" when this is recognized by others is a strong bargaining asset. (Snyder and Diesing 1977, 498–99)

A THEORY OF NORMS AND CRISIS BARGAINING

If there is some evidence that settlements can affect future dispute behav-ior, perhaps we should reexamine the costs of concluding settlements and their persuasive power as signals. My specific contention is that legitimate dispute settlements make it easier for defenders to protect the mutually

---

[6] See Rasmussen (1989) for a more detailed mathematical derivation of the solution to this problem. As one might expect, this situation implies that it will be more difficult to send persuasive signals about an issue that is of great value to both parties or where it is difficult to detect cheating by one of the parties. This result precisely parallels Jervis's expec-tation that cooperation in security will be more difficult than in areas such as international political economy where the costs of being exploited are lower. See Jervis in Krasner, ed. (1983). For a detailed analysis of when a state might attempt to undertake such a decep-tion, see Axelrod (1979).

agreed upon status quo for two complementary reasons. First, dispute settlements alter the challenger's interpretation of the defender's bargaining behavior in subsequent disputes by making coercive strategies appear more legitimate and less threatening. Second, dispute settlements, in combination with the defender's bargaining strategy, create substantial reputational costs for states that violate them.

Dispute Settlements as Normative Referents

I hypothesize that dispute settlements will act as normative referents that shape the interpretation of bargaining strategies. In particular, settlements provide the contracting parties with two important pieces of information that alter the context of subsequent crises. First, these agreements communicate to each state that its opponent is not fundamentally hostile. That is, they provide a focal point for resolving the crisis that both states recognize that their opponent prefers to an escalation of the conflict. As I noted earlier, the anarchic nature of international politics makes it difficult to determine the true preferences and intentions of other states (Mearsheimer 1994/1995, 2001). This pervasive uncertainty often generates strong fears on the part of national decision makers—especially with regard to their security affairs. The sensitivity of security interests makes state leaders extremely wary of exploitation in such matters. Consequently, state leaders are reluctant to make any concessions in international crises for fear that such concessions will be interpreted as signs of weakness which will cause the opposing state to escalate its demands. Such vigilance may successfully shield states from potential aggressors, but in doing so it often unnecessarily provokes hostile actions toward states that had no such aggressive intent (Jervis 1978). However, I hypothesize that dispute settlements can break this spiral of conflict by acting as a focal point that persuades each state that its opponent is not unalterably aggressive. In particular, if the defending state uses a highly coercive bargaining strategy following the violation of the settlement, the challenger can remain confident that the defender will not make demands for concessions that move beyond the previous settlement. This knowledge of the opponent's intentions alters the interpretation of subsequent crisis-bargaining behavior. Threatening and potentially aggressive behavior will no longer necessarily be categorized as a sign of aggressive intent. While outright aggression remains a possible interpretation for such actions, the fact that the opposing state has demonstrated its willingness to compromise will lead state leaders to search for other possible interpretations.

Second, I argue that dispute settlements introduce the concept of legitimacy into a relationship by defining for each of the contracting parties a set of acts that are proscribed. The anarchic nature of international politics has created a context in which notions of "right" and "wrong" are not useful categories for describing state behavior. Realist theory, for example, holds that states defend their interests, and argues that labeling such actions as "good" or "bad" is just beside the point (Walzer 1977; Carr 1946 is an exception). By consenting to a legitimate dispute settlement that proscribes a particular set of acts, however, the contracting parties create a normative dimension to their relations which gives them new categories for interpreting behavior. Because each contracting party recognizes this new normative dimension, I believe that the conclusion of a settlement enables state leaders to understand both their own actions and those of the opposing state as "legitimate" or "illegitimate" with regard to the issues covered by the settlement in a way that was not possible before its conclusion.

Dispute Settlements as Reputational Constraints

In addition to acting as normative referents, dispute settlements also inflict reputational costs on states that violate them. Robert Jervis (1970) has outlined a number of costs that states suffer by deceiving other states, most of which fall under the label of audience costs.[7] My argument focuses on the costs that international audiences (i.e., other governments) may impose on state leaders if they do not keep their commitments. In particular, such deception can have a devastating effect on states' bargaining reputations. Bargaining reputation is a crucial asset for states because it allows them to achieve many objectives that would otherwise be impossible. For example, deterrence theory focuses on the importance of a reputation for toughness to prevent international crises from escalating to the point of war. Despite the central role of a reputation for toughness in realist theories of crisis bargaining, these theories have often ignored the importance of other kinds of reputations. Cooperation theory, for example, focuses on the importance of a reputation for trustworthiness in resolving international crises (Oye 1985; Axelrod 1984). Just as the reputation for toughness is important in deterring an attack or escalation of force, a reputation for upholding one's word is critical if states are to convince others to cooperate with them (Larson 1992).

The notion that international agreements are powerful because states invest their reputations in them is not new. This argument implies that

[7] The concept of audience costs has received a great deal of attention in the literature on crisis bargaining. See for example, Schelling (1960, 1966); Jervis (1970); and Fearon (1994a). Much of the recent literature has focused on the influence of domestic audiences on crisis bargaining. See, for example, Bueno de Mesquita and Lalman (1992); Fearon (1994b); Schultz (1999); Gelpi and Griesdorf (2001); and Gelpi and Grieco (1999).

states should be wary of violating a dispute settlement because of the damage such violations would do to its reputation for trustworthiness. It has little to say, however, about the central focus of this work: the resolution of disputes *after* an agreement has been violated. By adding a corollary to this argument, however, I generate some hypotheses about how reputational concerns will affect bargaining *after* the violation of a dispute settlement. In particular, I hypothesize that the reputational costs of violating a settlement will depend significantly on the *response* of the injured party to the violation. For example, if the defending state makes no response to the violation, then the cheating state will suffer fewer reputational costs for at least three reasons. First, the lack of a vigorous response will limit the amount of international attention given to the violation. The event is more likely to be handled at a lower level of bureaucratic authority, and prominent decision makers in other states are not likely to spend much time considering the issue. Second, if the injured state does not object vehemently to the violation, others may view this response as tacit consent to the unilateral alteration of the settlement. Under these circumstances the damage to the trespassing state's reputation is limited because its actions are less likely to be viewed as illegitimate. Finally, in the absence of an attempt to enforce the previous settlement, it is difficult for others to infer how seriously the trespassing state takes its international commitments. Rather than inferring that the trespasser is a renegade state that cannot be trusted to uphold any agreement, for instance, states might make the more limited inference that the trespasser is willing to cheat on its obligations if it is *allowed* to do so. Such a state might be considered sufficiently trustworthy by another state that is willing to enforce the terms of any common understandings. According to this same logic, continuing to violate a settlement even after the injured state has vigorously tried to enforce the accord will involve much larger reputational costs for the trespasser. The strong response of the injured state is likely to draw greater international attention; no state could construe the trespasser's actions as a consensual revision of the previous agreement; and it would be clear to all that the trespassing state cannot be held to its obligations even through the threat or use of force.

THE REALIST APPROACH TO CRISIS BARGAINING

In presenting my specific hypotheses on crisis bargaining, I will begin by considering how challengers will respond to various bargaining strategies in the *absence* of a previous dispute settlement. After I have established the realist "null hypothesis" against which my argument about norms should be judged, I will turn my attention to how normative referents and reputational costs should alter the challenger's response to the defender's bargaining strategy.

Previous work on crisis bargaining has identified three strategies that may be ordered on a continuum from least to most coercive (Huth 1988; Leng and Wheeler 1979). A strategy of appeasement—which exerts little or no coercive pressure—consists of offering concessions to accommodate the challenger's demands. A firm-but-flexible strategy applies a moderate amount of coercive pressure by resisting the challenger's demands and threatening retaliation, while at the same time offering alternative compromise solutions. Finally, a bullying strategy—the most highly coercive of the approaches—consists of making counterthreats and demanding unconditional compliance.

States use these bargaining strategies in international crises to convey their resolve in defending their interests balanced with their desire to avoid war. In this work I focus on the effect of the defender's bargaining strategy on the challenger's response in a crisis. Thus I turn now to a description of the challenger's expected responses to each of the defender's possible bargaining strategies. Following the challenger's initiation of the crisis, a strategy of appeasement conveys an appearance of weakness on the part of the defender because it indicates that the defender's desire to avoid war outweighs its resolve to defend its security interests. Under these circumstances, the challenger is likely to view the crisis as an opportunity to improve its position. Thus appeasement is likely to make the challenger more insistent on overturning the status quo. A moderately coercive response, however, represented by the firm-but-flexible strategy, is more likely to be successful in persuading the challenger to back down. In his discussion of extended deterrence crises, Huth (1988) argues that the firm-but-flexible strategy succeeds by conveying a dual message to the challenger of both resolve and restraint.

> Opposition to the demands of the potential attacker demonstrates determination to support the protégé, whereas conditional offers of compromise signal to the potential attacker the possibility of reaching an agreement which protects its political position and bargaining reputation. If the potential attacker has decided to back down from its initial threat, the defender's offer of conditional compromise may provide the means to de-escalate. (Huth 1988, 52–53)

Thus the moderately coercive firm-but-flexible strategy conveys strength without triggering fears of aggression by the defender. Finally, bullying behavior should be less successful than a firm-but-flexible stance because it emphasizes the defender's resolve to stand firm without giving the challenger an acceptable way to extricate itself from the crisis. The challenger will fear making concessions in response to such strongly coercive tactics because such concessions may encourage additional demands by the defender. That is, the challenger fears developing a reputation for weakness which might result in future aggression. As a result, it becomes unwilling to make concessions, even to return to the status quo ante.

> HYPOTHESIS 1. *In the absence of a previous dispute settlement to guide their bargaining behavior, the relationship between the coerciveness of the defender's bargaining strategy and the challenger's insistence on overturning the* status quo *will be described by a concave curvilinear function. That is, appeasement will make the challenger highly insistent, a firm-but-flexible strategy will make the challenger less insistent, and bullying strategies will again make the challenger highly insistent on overturning the* status quo.

This hypothesis represents the conventional wisdom on international crisis-bargaining behavior and emerges from existing realist scholarship.[8] I do not wish to assert that the logic behind this argument is wrong, only that it is incomplete. This conventional view ignores both the role of norms as normative referents and the reputational costs of violating them. For both of these reasons, the bargaining strategies taken in response to the violation of a dispute settlement will elicit a different response from the challenger in a crisis.

HYPOTHESES ON NORMS AND CRISIS BARGAINING

While their roles as normative referents and reputational constraints represent two different ways in which dispute settlements can influence crisis bargaining, these arguments make identical predictions about the nature of crisis bargaining following the violation of a settlement. First, let us consider the influence of normative referents. In the absence of a previous settlement, I have argued that highly coercive bullying tactics on the part of the defender will cause the challenger to fear additional demands for concessions by the defender and to increase its insistence on overturning the status quo. If the challenger is in violation of a dispute settlement, however, bullying tactics should not result in intransigence by the challenger. To begin with, the previous settlement acts as a mutually recognized focal point for the solution of the current crisis. The chal-

---

[8] This hypothesized relationship follows from the works of Huth and Leng, among others, concerning crisis bargaining. Huth (1988) derives his expectation for this relationship from deterrence theory. Leng, on the other hand, attempts to distinguish this argument from realism and deterrence theory (Leng 1993; Leng and Wheeler 1979). Closer examination reveals, however, that Leng's version of realism includes some assumptions about the nature of the opposing state that are not central to realism or deterrence theory (Leng 1993, 6–10). Specifically, Leng appears to conflate what Jervis (1978) has labeled the "deterrence model" with deterrence theory. Thus his expectations about crisis bargaining are consistent with most realist approaches. For a critique of the conflation of deterrence theory with the "deterrence model," see Huth and Russett (1990).

lenger can feel safe backing down to terms of the previous settlement without running the risk of signaling to the defender that it will make even further concessions on the issue at hand. Moreover, the defender's consent to the previous settlement demonstrates that to the challenger that it is not inherently aggressive. Thus the challenger will reject the notion that the defender is aggressive and will search for alternative interpretations of the defender's bullying. As the challenger searches for these alternatives, the normative dimension to the relationship created by the dispute settlement will cause the challenger to reframe its own violation as an "illegitimate act." The defender's bullying, on the other hand, becomes a "legitimate" defense of the settlement and a *punishment* rather than an act of aggression. Thus if the defender uses a highly coercive strategy following the violation of a settlement, the challenger will retain its belief that the defender is not aggressive, but it will have learned that the defender remains vigilant. Consequently, it will comply with the defender's demands and yield in its challenge to the settlement.

Conciliatory responses to the violation of a settlement, on the other hand, will have precisely the opposite effect on the challenger's response. As I discussed earlier, appeasement is likely to be viewed as a sign of weakness if no previous settlement has been violated. If the challenger has violated a settlement, however, it did so recognizing that it was committing an act that both it and the defender had defined as illegitimate. Moreover, by appeasing a violation of the previous settlement, the defender is abandoning the mutually recognized focal point for the resolution of the crisis. Thus the challenger will view an appeasing response to the violation of a settlement as an even *stronger* sign of the defender's weakness than it would have in the absence of a settlement. Given such an opportunity for cheap gains, the challenger will remain stubborn in its bid to revise the status quo.

Finally, as was true without a dispute settlement, a moderately coercive firm-but-flexible strategy following the violation of a settlement should remain effective in persuading the challenger to yield. Such a strategy conveys vigilance in enforcing the norm without triggering fears of additional demands by the defender.

The reputational effects of dispute settlements should have an identical influence on subsequent crisis bargaining. First, bullying behavior by the defender in response to the violation of a settlement will inflict substantial reputational costs on the challenger if it remains intransigent. Other states will view the challenger as extremely untrustworthy under these circumstances because it has demonstrated that it cannot be held to its commitments even by the threat or use of force. Conceding to the defender, on the other hand, gives the challenger an opportunity to rehabilitate its reputation for upholding its word. While some reputational damage may be inevitable, by reestablishing compliance with the norm, the challenger can demonstrate that it is not unalterably aggressive and that it can be held to its word by a vigilant defender. In addition to salvaging the challenger's reputation for trustworthiness, offering concessions after violating a previous settlement does less damage to the challenger's reputation for toughness than it might in other contexts. The presence of a dispute settlement as a focal point for resolving the crisis makes it easier for the challenger to frame its concession as an act of compliance with the specific principles of the agreement rather than a general signal that it lacks resolve.

If the defender responds with appeasement following the violation of a settlement, however, we should expect the challenger to insist on overturning the status quo. Under these conditions, the violation will attract little international attention, and those states that do take notice either will infer that the challenger's revision has been tacitly consented to or will make a very limited inference about the challenger's trustworthiness. If the challenger chose to violate the settlement, it did so knowing that it was risking *some* damage to its reputation even if the defender responded with appeasement. Thus in the absence of any *additional* reputational damage beyond these expected costs, the challenger is likely to remain intransigent in its violation. Moreover, by agreeing to an international settlement, the defender has placed *its* reputation for toughness on the line by explicitly committing itself to the status quo. Once again, I hypothesize that failure to enforce the violation of a settlement should be an even stronger sign to the challenger of the defender's weakness than if no settlement had existed. This weakness should encourage the challenger to become even more insistent on overturning the status quo.

Finally, as was the case without a dispute settlement, a firm-but-flexible strategy should persuade the challenger to yield. A firm-but-flexible response by the defender will be successful in attracting international attention to the violation, and continued intransigence in the face of such a response would do severe damage to the challenger's reputation for trustworthiness. Specifically, such intransigence would indicate that the challenger is entirely untrustworthy and cannot be held to its word even by force. If the challenger chooses to concede, on the other hand, the presence of the settlement and the face-saving compromises incorporated in the defender's firm-but-flexible strategy will limit the damage to the challenger's reputation for toughness.

HYPOTHESIS 2. *When a challenger has violated a dispute settlement and the defender responds with* appeasement, *the challenger's resistance will be* higher *than if no previous settlement had existed.*

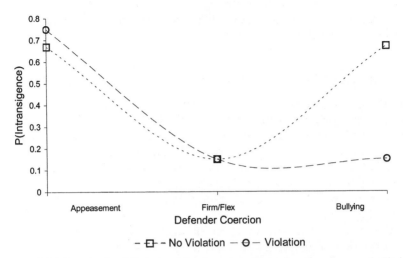

Depending on Violation of Previous Settlement

- ❑ - No Violation — ⊖ — Violation

Figure 3A Hypothesized Relationships between Defender Coercion and Challenger Resistance, Depending on Violation of Previous Settlements

HYPOTHESIS 3.   *When a challenger has violated a dispute settlement and the defender responds with a* bullying *strategy, the challenger's resistance will be* lower *than if no previous settlement had existed.*

HYPOTHESIS 4.   *When a challenger has violated a dispute settlement and the defender responds with a* firm-but-flexible *strategy, the challenger's resistance will be* at least as low *as if no previous settlement had existed.*

The competing predictions of the conventional crisis-bargaining model and my norm-based argument concerning the relationship between the defender's bargaining strategy and the challenger's insistence on overturning the status quo are displayed in figure 3A. The dotted line reflects the conventional argument, which holds that both very weak and very coercive strategies will result in intransigence by the challenger, while moderately coercive strategies will persuade the challenger to yield. My model suggests that this prediction will only be correct for cases in which no previous dispute settlement has been violated. If the challenger has violated a settlement, I predict that the relationship between the defender's strategy and the challenger's response will shift to the one described by the dashed line. In this case very weak strategies will make the challenger even more insistent on overturning the status quo. The influence of moderately coercive strategies will remain relatively unchanged, but highly coercive strategies will become effective in persuading the challenger to yield to the previous status quo.

THE REALIST ALTERNATIVE–RATIONAL COERCION THEORY

In testing my argument about the influence of norms, it is important to control for the prominent realist alternatives to this approach. Deterrence theory and coercion theory stand as the most clearly established competitors to my argument (Ellsberg 1968; Schelling 1966; Schelling 1960). In addition, since my hypotheses concern behavior in reinitiated crises, it is also important to consider realist arguments that focus on the evolution of conflict over time—such as those that emerge from the literature on enduring rivalries.[9]

Deterrence refers to a situation in which an actor attempts to use a combination of threatened punishments and promised rewards to prevent another actor from taking some action that it would otherwise take. Coercion refers to a similar situation, but in this case the actor is attempting to force its opponent to *reverse* some action that it has already taken (Schelling 1966, 78–91). Perhaps because of their focus on the prevention rather than the conduct of war, international relations scholars have devoted much more time and effort to studying the problems of deterrence than they have to coercion. The subject of this work, however, is the use of coercive behavior once a conflict has erupted to reestablish cooperative relations and prevent future disputes. Consequently, a theory of coercion is more directly relevant here.

Fortunately, although deterrent and coercive situations differ in some structural aspects, the logic by which realists assert that states may deter and coerce one another is identical. For example, many authors have argued that coercion is inherently more difficult than deterrence because a state must force its opponent to *do* something, rather than *not* to do something. While this distinction may be valid, it does not imply that different variables will be important in understanding these two processes.

[9] Despite the obvious importance of rivalries in international politics, this literature is still in its relatively early stages of development. Moreover, as Hensel (1994) and Goertz and Diehl (1992) note, much of the existing literature on enduring rivalries use this concept as a case selection device to test arguments that are not directly related to the concepts of rivalry (Huth and Russett 1993; Huth, Bennett, and Gelpi 1992). Thus my hypotheses are restricted to some of the very basic concepts that underpin the notion of rivalries, such as a concern with reputation for toughness and the possibility of a positive feedback cycle that drives conflict escalation.

Perhaps the clearest way to see the identity between rational theories of deterrence and coercion is to compare prominent works from each of these areas. For example, in his article "Pearl Harbor: Deterrence Theory and Decision Theory," Bruce Russett presents a rational model of deterrence that predicts when deterrent threats made by defenders will succeed or fail in protecting a third party "pawn" from an attack (Russett 1967). In addressing a topic that appears—at least superficially—to be somewhat different, Daniel Ellsberg has presented a rational theory of coercive threats that has been referred to as the "critical risk" model (Ellsberg 1968). Upon closer inspection, however, it becomes clear that these two formulations regarding the workings of deterrence and coercion are mathematically equivalent.

First, Russett states the core of this theory in the following manner:

$$\text{If } A(S) \,+\, W(1-S) > P, \text{ then deterrence fails.}$$

Where A = value of success to the potential attacker (value of an attack *without* defender intervention); W = costs of failure to the potential attacker (attack *with* defender intervention—i.e., war); P = value of peace to the potential attacker (costs of inaction); and S = probability of successful attack (probability of attack without defender intervention). (Russett 1967)

Success and failure here refer to the defender's intervention (i.e., success or failure of deterrence), not the outcome of attack on the pawn. In addition, the military costs of attacking the pawn alone are subsumed under the value of success. Finally, these military costs combined with the values at issue in the dispute must exceed the value of peace, otherwise there is no deterrent encounter.

Ellsberg's model, on the other hand, states:

$$\text{If } Pr > \frac{T - S}{T - P}, \text{ then coercion succeeds.}$$

Where Pr = probability of punishment (probability that blackmailer will carry out threat if victim resists); T = value of resistance (value of resistance *without* punishment); S = value of compliance (value of conceding without punishment); and P = value of punishment (value of resisting and being punished).

The values in this equation are payoffs for the victim because in Ellsberg's model of coercion, the victim takes the place of a potential attacker in a deterrence model. Ellsberg makes this reversal because in a coercive situation it is the victim's behavior that is being manipulated. In the cases that I examine, the challenger will also be the "victim" of the defender's coercive attempts.

To equate these two models, we must first translate their symbolic language into compatible terms. It is not difficult to see that this translation should be completed as follows:

Ellsberg		*Russett*	
Pr	$=$	$1-S$	$P(\text{Punishment}) = P(\text{War})$
T	$=$	A	$\text{Value}(\text{Resist}) = \text{Value}(\text{Success})$
S	$=$	P	$\text{Value}(\text{Compliance}) = \text{Value}(\text{Peace})$
P	$=$	W	$\text{Value}(\text{Punish}) = \text{Value}(\text{War})$

Because Ellsberg's model predicts when threats will *succeed* while Russett's formulation predicts when threats will *fail*, the direction of the inequality in Russett's model must be reversed so that the two equations are attempting to predict the same outcome. Thus Russett's equation written in Ellsberg's terminology is as follows:

If $T(1 - Pr) + P(Pr) < S$, then the threat will succeed.

Now, some simple algebraic manipulations allow us to reformulate this statement:

$$T - T(Pr) + P(Pr) < S$$
$$T - S - T(Pr) + P(Pr) < 0$$
$$T - S < T(Pr) - P(Pr)$$
$$T - S < (T - P)Pr$$
$$\frac{T - S}{T - P} < Pr$$

This last formulation *is* Daniel Ellsberg's equation for critical risk, demonstrating that his approach is identical to Russett's. As I mentioned earlier, the situation that I am examining is essentially a coercive one, and so I shall frame my discussion and hypotheses in terms of a theory of coercion. But since rational theories of deterrence and coercion incorporate the same variables and make the same predictions concerning their effects, I shall draw on the insights of deterrence theory as well in constructing my argument.

Rational coercion theory describes a relationship between two actors. The first party—the "blackmailer"—must use some combination of threats and rewards in an attempt to convince the second party—the "victim"—to comply with its wishes. The focus of this approach is exclusively on dyadic level variables—to the exclusion of domestic influences on conflict behavior. In its simplest form, this approach asserts that the victim compares the expected costs and benefits of continuing a dispute to the costs and benefits of changing its behavior to meet the demands of the blackmailer. For coercion to succeed, the following condition must hold:

$$\text{Value of Compliance} < \left[P(\text{Win}) \times \text{Value of Victory} + (1 - P(\text{Win})) \times \text{Value of Defeat} \right]$$

Coercion theory argues that the credibility of threats is central in determining the success or failure of blackmail. A credible threat implies that the blackmailer has both the capability to impose high costs on the victim and the willingness to do so. Consequently, credibility is a function of two conceptual variables: (1) the balance of capabilities between blackmailer and victim, and (2) the blackmailer's and victim's levels of resolve. The balance of capabilities, for example, affects the victim's probability of prevailing as well as the value it places on victory and defeat. As the balance of capabilities shifts in favor of the blackmailer, it becomes more likely that the blackmailer will prevail if the conflict continues. Additionally, under these circumstances, the victim's costs of continuing the conflict increase—decreasing its net utility for standing firm. Similarly, the blackmailer's and victim's resolves are a function of the value they place on victory, defeat, and the value of compliance. Thus as the victim places a larger value on victory relative to the value of compliance, it becomes more resolved to continue the conflict.

Theories of coercive behavior have been developed by many scholars over the past several decades. As one might expect, each of these efforts has emphasized its own particular aspects of the coercive relationship, but a number of important sources of coercive leverage have continued to surface as central to any realist theory of coercion.

Drawing on these three literatures, I have developed a list of variables that I believe are central to any realist explanation of crisis outcomes. These variables—which I shall include as controls on my analysis—are as follows: (1) bargaining behavior, (2) the balance of conventional military forces, (3) the interaction between bargaining behavior and the balance of conventional military forces, (4) the possession of nuclear weapons, (5) the interests at stake in the dispute, (6) concurrent involvement in other disputes, (7) behavior in previous disputes between the same adversaries, (8) the number of times that these adversaries have been involved in previous disputes, and (9) the change in the balance of military capabilities since the most recent dispute between the adversaries.

Crisis-Bargaining Behavior

The realist argument about bargaining behavior is described in hypothesis 1. Thus coercion theory's predictions concerning bargaining behavior are identical to those of my normative model *in the absence of a dispute settlement*. The crucial difference between these two approaches is that coercion theory does *not* incorporate the possible construction of norms or the way that they can alter crisis bargaining. In fact, rational coercion theory explicitly rejects the notion that the standards of legitimacy constructed by dispute settlements will have any effect on crisis behavior (Mearsheimer 1994/1995).

The Balance of Conventional Military Capabilities

The balance of military capabilities represents perhaps the most basic variable in any realist approach to international conflict. States with an advantage in military capabilities relative to those of their adversaries face lower costs in the event of military conflict than do the disadvantaged states. Consequently, dominant states may exploit their position by coercing others into making concessions, or simply impose their will through victory on the battlefield. States that are in a position of weakness, on the other hand, may make concessions to appease their powerful adversaries and to avoid the costs of military conflict.

Crisis Bargaining and the Balance of Forces

Although a disadvantage in relative military capabilities will have some impact on a state's behavior, this effect may not be substantial if the more powerful state does not demonstrate the willingness to use its capabilities. Engaging in military conflict always entails some costs, even for a very powerful state. As a result, a very weak state need not make concessions to a powerful one because it fears the costs of war unless the powerful state has indicated that it is willing to use force. This argument suggests that military capacity will be more effective in extracting concessions from the opposing state when it is complemented by highly coercive bargaining tactics.

Possession of Nuclear Weapons

Although a nuclear capability undoubtedly contributes to a state's military capabilities, the fundamentally different nature of nuclear weapons has caused most students of international conflict to treat these weapons separately from the analysis of conventional armaments (Glaser 1990;

Powell 1990; Zagare 1987). One central argument of this literature relates to the possession of first-strike capacities. A first-strike capacity refers to the ability to destroy or disable all of the opponent's deliverable nuclear warheads by launching first. The defender's possession of a first-strike capability has obvious and damaging implications for the challenger. Such a capacity sharply increases the costs that the challenger will suffer in the event of military conflict. Additionally, the defender's possession of a first-strike capability undoubtedly lowers the likelihood that the challenger will prevail on the battlefield. Both of these factors will lead the challenger to make concessions to avoid an escalation of the conflict.

Interests at Stake in the Dispute

A number of scholars have drawn attention to the importance of the interests at stake in a particular dispute (Jervis 1984; George and Smoke 1974; Betts 1987). If the defender has substantial interests at stake, it will be willing to suffer greater costs to achieve its goals. Acquiescing to the challenger's revision of the status quo, on the other hand, becomes less attractive. As a result, the challenger will be cautious in altering the status quo on issues that concern the defender's core values because of its belief that the defender will be willing to suffer substantial costs rather than concede. When disputes arise over such issues, the challenger will be more likely to yield.

Involvement in Other Disputes

The resources that the defender may direct toward a confrontation with the challenger also depend, in part, on the defender's involvement in disputes with third parties (Huth, Gelpi, and Bennett 1993; Huth and Russett 1993; Huth, Bennett, and Gelpi 1992). A state that is occupied with a war on one of its borders, for example, is less likely to be willing or able to threaten force against another neighbor. Consequently, the fact that the defender has committed diplomatic, political, and military resources to another dispute makes it less likely that it will be in a favorable position to prevail in the current disagreement with the challenger.

Previous Dispute Behavior

Much of the work on deterrence and coercion—in theory and practice—is directly concerned with the importance of bargaining reputation.[10] If a state capitulates during a crisis, it does so knowing that it is damaging its

[10] The literature on this point is far too extensive to cite exhaustively, but perhaps the most influential works in this regard are Schelling (1960, 1966) and Fearon (1994a).

bargaining reputation. As a result, a state's backing down in a previous crisis will be viewed by others as a reliable signal that it is weakly resolved (Nalebuff 1991; Powell 1990; Schelling 1966). Since the challenger should perceive the previous capitulation of the defender as a sign of general weakness, it will take an intransigent stance in subsequent encounters with the same defender, confident of its ability to prevail.

History of Previous Conflict

The literature on enduring rivalries has demonstrated that a relatively small number of interstate dyads account for a substantial share of all international militarized conflicts (Goertz and Diehl 1992; Gochman and Maoz 1984). This observation has led to speculation about whether the dynamics of repeated conflict may create a cycle in which disputes become increasingly frequent and violent over time (Hensel 1994). In presenting his "modified realist" model of territorial rivalries, for example, Huth (1996) argues that rivalries become embedded in the domestic political debates within the disputing states. Thus, as a conflict persists, it becomes increasingly difficult for state leaders to make any kind of concessions to their adversaries because of the domestic repercussions. Taking a slightly different approach to the same question, Leng (1983) argues that states tend to learn "realist" lessons about the dynamics of international conflict as they engage in repeated disputes. These lessons cause states to rely on increasingly coercive bargaining strategies as crises recur. Both of these arguments suggest that challenging states will be more likely to remain intransigent if an extensive history of conflict exists between the challenger and defender.

Change in Balance of Military Capabilities

Finally, according to realist theory, the status quo established by the outcome of a crisis reflects the relative power of the two states at the time of that crisis. As a result, realist theory would suggest that if the balance of military capabilities has changed between a previous crisis and a current one, then the state that has become more powerful should be able to improve its position relative to the status quo.[11] Thus, if the balance of military capabilities has shifted in favor of the challenger since the previous crisis, the challenger should become more likely to remain intransigent in the current crisis as it insists on improvements in the status quo to reflect its increased capabilities. If the defender has become more pow-

---

[11] I would like to thank Chris Achen and Stephen Krasner for bringing this argument to my attention.

erful since the previous dispute, on the other hand, the challenger should be more likely to abandon its challenge to the status quo in the current dispute and comply with the defender's demands.

CONCLUSIONS

In this chapter I developed an institutionalist framework for thinking about the impact of norms on crisis bargaining. This framework focuses on the information that norms provide to the disputants and the way in which that information shapes the disputants' perceptions of bargaining behavior. From this framework I derived specific hypotheses about the way in which norms would cause behavior to deviate from the expectations of the conventional realist approach to crisis bargaining. In addition, I derived a series of hypotheses based on rational theories of deterrence and coercion. Having derived my contrasting expectations about the crisis bargaining and the outcomes of international crises, I now turn my attention to the development of appropriate methods for testing these hypotheses.

CHAPTER 4

Structuring the Analysis of International Norms

$\mathbf{I}$n the previous chapter I derived the hypotheses from both a realist and an institutionalist approach to crisis bargaining. In this chapter I turn my attention to creating a properly structured test for these hypotheses. As discussed earlier, I am investigating the role of legitimacy in shaping international security affairs. International security is an extremely broad issue area, however, which incorporates a wide variety of specific issues. Since I cannot possibly examine all of these topics, I select one particular security issue for analysis. Specifically, I will focus my attention on militarized dispute settlements and their role in creating legitimate norms and standards of behavior that affect bargaining in future crises over the same issue.

International crises and dispute settlements represent a good place to focus my analysis of the role of legitimacy in security affairs for several reasons. First, since the disputing states have actively constructed these settlements through a process of negotiation, the contracting parties may reasonably be described as having consented to the agreements. As a result, the concept of legitimacy may be meaningfully invoked in this context. Second, crisis-bargaining behavior has been a central substantive concern in the contemporary research on security affairs. For obvious normative reasons, international relations scholars and policy makers have spent much of their time finding ways to prevent crises from becoming wars. Following in this tradition, I hope to discover whether or not international norms can play a role in accomplishing this task and in restoring more cooperative relations. Finally, as Jervis (in Krasner 1983) has pointed out, security affairs represents a "hard case" for the operation of international norms.

Within the area of security affairs, arms control negotiations concerning nuclear weapons might represent the easiest case for legitimate agreements to operate in the security area. In this situation, the mutual interest in avoiding nuclear war is fairly strong, and the cost of being exploited by one's partner is fairly low, since a secure second-strike capability can be made quite robust against marginal changes in the opponent's arsenal. The operation of postwar agreements such as the Versailles treaty, on the other hand, might represent the most difficult case for norms to have an effect. In this case the defeated parties' consent to the agreement may seriously be contested, and there exist few common interests in maintaining the agreement. Moreover, the costs of failing to detect or respond to cheating on the agreement may—as France, Britain, and their allies discovered with the outbreak of World War II—be quite high.

Crisis bargaining represents something of a midpoint between these extremes. As I mentioned previously, the disputing parties may reasonably be described as consenting to their settlement agreements, and the fact that these settlements result from a negotiation process suggests that some common interests do undergird them. Nonetheless, the costs of being cheated by an opponent can—in some circumstances—be quite high. As a result, international crises represent a good starting point for investigating the role of legitimacy in security affairs more generally.

Of course, there are various subsequent stages of crisis bargaining at which one might try to measure the impact of legitimate dispute settlements. Most obviously, one might investigate whether crises that end in legitimate dispute settlements are less likely to experience renewed military conflict. As I discussed in chapter 2, however, demonstrating such a causal relationship is plagued with problems of spuriousness. That is, the presence of a legitimate dispute settlement might indicate a greater degree of common interests between the adversaries regarding the issue in dispute. Thus a lack of renewed conflict in the wake of a settlement might easily be attributed to the greater common interests rather than any normative impact of the settlement per se.

A second stage at which settlements might influence subsequent bargaining is by altering the response of the defending state. For example, defenders might be more likely to offer a highly coercive response if the challenger is in violation of a previous settlement than if no violation occurred.[1] Such an analysis is worthy of further study, but it does not address my central concern over whether norms can constrain the behav-

---

[1] For example, constructivists might argue that the violation of a legitimate settlement gives the defender a greater (moral) interest in a coercive response (Tannenwald 1999; Welch 1993). Institutionalist expectations regarding the defender's response are not as clear. While norms may create a reputational interest in a coercive response, institutionalists also assume that norms do not shape state interests. Consequently, norms may be plagued by enforcement problems because actors may be reluctant to pay the costs of punishing violations (Axelrod 1986; Downs and Rocke 1995). A brief examination of my data set (see table 4A) reveals no relationship between the violation of a settlement and the defender's response. When no settlement was violated, 25 percent of defenders responded with appeasement, 24 percent with a firm-but-flexible strategy, and 51 percent with bullying. After a settlement was violated the respective frequencies were 24 percent, 33 percent, and 43 percent. These differences of proportions do not approach statistical significance ($p < .53$) Nonetheless, this is an avenue of inquiry that may merit more detailed attention in future research.

ior of dissatisfied states. If a defender makes a strongly coercive response to the violation of a norm, but the challenger does not respond to this coercion any differently from the way it would in any other context, then one cannot conclude that bargaining is guided by norms of legitimate behavior. In this case the *defender's* behavior may be guided by standards of legitimacy, but unless the challenger is also guided by these standards, then the norm has failed in a crucial sense.

Thus I focus my investigation on the challenger's responses to the defender's coercive behavior. I do so because I believe that the normative impact of legitimate dispute settlements can most clearly be observed by examining the challenger's response to coercive behavior in differing normative contexts. This empirical focus avoids the problems of spuriousness in distinguishing the impact of norms on state behavior, while also examining the critical link between standards of legitimacy and the willingness of dissatisfied states to alter their behavior.

I hope that future research may build on the results of this study to map out in greater detail where international security norms can and cannot have an effect. In chapter 7 I take the first steps toward extending my analysis in that manner.

IDENTIFYING INTERNATIONAL CRISES AND CRISIS ACTORS

The specific population from which I draw my cases has been identified by Michael Brecher, Jonathan Wilkenfeld and Sheila Moser in the International Crisis Behavior (ICB) Project (Brecher and Wilkenfeld 1997). The more commonly used data set for this type of analysis is the Correlates of War (COW) Militarized International Dispute (MID) data set, which covers the period from 1816 to 1992. MID and ICB data sets differ somewhat in their specific criteria for including a militarized encounter, but the essential substantive difference between the two is that the ICB set consists only of what might be considered the more "serious" militarized international encounters. The MID data set, on the other hand, includes a number of disputes that are essentially minor airspace violations, border violations, or boating incidents. Although the MID includes many more cases than the ICB project, I chose to select my cases from the latter data set because it provides much more detailed information about each of the crises that it covers—including a brief historical summary of each case. Some of the measurement issues involved in testing my hypotheses—such as establishing the presence of a legitimate agreement—require a fairly detailed and descriptive history of the relevant international crises. Consequently, I felt it was important to obtain a more detailed and precise measurement of the concepts I am interested in, even at the expense of including a smaller number of crises in my analysis.

Because of the research necessary to identify the presence of a legitimate dispute settlement and to categorize the bargaining strategies used by the disputants, I draw my cases from the crises that the ICB data set identifies between 1929 and 1979. Although focusing the analysis on a relatively narrow fifty-year period might appear limiting, Brecher, Wilkenfeld, and Moser note that this period includes a very wide variety of crisis actors, issues, and contexts. In particular the authors defend their population of cases by noting that

> the choice of that half-century provides several research benefits. It facilitates comparison: across types of international systems (multipolar, bipolar, and polycentric) and international security organizations; across diverse actor attributes (age size, regime, etc.); and across levels of economic development and military power, from the United States and the Soviet Union as superpowers to the weak, developing states of post-colonial Africa in the 1960's and 1970's. (Brecher, Wilkenfeld, and Moser 1988, 1)

And in fact, I, too, find that the population of crises that remains does appear to include a broad cross section of crisis participants and contexts.

Brecher, Wilkenfeld, and Moser define international crises in terms of three important criteria. "Viewed from the perspective of a state," the authors write,

> a crisis is a situation with three necessary and sufficient conditions deriving from a change in its external environment. All three conditions are perceptions held by the highest level decision makers: 1) *a threat to basic values*, with a simultaneous subsequent awareness of 2) *finite time for response*, and of the 3) *high probability of involvement in military hostilities*. (Brecher, Wilkenfeld, and Moser 1988, 2)

It is from this set of events that I begin to define the population of cases for my analysis. To fit the requirements of my research question, I make five adjustments to the ICB data set. First, I exclude from my analysis international crises that take place within the context of a total war. The theories I have discussed are concerned with political decision making about the use of force and bargaining within a crisis. During a total war, however, decisions cease being driven primarily by politics as military strategy and tactics take precedence.[2] Total wars have become exercises in military tactical and strategic prowess, but such is not the case for crises embedded in *limited* wars. In fact, the decision to escalate or deescalate a limited war is often driven by political rather than military needs. Thus in

[2] For a detailed discussion of the concept of "total" versus "limited" wars, see Organski and Kugler (1980).

selecting my cases, I include crises that entail the escalation of a limited conflict, but I exclude crises in which the highest levels of military conflict have already been reached.

These coding rules may be more clearly understood through the presentation of some examples. During the slow burning War of Attrition in 1970, Israel decided to escalate the conflict by beginning deep penetration bombing of Egypt. I included this case in my analysis (War of Attrition II), since Israel's decision represented a political choice to escalate the conflict in the hope of forcing a resolution. During World War II, on the other hand, the success of the Soviet counteroffensive at Stalingrad created what the ICB codes as a crisis for Germany as the tide began to turn against them. I do not include this case in my list of crises because the German-Soviet conflict had already reached the status of a total war. The Soviet counteroffensive was not a political decision to escalate the conflict, but a military one concerning the best way to defeat the Germans on the battlefield. The situation was no longer one of crisis bargaining but of pure brute force.[3]

Second, for each of the remaining international crises I identify the primary challenger and defender for each encounter. The challenger is defined as the first state to take militarized action to overturn the status quo with regard to the issue at stake in the crisis. I use the "challenger" label as a purely descriptive rather than pejorative term. My designation of the challenger concerns the legal or moral validity of the challenger's claims only in relation to its violation of any existing agreement. If such an agreement was violated, the "challenger" label only identifies the state that broke the agreement. If no previous agreement existed, then the "challenger" label simply indicates which state was the first to take action to change the status quo. It is not intended to make any claim about the just or unjust nature of that status quo.[4] The defender, on the other hand, is defined as the primary state against which the challenger's militarized act is aimed. Thus in the terms Brecher, Wilkenfeld, and Moser use to identify the cases, the defender is generally the first crisis actor to have its values threatened by the challenger. The challenger's actions may subsequently be threatened by the defender's response. This is not always the case, however, since the challenger's values may be threatened first by some nonmilitary act on the part of the defender.[5]

---

[3] Thomas Schelling draws a similar distinction between the political use of violence in coercion and the apolitical use of brute force. See Schelling (1966), chapter 1.

[4] For a more detailed discussion of this issue, see Huth and Russett (1990).

[5] One example of this pattern occurs in the fourth crisis between the United States and the PRC over Taiwan. The PRC is threatened by the signing of a defense pact between the United States and Taiwan, but the PRC is labeled the challenger, since it responds to this development by resuming the shelling of the offshore islands.

Third, after designating a primary challenger and defender, I identify other states that may play supporting roles in a crisis. This level of support may vary from diplomatic support and moral exhortation through economic and military aid to direct militarized action in the crisis. I am primarily interested in supporting states because they may shift the balance of military capabilities between the challenger and defender during the crisis at hand. Diplomatic support and economic aid, however, can have little direct effect on the available military capabilities for the challenger and defender during the crisis at hand. As a result, I will only include a state as a supporting actor on either side if it takes some direct militarized action on behalf of one of the disputing parties or if it threatens to take some military action.

Using these rules, the identification of the challenger, defender, and their supporting parties is generally relatively straightforward. Some international crises that are also cases of extended deterrence, however, are more complex. In particular, cases in which a Great Power practices extended deterrence on behalf of a minor power require some adjustments in coding the identity of the defender. One might think, for example, that the minor power protégé would be coded as the defender and the Great Power as a supporting actor. In such extended deterrence cases where the Great Power's military forces are directly engaged, however, the outcome of the crisis is affected much more directly by the Great Power's behavior than it is by the actions of the minor power. My statistical model includes the bargaining behavior of the defender, but not that of its supporting actors. In such cases, coding the Great Power as a mere supporting actor would severely misrepresent the crisis. As a result, in these cases the Great Power is coded as the defender and the minor power is coded as a supporting actor.

Fourth, many of the agreements and crises that I will analyze are multilateral in nature. Modeling such complex interactions raises some difficult but not insurmountable methodological problems. Most important, I must determine whether the outcomes of the interactions between the various actors can be determined independently. If the outcomes can be determined independently, then I break the multilateral crisis down into several dyads which are included separately in the analysis. If the outcomes are codetermined, however, then the crisis remains as a single case, and I must determine which actors represent the primary challengers and defenders. For example, Syria and Egypt fought together against Israel in the Yom Kippur War of 1973. Since the two states fought on separate fronts, I argue that the outcomes of these two conflicts are not codetermined. Although both Syria and Egypt were unsuccessful, the combat did take different courses on the separate battlefields, and it is possible that one challenger could have been defeated while the other prevailed.

As a result, I code this conflict as two separate cases for my analysis.[6] In the conflicts between the United States, South Vietnam, and North Vietnam, however, I argue that the outcomes of these crises are codetermined. The United States and South Vietnam did not fight on separate fronts, their military activities were closely coordinated, and their military-strategic goals were identical. As a result, it is impossible to imagine the United States prevailing over North Vietnam while the South was defeated. Thus I preserved crises such as the Christmas bombing of 1972 as a single case with the United States as the defender and South Vietnam as a supporting actor.[7]

Finally, I selected crises from this group that occurred between 1919 and 1979 that were *reinitiations* of previous crises that also occurred between 1929 and 1979. Thus my research design compares crises in which a previous dispute settlement has been violated to other international crises that are *also* reinitiations of previous disputes over the same issue but lack any previous settlement. It is important to compare crises that involve violations to other reinitiated crises—as opposed to all other international crises—because the failure to do so would conflate the influence of international norms with the simple salience of the status quo. One might expect, for example, that once an issue has been bargained over to a particular solution, the status quo that was established would become a salient point for settling subsequent crises regardless of whether that status quo was one to which both parties had consented. By comparing violations to other reinitiations, I am able to separate the normative content of consensual dispute settlements from the simple salience effect of the previous status quo.

The application of these five rules and procedures to the ICB data set generated a final population of 122 international crises between 1929 and 1979, which are reinitiations of previous crises that also occurred between 1929 and 1979. Sixty-seven of these reinitiations represent violations of previous settlements, while fifty-five of them involve no such violation. These cases are listed and described in table 4A.

The specific actions that I identify as "violations," of course, must vary by each particular agreement. Most of the agreements in my data set (84 percent) are explicitly codified or publicly stated. In these cases identifying acts that constitute a violation is relatively straightforward. The other 16 percent of the agreements, however, are tacit, and these are necessarily more tricky. I have attempted to determine the substantive core of

---

[6] Although the crisis is coded as two cases, I do include Syria as a supporting actor in Egypt's Yom Kippur War and Egypt as a supporting actor in Syria's conflict. Thus both of these cases account for the fact that Israel was fighting a two-front war in this crisis.

[7] The United States is coded as the primary defender rather than South Vietnam according to the rule concerning Great Power extended deterrence discussed previously.

the tacit pact, and I code a crisis as a violation if some action in the crisis conflicts with this core. In practice this process is less difficult than it might appear, since the central component of most of these settlements—both tacit and explicit—is the establishment of some policy which the parties agree not to attempt to overturn by force. Thus the reinitiation of a crisis over the same issue itself generally constitutes a violation. For example, a crisis between Czechoslovakia and Germany in May of 1938 ended with a German pledge that it will forward no territorial claims against its neighbor. Thus Germany's reinitiation of this dispute in the Munich crisis in and of itself constitutes a violation of the previous understanding.

DATA AND MEASUREMENTS

Having identified the population of crises that I will use in my analysis, I shall devote the following section to my discussion of the specific measures that I will use to operationalize my theoretical model for testing.

The Challenger's Response

The challenger's response to the defender is the dependent variable in my analysis. My coding refers to the challenger's *final* response to the defender in the crisis. In other words, it essentially refers to the outcome of the crisis.

The coding procedure for this variable draws on Leng and Wheeler (1979). It is coded on a three-point ordinal scale reflecting increasing insistence by the challenger on altering the status quo. The three categories are compliance, compromise, and intransigence. *Compliance* involves two kinds of responses by the challenger. First, of course, the challenger may comply with all of the defender's demands. In addition, if the challenger attempts to *placate* the defender by giving in to some demands and/or offering alternative concessions without making any threatening actions, I coded this as compliance. I coded a *compromise* outcome if the challenger concludes the crisis by offering some concessions while remaining firm in other aspects of its challenge. There are two substantial distinctions between placation, which is coded as compliance, and compromise. First, in compromise outcomes the challenger's refusal to comply completely with the defender's demands is backed up by the threat of force. Second, the concessions offered as placation are substantively comparable to those demanded by the defender, while compromise implies that the challenger offers less than demanded by the defender. Finally, *intransigence* includes two possible responses by the challenger. First, the challenger may simply *ignore* the defender's demands and refuse to alter

TABLE 4A

Reinitiated International Crises, 1929–1979

Crisis Name	Year	Challenger	Defender	Challenger Resistance	Defender Coercion	Settlement Violation	Previous Crisis Name	Previous Year
Chaco II	1932	Bolivia	Paraguay	Intran	Appease	Yes	Chaco I	1928
Jehol Campaign	1933	Japan	China	Intran	Bully	No	Mukden Incident	1931
Bulgaria-Turkey II	1935	Turkey	Bulgaria	Compro	Firm/Flex	Yes	Bulgaria-Turkey I	1935
Ethiopian War	1935	Italy	Ethiopia	Intran	Appease	No	Wal Wal	1934
Marco Polo Bridge	1937	China	Japan	Intran	Bully	Yes	Jehol Campaign	1933
Anschluss	1938	Germany	Austria	Intran	Appease	Yes	Austrian Putsch	1934
Czechoslovakia Crisis	1938	Germany	Czechoslovakia	Comply	Firm/Flex	No	Remilitarize Rhine	1936
Changkufeng	1938	USSR	Japan	Intran	Appease	Yes	Amur River Incident	1937
Munich	1938	Germany	Czechoslovakia	Intran	Appease	Yes	Czech May Crisis	1938
Italy Threatens France	1938	Italy	France	Comply	Bully	Yes	Ethiopian War	1935
Czechoslovakia Annexation	1939	Germany	Czechoslovakia	Intran	Appease	Yes	Munich	1938
Memel	1939	Germany	Lithuania	Intran	Appease	Yes	Kaunas Trials	1935
Nomonhan	1939	USSR	Japan	Intran	Bully	Yes	Changkufeng	1938
Entry into WWII-Poland	1939	Germany	Poland	Intran	Bully	No	Danzig	1939
Entry into WWII-Lithuania	1939	Germany	Lithuania	Intran	Appease	Yes	Memel	1939
Soviet Occupation-Estonia	1939	USSR	Estonia	Intran	Appease	No	Entry into WWII	1939
Soviet Occupation-Latvia	1939	USSR	Latvia	Intran	Appease	No	Entry into WWII	1939
Soviet Occupation-Lithuania	1939	USSR	Lithuania	Compro	Firm/Flex	No	Entry into WWII	1939
Invasion Scandinavia	1940	Germany	Norway	Intran	Bully	No	Entry into WWII	1939
Fall of Western Europe	1940	Germany	France	Intran	Bully	No	Entry into WWII	1939
Closure of Burma Road	1940	Japan	Britain	Intran	Appease	Yes	Tientsin	1939
Romanian Territories	1940	USSR	Romania	Compro	Appease	No	Entry into WWII	1939
E. African Campaign	1940	Italy	Britain	Intran	Bully	No	Ethiopian War	1935
Balkan Invasions	1940	Italy	Britain	Intran	Appease	No	Invasion of Albania	1939
Barbarossa	1941	Germany	USSR	Intran	Appease	Yes	Entry into WWII	1939
Maranon II	1941	Peru	Ecuador	Intran	Appease	Yes	Maranon I	1935
Pearl Harbor-USA	1941	Japan	USA	Intran	Bully	Yes	Panay Incident	1937
Pearl Harbor-UK	1941	Japan	Britain	Intran	Bully	No	Closure of Burma Rd	1940

Iran	1944	USSR	Iran	Comply
Azerbaijan	1945	USSR	Iran	Comply
Turkish Straits	1946	USSR	Turkey	Comply
Indonesia Independence II	1947	Netherlands	Indonesia	Comply
Indonesia Independence III	1948	Netherlands	Indonesia	Comply
Sinai Incursion	1948	Israel	Egypt	Comply
Korea II	1950	USA	PRC	Intran
Tel Mutilah	1951	Syria	Israel	Intran
Korea III	1953	PRC	USA	Comply
Trieste II	1953	Yugoslavia	Italy	Compro
Dien Bien Phu	1954	North Vietnam	France	Intran
Taiwan Straits I	1954	PRC	USA	Comply
Costa Rica-Nicaragua II	1955	Nicaragua	Costa Rica	Comply
Gaza Raid	1955	Israel	Egypt	Intran
Pushtunistan II	1955	Afghanistan	Pakistan	Comply
Suez Nationalized-UK	1956	Egypt	Britain	Intran
Hungary Liberalized	1956	USSR	Hungary	Intran
Suez-Sinai-UK	1956	Britain	Egypt	Comply
Suez-Sinai-Israel	1956	Israel	Egypt	Comply
Poland Liberalized	1956	USSR	Poland	Compro
Nicaragua-Honduras	1957	Nicaragua	Honduras	Comply
Berlin Deadline	1958	USSR	USA	Compro
Tunisia-France II	1958	France	Tunisia	Comply
Taiwan Straits II	1958	PRC	USA	Comply
Cuba-Central America II	1960	Cuba	Nicaragua	Intran
Pushtunistan III	1961	Afghanistan	Pakistan	Intran
Bizertia	1961	France	Tunisia	Comply
Berlin Wall	1961	USSR	USA	Intran
West Irian II	1961	Netherlands	Indonesia	Comply
Goa II	1961	India	Portugal	Intran
Taiwan Straits III	1962	Taiwan	PRC	Comply
Pathet Lao Offensive II	1962	North Vietnam	USA	Compro
India-PRC Border I	1962	PRC	India	Intran
Ogaden I	1964	Somalia	Ethiopia	Comply

Occupation of Iran	1941	Yes	Bully	Comply
Iran	1944	Yes	Firm/Flex	Comply
Kars Ardahn	1945	No	Firm/Flex	Comply
Indonesia Independence I	1945	Yes	Firm/Flex	Comply
Indonesia Independence II	1947	Yes	Firm/Flex	Comply
Israel Independence	1948	No	Bully	Intran
Korean War I	1950	No	Bully	Intran
Israel Independence	1948	Yes	Bully	Comply
Korean War II	1950	Yes	Bully	Intran
Trieste I	1945	Yes	Bully	Compro
Invasion of Laos I	1953	No	Bully	Intran
China Civil War	1948	Yes	Firm/Flex	Comply
Costa Rica-Nicaragua I	1948	Yes	Firm/Flex	Comply
Sinai Incursion	1948	No	Appease	Intran
Pushtunistan I	1949	No	Bully	Intran
Suez Canal	1951	No	Bully	Intran
Communism in Hungary	1947	No	Bully	Intran
Suez Nationalization	1956	No	Appease	Comply
Gaza Raid	1955	No	Appease	Comply
Communism in Poland	1946	No	Firm/Flex	Compro
Postage Stamp	1937	Yes	Firm/Flex	Comply
Berlin Blockade	1948	Yes	Firm/Flex	Compro
Tunisia-France I	1957	Yes	Firm/Flex	Comply
Taiwan Straits I	1950	Yes	Firm/Flex	Comply
Cuba-Central America I	1959	Yes	Firm/Flex	Intran
Pushtunistan II	1955	No	Bully	Intran
Tunisia-France II	1958	Yes	Bully	Comply
Berlin Deadline	1957	Yes	Appease	Intran
West Irian I	1957	No	Appease	Intran
Goa I	1955	Yes	Firm/Flex	Comply
Taiwan Straits II	1958	Yes	Appease	Intran
Pathet Lao Offensive I	1961	Yes	Firm/Flex	Comply
India-PRC Border I	1959	Yes	Bully	Compro
Ethiopia-Somalia	1960	No	Firm/Flex	Comply

TABLE 4A (*Continued*)

Crisis Name	Year	Challenger	Defender	Challenger Resistance	Defender Coercion	Settlement Violation	Previous Crisis Name	Previous Year
Yemen War II	1964	South Arabia	Yemen	Compro	Firm/Flex	Yes	Yemen War I	1962
Gulf of Tonkin	1964	USA	North Vietnam	Intran	Bully	No	Vietcong Attack	1961
Yemen War III	1964	South Arabia	Yemen	Compro	Firm/Flex	Yes	Yemen War-II	1964
Pleiku	1965	North Vietnam	USA	Intran	Bully	No	Gulf of Tonkin	1964
Kashmir II	1965	Pakistan	India	Comply	Bully	Yes	Kashmir I	1947
Yemen War IV	1966	Yemen	South Arabia	Compro	Bully	Yes	Yemen War-III	1964
El Samu	1966	Israel	Jordan	Intran	Bully	Yes	Israel Independence	1948
Six-Day War-Egypt	1967	Egypt	Israel	Intran	Bully	Yes	Suez-Sinai Campaign	1956
Six-Day War-Jordan	1967	Jordan	Israel	Intran	Bully	No	El Samu	1966
Six-Day War-Syria	1967	Israel	Syria	Intran	Bully	Yes	Tel Mutilah	1951
Cyprus II	1967	Greece	Turkey	Comply	Bully	Yes	Cyprus I	1963
Tet Offensive	1968	North Vietnam	USA	Intran	Appease	No	Pleiku	1965
Prague Spring	1968	USSR	Czechoslovakia	Intran	Appease	No	Communism in Czechoslovakia	1948
Pre-War of Attrition	1968	Egypt	Israel	Comply	Bully	Yes	Six-Day War	1967
Vietnam Spring Offensive	1969	North Vietnam	USA	Intran	Appease	Yes	Tet Offensive	1968
War of Attrition I	1969	Egypt	Israel	Comply	Bully	No	Pre-War of Attrition	1968
Shat-Al-Arab II	1969	Iraq	Iran	Comply	Bully	Yes	Shat-Al-Arab I	1959
War of Attrition II	1970	Israel	Egypt	Compro	Firm/Flex	No	War of Attrition I	1969
Invasion of Cambodia	1970	North Vietnam	USA	Intran	Bully	No	Vietnam Spring Offensive	1969
Cienfuegos	1970	USSR	USA	Comply	Bully	Yes	Cuban Missiles	1962
Invasion of Laos II	1971	USA	North Vietnam	Intran	Bully	Yes	Pathet Lao Offensive II	1962
Vietnam Ports Mining	1972	North Vietnam	USA	Compro	Firm/Flex	Yes	Invasion of Cambodia	1970
Uganda-Tanzania II	1972	Tanzania	Uganda	Compro	Bully	Yes	Uganda-Tanzania I	1971
Christmas Bombing	1972	North Vietnam	USA	Compro	Bully	Yes	Vietnam Ports Mining	1972
Zambia	1973	Rhodesia	Zambia	Intran	Bully	No	Rhodesia's UDI	1965
Iraq Invasion Kuwait	1973	Iraq	Kuwait	Compro	Firm/Flex	Yes	Kuwait Independence	1961
Yom Kippur War-Egypt	1973	Egypt	Israel	Intran	Bully	Yes	War of Attrition II	1970
Yom Kippur War-Syria	1973	Syria	Israel	Intran	Bully	Yes	Six-Day War	1967
Cyprus III	1974	Greece	Turkey	Comply	Bully	Yes	Cyprus II	1967

Panel 1

Crisis	Year	State A	State B	Outcome	Response
Final Vietnam Offensive	1974	North Vietnam	South Vietnam	Intran	Bully
Cod War II	1975	Iceland	Britain	Compro	Firm/Flex
Nouakchott I	1976	Algeria	Mauritania	Comply	Bully
Nagomia Raid	1976	Rhodesia	Mozambique	Intran	Bully
Mapai Seizure	1977	Rhodesia	Mozambique	Intran	Bully
Belize II	1977	Guatemala	Britain	Comply	Firm/Flex
Nouakchott II	1977	Algeria	Mauritania	Intran	Bully
Ogaden II	1977	Somalia	Ethiopia	Intran	Bully
Rhodesia Raids	1977	Rhodesia	Zambia	Intran	Bully
Vietnam Invades Cambodia	1977	Vietnam	Cambodia	Intran	Bully
Chimoio-Tembue Raids	1977	Rhodesia	Mozambique	Intran	Firm/Flex
Chad-Libya II	1978	Libya	France	Compro	Firm/Flex
Lebanon Civil War II	1978	Syria	Lebanon	Intran	Bully
Sino-Vietnam War	1978	Vietnam	Cambodia	Intran	Appease
Litani Operation	1978	Israel	Lebanon	Compro	Firm/Flex
Chad-Libya III	1978	Libya	France	Compro	Firm/Flex
Cassinga Incident	1978	South Africa	Angola	Intran	Appease
Shaba II	1978	Angola	Zaire	Comply	Appease
Air Rhodesia Incident	1978	Zambia	Rhodesia	Comply	Bully
Beagle Channel II	1978	Argentina	Chile	Compro	Firm/Flex
Fall of Amin	1978	Uganda	Tanzania	Comply	Bully
Tan Tan	1979	Algeria	Morocco	Intran	Firm/Flex
Raids on Zipra	1979	Rhodesia	Zambia	Compro	Appease
North-South Yemen II	1979	North Yemen	South Yemen	Intran	Bully
Raids on SWAPO	1979	South Africa	Angola	Compro	Appease
Chad-Libya IV	1979	Libya	France	Intran	Firm/Flex
Goulimime-Tarfaya Raids	1979	Algeria	Morocco	Comply	Bully
Rhodesia Settlement-Zambia	1979	Rhodesia	Zambia	Comply	Firm/Flex
Rhodesia Settlement-Botswana	1979	Rhodesia	Botswana	Comply	Firm/Flex
Rhodesia Settlement-Mozambique	1979	Rhodesia	Mozambique	Comply	Firm/Flex
Raids on Angola	1979	South Africa	Angola	Intran	Appease

Panel 2

Crisis	Year	Outcome	Response	Super
Christmas Bombing	1972	Intran	Bully	Yes
Cod War I	1973	Compro	Firm/Flex	Yes
Sahara	1975	Comply	Bully	No
Operation Thrasher	1976	Intran	Bully	No
Nagomia Raid	1976	Intran	Bully	No
Belize I	1975	Comply	Firm/Flex	Yes
Nouakchott I	1976	Intran	Bully	No
Ogaden I	1964	Intran	Bully	Yes
Zambia	1973	Intran	Bully	No
Final Vietnam Offensive	1974	Intran	Bully	No
Mapai Seizure	1977	Intran	Firm/Flex	No
Chad-Libya I	1971	Compro	Firm/Flex	Yes
Lebanon Civil War I	1976	Intran	Bully	No
Vietnam Invades Cambodia	1977	Intran	Appease	No
Beirut Airport	1968	Compro	Firm/Flex	No
Chad-Libya II	1978	Compro	Firm/Flex	Yes
War in Angola	1975	Intran	Appease	Yes
Shaba I	1977	Comply	Appease	No
Rhodesia Raids	1977	Comply	Bully	Yes
Beagle Channel I	1972	Compro	Firm/Flex	Yes
Uganda-Tanzania II	1975	Comply	Bully	Yes
Sahara	1978	Intran	Firm/Flex	No
Air Rhodesia	1972	Compro	Appease	Yes
North-South Yemen I	1978	Intran	Bully	Yes
Cassinga Incident	1978	Compro	Appease	Yes
Chad-Libya III	1978	Intran	Firm/Flex	Yes
Tan Tan	1979	Comply	Bully	No
Raids on Zipra	1979	Comply	Firm/Flex	No
Operation Tangent	1976	Comply	Firm/Flex	No
Chimoio-Tembue Raids	1977	Comply	Firm/Flex	No
Raids on SWAPO	1979	Intran	Appease	No

its behavior. Second, the challenger may actually *defy* the defender by escalating its demands or military activities in response. In coding the challenger responses, I relied primarily on the sources and case summaries provided by the ICB data set as well as *Keesing's Contemporary Archives*.

The Defender's Bargaining Strategy

The defender's bargaining strategy is coded according to the three-category framework used in previous research on crisis bargaining by Huth (1988). The three categories—appeasing, firm-but-flexible, and bullying—reflect increasing coerciveness in the defender's bargaining strategy. In general, defenders using bullying strategies respond to any challenger behavior other than compliance by continuing or escalating their threatening actions. Defenders using firm-but-flexible strategies respond to compliance or placation by repeating their position or offering further inducements, but they escalate their level of hostility in response to defiance or being ignored by the challenger. Huth (1988, 65) writes that the "critical difference between the bullying and firm-but-flexible strategies is that in the latter case the defender does more than react negatively to the demands of the potential attacker: it also initiates proposals for compromise." Finally, defenders using appeasing strategies respond to anything but compliance by offering further inducements to the challenger.

To code this variable, each crisis was broken down into a series of actions and counteractions. Relying on the procedures used by Huth and developed by Leng to categorize each coercive strategy, I examined each response of the defender to the bargaining position of its adversary (Leng 1993, 1989; Leng and Wheeler 1979).[8]

Leng actually begins with five categories—adding "trial and error" and "stonewalling" to the strategies discussed previously. Conceptually, however, each of these categories includes within it two or more different kinds of behavior. Trial and error strategies, for example, may begin with any type of coercive response. If the strategy appears to be successful the state will continue its behavior, whereas if it appears to fail the state will select a new strategy. In principle, this can result in five very different patterns of behavior: (1) states that remain highly coercive throughout,

---

[8] Having identified the move/countermove sequence of each crisis, I relied on Leng's coding procedures (Leng and Wheeler 1979; Leng 1989). My codings cannot, however, be considered a duplication of the Behavioral Correlates of War (BCOW) data-gathering effort. In particular, BCOW utilized primary sources and multiple coders to test for intercoder reliability. Resource constraints, however, forced me to rely on the ICB case summaries, secondary sources cited by ICB coders, *Keesing's Contemporary Archives*, and *Facts on File* in identifying the sequence of moves in each crisis.

(2) states that begin with low levels of coercion and increase it as the challenger continues to resist, (3) states that begin with high levels of coercion and back down as the challenger continues to resist, (4) states that use very low levels of coercion throughout, and (5) states that fluctuate aimlessly in their level of coercion, unable to find a strategy that works. The first of these types of cases I recoded as a "bullying" strategy, the second as "firm-but-flexible," and the third, fourth, and fifth as "appeasing." Similarly, the "stonewalling" category can in principle refer to one of two very different situations: (1) the defender ignores the challenger's threatening actions while the challenger is unable to accomplish its goals; and (2) the defender ignores the challenger while the challenger achieves its goals in the face of the defender's inaction. The first of these situations I recoded as a "bullying" strategy; the second situation I recoded as "appeasement."[9]

Violation of a Legitimate Settlement

For each case in my data set I determined whether or not the previous crisis had resulted in a legitimate dispute settlement.[10] Legitimate dispute settlements include two types of crisis outcomes. The first category includes various types of *explicit settlements* including a treaty, armistice, cease-fire, and so on. The agreement may have come in the form of a formal document, a public letter, or an oral declaration, but the conditions of the settlement are explicitly stated. The second category represents *tacit settlements* that are mutual understandings by the adversaries that are neither publicly written nor stated. All other results of previous crises were coded as lacking a legitimate settlement. These outcomes also fall into two categories. First there are imposed outcomes in which one actor emerges as the clear victor in the crisis and imposes its desired outcome on its adversary. This imposed solution may or may not be couched in terms of a treaty settlement. I did not include such imposed treaties as dispute "settlements," since such agreements are not likely to be viewed as legitimate by the defeated party. Dispute settlements are differentiated from imposed outcomes by the presence of bargaining between the adversaries over the policies included in the settlement. If such a "settlement" did not reflect any responsiveness to the preferences of one of the states, I coded the outcome as imposed. Second, the previous

[9] In terms of the actual cases in my data set, all of the stonewalling cases were recoded as "appeasement." I did not encounter any of the other possible patterns of behavior.

[10] The previous outcomes were coded on the basis of the "Form of Outcome" variable in the ICB data set. I then reviewed each of the cases myself to determine: (1) whether a settlement was present, (2) whether it was "legitimate," and (3) whether it had been violated.

crisis may have ended in a stalemate in which the dispute simply fades without any change in the status quo or any agreement—imposed or otherwise.

After having determined whether or not a previous legitimate settlement existed, I then identified the cases in which that settlement was violated by the challenging state. For each case I reviewed the relevant documents or statements and determined the substance of the settlement.[11] If the challenging state violated the terms of that understanding, either through the reinitiation of the crisis or at any time during the crisis, I coded it as in violation of the settlement. In practice this process is less difficult than it might appear, since the central component of most of these settlements—both tacit and explicit—is the establishment of some policy (often a territorial boundary) that the parties agree not to attempt to overturn by force. Thus the reinitiation of a crisis over the same issue itself generally constitutes a violation. I coded the challenger as not in violation of a previous legitimate settlement for all crises in which no such settlement existed. The challenger is also coded as not in violation if a settlement existed but the actions of the challenger in the subsequent dispute did not violate the specific terms of the settlement.

Interaction of Bargaining and Settlement

The three possible defender bargaining strategies combine with the presence or absence of a previous settlement to define six possible actions by the defender: (1) appeasement without a previous settlement, (2) appeasement after a violation of a previous settlement, (3) firm-but-flexible without a previous settlement, (4) firm-but-flexible after a violation of a previous settlement, (5) bullying without a previous settlement, and (6) bullying after a violation of a previous settlement. To avoid severe problems of multicollinearity in testing a curvilinear relationship combined with an interaction, I test hypotheses 1 through 4 with a series of dummy variables. Using firm-but-flexible without a previous settlement as the excluded category, I include five dummy variables to capture each of the possible interactions of previous settlements and the defender's bargaining strategy.[12]

[11] In selecting primary and secondary sources for evaluating the settlements, I relied on the bibliographies and crisis summaries in Brecher and Wilkenfeld (1997); and Brecher, Wilkenfeld, and Moser (1988).

[12] An alternative specification of the relationship would be to include the three-category scale of the coerciveness of the defender's bargaining strategy along with its square to capture the curvilinear effect predicted by hypothesis 1. The effects of international norms could be estimated by interacting each of these variables with the dummy variable marking the violation of a previous settlement. This specification of the model yields predicted ef-

The Balance of Conventional Military Capabilities

There has been some debate as to which resources should be included in the balance of military capabilities. A.F.K. Organski and Jacek Kugler, for example, have focused on the long-term capabilities that a state may mobilize in an extended total war, and thus they conceive of capabilities as the interaction of a nation's gross national product (GNP) and the government's ability to mobilize those resources (Organski and Kugler 1980). The COW data set on military capabilities, on the other hand, includes both long-term aspects of capability—such as population, energy consumption, and iron and steel production—as well as aspects of capability that can be mobilized and utilized in a much shorter period of time—such as current military expenditure and personnel. More recent research into crisis-bargaining behavior suggests that states tend to act according to a fairly short time horizon in such situations (Mearsheimer 1983; Huth 1988). Generally, when thinking about using military force, state leaders appear to be concerned with whether or not they can prevail quickly in a relatively brief conflict. The prospect of fighting a drawn-out war is unattractive to all political leaders, since their constituents (whether mass or elite) are likely to tire of the effort. These findings suggest that states tend to avoid involvement in conflicts that they do not believe they can win quickly. As a result, short-term military capabilities should be of greater consequence in shaping crisis bargaining than are long-term capabilities. My indicator of conventional military resources includes three separate components that all measure short-term capabilities: (1) military expenditures, (2) military personnel, and (3) the ratio of expenditures to personnel.[13]

In addition to the capabilities of the challenger and defender, however, I must also consider the distance over which those capabilities must be projected. Engaging in conflicts over long distances has obvious taxing effects on a state's military capacity. Moving supplies to the point of con-

---

fects that are nearly identical to those described here. Very high levels of multicolinearity, however, prevent the coefficients in that model from achieving statistical significance. The auxiliary r-squares for the normative variables in that specification model exceed 0.99.

[13] This ratio of spending per soldier is included as a crude measure of troop quality. Spending per soldier is likely to capture the amount of resources spent on equipment, training, and support serves for each soldier. For a more detailed discussion of this measure, see Huth, Bennett, and Gelpi (1992). The data for this measure is taken from the COW data set on military capabilities. Because of obvious informational constraints—this data has been aggregated to annual observations. For crises that occur early in a particular year, however, military spending and personnel figures that derive largely from actions taken following the crisis are not relevant as indicators of the balance of forces. Consequently, for crises that occur in the first quarter of a year, I use the previous year's data as a more accurate reflection of a state's military capacity in the early part of the following year.

flict becomes more burdensome, and the supply lines themselves must also be defended, causing a further drain on personnel and equipment. Consequently, the capabilities of all parties involved in the crisis are discounted for the distance from each state's homeland to the point of conflict. I shall use the discounting procedure developed by Bruce Bueno de Mesquita, since it has proved fruitful in previous research efforts in this area.[14]

After accounting for the effects of distance, I sum up the capabilities of both the challenger and its supporting states and the defender and its supporters for each of the three components of capabilities listed earlier. Then, for each component I compute the defending sides' proportion of the total dyad's capabilities in the following manner:

$$\frac{\text{Defender} + \text{Supporting Capabilities}}{(\text{Defender} + \text{Supporting Cap}) + (\text{Challenger} + \text{Supporting Cap})}$$

The average of these three ratios determines the balance of conventional military capabilities for the crisis.

Interaction of Military Capabilities and the Defender's Bargaining Strategy

To test the hypothesis that the balance of military capabilities has a greater impact when the defender shows willingness to use force, I included the measure of balance of forces interacted with a dummy variable identifying when the defender used a bullying strategy.

Possession of Nuclear Weapons

I began my coding based on the ICB data set and referred to additional sources to fill in missing data (Goldschmidt 1982; Betts 1987). Using this information, I created a three-point nuclear scale for each state (1 = no capability, 2 = rudimentary, 3 = developed). The essential difference between a rudimentary and developed nuclear capacity is the pos-

---

[14] The method I use was developed in Bueno de Mesquita (1981). It simply discounts capabilities by a varying amount per mile depending on the historical time period. As one moves closer to the present, the distance discount decreases to allow for the improvements in transportation technology. The ability to project power varies widely according to geographic terrain and technological development, and so this measure is flawed in the sense that it does not account for these changes in the miles/day projection ratio. However, the data necessary for generating this ratio independently for each actor in each crisis is prohibitive. Although Bueno de Mesquita's indicator is crude and does not allow for variations in projection capability between nations, it has been used successfully in numerous other projects. See, for example, Bueno de Mesquita (1985) or Huth, Gelpi, and Bennett (1993).

session of a secure second-strike force with regard to the opposing state in the current dispute. States with a rudimentary capability have nuclear warheads and the capacity to deliver them onto the territory of their adversary, but they lack sufficient numbers of warheads and/or basing capabilities to be assured of a second strike. One example of a state with a "rudimentary" nuclear capability would be the People's Republic of China (PRC) during the late 1960s. Finally, I used this three-point scale to create a dummy variable marking first-strike capabilities for the defender. The defender is coded as having a first-strike capacity (value of 1) if its nuclear score is greater than the challenger's, and the variable is coded zero otherwise.

Issues at Stake in the Crisis

Once again, I based my codings for this variable on the ICB data set. In particular, Brecher, Wilkenfeld, and Moser use a six-category framework to identify the "gravity of the value threatened" for each state in the crisis. The first issue category that the ICB data set identifies is "low level of threat," which refers to crises that represent a threat to the economic or social activities of the state or population. The second category includes crises that pose political threats to the viability of the state's current regime or leadership. The third category identifies crises that threaten a state's territorial integrity. The fourth category includes cases in which the actor views the crisis as a threat to its influence with its adversaries or allies within the international system or a regional subsystem. The fifth set of crises identify those that threaten "grave damage," such as large casualties in war, or mass bombings. Finally, a crisis may threaten the very existence of a state as a political unit or the survival of its entire population. If a crisis threatened more than one type of value, the more severe threat was coded. I referred to *Keesing's Contemporary Archives* to fill in data points that were missing from the ICB data set.

This variable is included in my analysis as part of a realist theory of coercion. Realist theories argue that the fundamental interests of all states are identical: (1) the continued survival of the state and its government, and (2) the maintenance of the territorial integrity of the state (Waltz 1979). In one respect, however, Brecher, Wilkenfeld, and Moser's scale does not reflect these priorities. According to realist theory, the fourth category—international influence—should not be considered a more serious issue than the territorial integrity of the state itself or the political stability of the government in power. Thus I switch the positions of the second and fourth categories of Brecher, Wilkenfeld, and Moser's scale for its use in my analysis.

Previous Bargaining Behavior

As with the two preceding variables, I begin my measurement of previous bargaining behavior by building on indicators included in the ICB data set. In particular, the variables I rely on are the "centrality of violence" to an actor's bargaining strategy, and the "substantive outcome" of the crisis in terms of the actor's success or failure in achieving its goals. Brecher, Wilkenfeld, and Moser code both variables as four-point scales. First, violence may play no role, a minor role, an important role, or a preeminent role in a state's bargaining strategy. Second, the substantive outcome for a state may be coded as a victory, compromise, stalemate, or defeat. Once again, missing data points were filled in by referring to *Keesing's Contemporary Archives*.

Conceptually, this variable captures a state's willingness to use force in defense of its interests. To measure this willingness, I examine both a state's bargaining behavior in the previous crisis with the same adversary over the same issue and its success in achieving its objectives. At first glance, one might think that simply measuring whether or not a state used force in the previous crisis would be sufficient indicator of its "toughness." However, we would not want to categorize a state as "weak" if it is able to prevail in a crisis without having to use force. On the contrary, this ability may be a sign of great strength. Similarly, we would not wish to categorize a state as "unwilling" to use force if it was defeated in a previous encounter but fought to protect its interests. Such states might not be as militarily powerful as their adversaries, but it is willingness to fight rather than military capacity which this variable is supposed to capture. Thus I use a combination of the "centrality of violence" and "content of crisis outcome" variables to identify actors that were *defeated* in their previous crisis with the adversary *and* which *did not use force* or only used a *minor amount of force* to avoid this defeat.[15] Such states are coded as having capitulated in the previous dispute (value of 1). Otherwise a value of zero was coded.

Involvement in Other Disputes

I code this variable based on the COW data set on Militarized International Disputes. In this case I chose to use the COW data set instead of the ICB because the COW MID data include a large number of conflicts that represent a drain on state resources but which do not reach the

[15] As noted, this coding procedure separates out military strength—which is measured in the balance of conventional capabilities and the possession of a nuclear capacity—from a state's willingness to use force to defend its interests.

"crisis" proportions of the cases in the ICB data set. In addition, since I do not require detailed information about each of these "other" disputes beyond the dates of each state's involvement, there are few costs to relying on the COW data. However, the COW data set includes a number of cases that are of such low intensity that I do not wish to include them in my analysis because they represent no significant drain on state resources. Thus, to count it as a dispute, I require that a conflict must last at least one week, and there must be some militarized action or threat of such action by both parties to the conflict. I code this variable simply as the number of militarized disputes that a state is involved in both during the crisis of interest and during the six-month period preceding that crisis.[16]

History of Previous Conflict

This variable is coded on the basis of the crises in the ICB data set. I coded the number of times that the challenger and defender have been identified as the primary disputants in international crises prior to the current crisis.[17] Since this variable reflects either the domestic political implications of engaging in conflict or the lessons that leaders learn from a pattern of hostile interaction, I included all previous crises between the challenger and the defender between 1929 and 1979, regardless of whether the issues at stake in the previous crises matched those in the current crisis and regardless of which state was identified as the challenger in the previous crises.

Change in the Balance of Conventional Military Capabilities

This variable is coded as the change in the proportion of dyadic capabilities that belong to the challenger in the current crisis since the most recent crisis over the same issue. First I determined the defender's proportion of the dyadic balance of military capabilities for the previous crisis in an identical manner to the procedure described earlier. I then subtracted the defender's proportion of dyadic capabilities in the current crisis from the value for the previous crisis. Thus positive values on this

[16] Involvement in an interstate war counts as involvement in another dispute if the war lasted until at least one year before the beginning of the current dispute.

[17] Generally, of course, all cases will score at least a 1 on this variable. Some cases may be coded zero, however, if the challenger and defender were not the *primary* disputants in any previous crises. Such crises are properly coded as reinitiations, for the purposes of inclusion in my data set, since the two disputants were participants in the previous crises. For this variable, however, I identify the number of times that these states have been *primary* disputants, because both the Huth (1996) and Leng (1983) arguments suggest that the influence of previous conflicts should be stronger if the two states were the primary disputants with the most critical issues at stake.

variable reflect an increase in challenger capabilities between the previous
and current disputes.

CASE STUDY RESEARCH

Although I believe that my statistical model makes a significant contribution to the study of norms in terms of testing theoretical propositions in a
comparative and generalizable manner, such quantitative methods should
not represent the only research approach to these questions. In particular,
it seems important that quantitative analyses such as this one be supple-
mented by case studies of international norms. Many political scientists—
especially those studying international relations—seem to have become
trapped in a fruitless debate concerning the relative merits of quantitative
and historical research. Rather than hurling epithets at one another, students of world politics would be better served by adopting multiple
methods of research that allow one to benefit from the very different
strengths and weaknesses of statistical techniques and historical analysis.
Statistical work allows the researcher to make statements about the external validity of his or her findings. That is, statistical research and probability theory allow one to make probabilistic generalizations to a broad
universe of cases. Case studies, on the other hand, bring a greater degree
of internal validity to the results of a research project.

In chapter 5 I will present the results of my quantitative analysis, and
in chapter 6 I will investigate two of these crises in greater depth. In
general, I hope that the discussion of these historical examples will add to
the quantitative analysis in several ways. First, these case studies will ex-
plicate and illustrate the findings of the quantitative model. A table of
statistical results may not provide a good grasp of what the results really
mean in practice. Reviewing some examples may clarify these problems
and help us to apply the findings properly. Second, case studies represent
an important check on the measurements used in the statistical model.
Are the variables that seem to have an effect in the historical cases captured in my quantitative measures? Although I believe that the measures
I have presented all have a respectable level of face validity, it is important
to examine these measures more carefully and adjust them if necessary.
Third, case studies will allow me to trace the bargaining process in
greater detail to determine whether the causal process that I have hypothesized remains a plausible explanation of events as they actually un-
folded. Quantitative analyses are conducted at a very high level of ab-
straction on brief summary measures of each case. Consequently, it is
always reassuring to find that the explanation constructed on a very abstract level continues to make sense when one examines historical cases in

more detail. Finally, case studies can be useful for generating new hypotheses that serve as a spark to future research.

CONCLUSIONS

In this chapter I outlined the structure of the test for my hypotheses. I began by defining the events for study and identifying the population of cases for my analysis. These procedures led me to identify a population of 122 reinitiated international crises that will serve as the foundation for my quantitative analysis. Next, I developed operational measures that I will use to test the hypotheses I presented in chapter 3. Finally I discussed my presentation of case studies as a supplement to my quantitative approach, and the role that I hope these studies will play in my research. Now let us turn our attention to investigating the empirical influence of norms on crisis bargaining.

CHAPTER 5

Testing the Power of Legitimacy:
Dispute Settlements from 1929 to 1979

In the two previous chapters I have derived hypotheses from realist and institutionalist approaches to crisis bargaining and constructed tests for these hypotheses. In this chapter I carry out these statistical tests on the population of reinitiated international crises from 1929 to 1979. Then, in the subsequent chapter, I will extend these tests by examining two of the individual crises from my data set in greater detail.

The statistical analysis is conducted through the use of ordered probit analysis. This process is analogous to ordinary regression, but is the appropriate statistical tool for dependent variables with three or more ordinally ranked categories (Hanushek and Jackson 1977; King 1989).[1] As I discussed earlier, the interaction of the defender's bargaining strategy and the violation of a previous settlement is represented with five dummy variables with firm-but-flexible, no settlement as the excluded category. Recall that hypothesis 1 predicts a concave *curvilinear* relationship between the coerciveness of the defender's strategy and the challenger's insistence on overturning the status quo in the absence of a previous dispute settlement. This relationship is represented in the statistical model through the combination of two variables: appeasement with no settlement and bullying with no settlement. I expect to find a positive coefficient on both of these variables, since, in the absence of a previous settlement, both appeasement and bullying should result in more challenger resistance than with a firm-but-flexible strategy. Hypothesis 2 predicts that if defenders are appeasing, challengers will be more insistent if they have violated a settlement than if they have not. This effect will be reflected in a positive coefficient on the dummy variable for defender appeasement after a previous settlement that is substantively larger than

---

[1] Because my dependent variable has three categories, the statistical model must estimate a constant term and two threshold boundaries between the categories. Since the dependent variable in an ordered probit has no metric scale, one of these values must be held constant while all other coefficients are calculated in relation to that constant value. The statistical software accomplishes this estimation by assuming that the coefficient for the constant term is zero. The first and second thresholds are then estimated as parameters in the model along with those for the independent variables. These estimated thresholds between the categories appear in the results in table 5A.

the coefficient for appeasement with no settlement. Hypothesis 3 predicts that the challenger will yield if the defender's coercive behavior represents a punishment for the violation of a previous settlement. This hypothesis predicts that bullying following the violation of a previous settlement does *not* have a significantly different impact on the challenger's response than that of a firm-but-flexible strategy without a previous settlement. Consequently, the coefficient for this variable should be much smaller than the coefficient for bullying without a previous settlement, and it should not be statistically significant. Finally, hypothesis 4 predicts that firm-but-flexible strategies following the violation of a previous settlement will be at least as effective in persuading the challenger to yield as they will without a settlement; therefore, the coefficient on this variable should be either zero or negative.

My expectations for the realist control variables are relatively straightforward and follow directly from rational coercion theory and the enduring rivalries literature. I expect negative coefficients both on the balance of conventional military capabilities, and on the interaction between a bullying strategy and the balance of forces. The latter coefficient reflects the realist expectation that the effectiveness of military capability will depend on the perceived willingness to use it. Next, I expect negative coefficients on the defender's issues at stake and the defender's possession of a nuclear first-strike capability because both highly motivated defenders and those with nuclear advantages should be more capable of forcing challengers to yield. Finally, I expect positive coefficients on the variables marking a previous capitulation by the defender, the defender's involvement in other disputes, the number of previous crises between challenger and defender, and the change in the challenger's proportion of dyadic conventional military capabilities, since each of these factors should make challengers more insistent on overturning the status quo. The results of the probit analysis are presented in table 5A.[2]

Overall, the statistical performance of this model is quite good. It predicts the outcome of 67 percent of the 122 cases correctly. The model produces a 28 percent reduction in error over a null model that simply

---

[2] By using dummy variables, I was able to keep the multicollinearity among my normative variables reasonably low. Specifically, the auxiliary r-squares for bullying with a previous settlement and bullying without a settlement were approximately .84. The auxiliary r-squares for the other normative variables ranged from .49 to .62. The auxiliary r-squares for the balance of forces was .57, and its interaction with bullying strategies was slightly higher at .84. The auxiliary r-squares for the other realist variables ranged from .10 to .30. Thus multicollinearity cannot be forwarded as an explanation for the generally weak results on the realist variables. In addition, reestimation of this equation with the insignificant variables dropped yielded no change in the substantive size of the remaining coefficients or their statistical significance.

TABLE 5A
Probit Analysis Predicting Challenger Response: Normative and Realist Variables

Explanatory Variables	Coefficient	Standard Error	Significance Level
Normative Variables			
Bully, No Settlement	1.73	0.70	0.007
Bully, Settlement Violated	0.61	0.65	0.35
Firm/Flex, Settlement Violated	−0.26	0.47	0.57
Appease, No Settlement	1.12	0.49	0.01
Appease, Settlement Violated	1.98	0.59	0.0005
Realist Coercion Variables			
Balance of Military Capabilities	−0.65	0.68	0.17
Balance of Military Capabilities × Bully	−0.15	1.01	0.44
Defender First-Strike Capability[a]	0.78	0.40	0.05
Defender Issue at Stake[a]	0.13	0.08	0.10
Defender Number of Other Disputes	0.03	0.12	0.41
Defender Previous Capitulation	0.45	0.39	0.13
Number of Previous Disputes	−0.02	0.08	0.39
Change in Balance of Military Capabilities	−0.99	1.45	0.25
First Threshold	0.33	0.59	Ancillary
Second Threshold	1.00	0.59	Parameters

Note: Number of observations = 122; number of observations correctly predicted = 82; percent correctly predicted = 67.2%; proportional reduction in error = 28.1%; initial log likelihood = −122.91; log likelihood at convergence = −95.01.
[a] = Two-tailed test for significance. All other tests are one-tailed.

predicts intransigence by the challenger in every case.[3] Moreover, one should keep in mind that predictive success is often largely a function of the distribution of the dependent variable. It is easy, for example, to predict 90 percent of the cases correctly when over 80 percent of the outcomes fall into a single category. This model predicts fairly well despite the fact that the outcomes are widely distributed across the categories.

In addition to fitting the dependent variable fairly well, the results strongly support my argument concerning the role of norms and dispute settlements. As predicted by both frameworks, increases in the coerciveness of the defender's strategy have a curvilinear effect on the challenger's

[3] Intransigence is the modal category for challenger resistance and thus represents the "best guess" prediction of a null model. Specifically, my data set contains thirty-six cases of compliance, twenty-two of compromise, and sixty-four of intransigence.

insistence on overturning the status quo when no settlement has been violated. The positive coefficient on appeasement with no settlement indicates that appeasement in the absence of a previous settlement will cause the challenger to insist more firmly on an alteration of the status quo relative to the firm-but-flexible, no settlement excluded category. The positive coefficient on the variable for bullying with no settlement indicates that highly coercive strategies without the existence of a previous settlement will also make challengers highly insistent. These findings confirm the realist conventional wisdom concerning crisis bargaining reflected in hypothesis 1. While both realism and my normative approach predict this curve, coercion theory is *unable* to account for the sharp differences in the challenger's response to the defender's bargaining strategy when a previous dispute settlement has been violated.[4] First, consistent with hypothesis 2, the coefficient on the dummy variable marking appeasement following the violation of a settlement is positive and almost twice the size of the coefficient for appeasement in the absence of a settlement. This result indicates that when defenders are appeasing, challengers will be more insistent on changing the status quo if this appeasement follows the violation of a settlement. Second, the insignificant coefficient on the dummy variable for bullying following the violation of a settlement indicates that these cases are not statistically different from cases of firm-but-flexible with no settlement. Moreover, the coefficient for bullying after the violation of a previous settlement, while positive, is one-third the size of the coefficient for bullying in the absence of a previous settlement. This finding supports hypothesis 3, which predicted that challengers will be more compliant in the face of bullying behavior when the defender's actions represent punishment for the violation of a previous settlement. Finally, consistent with hypothesis 4, the coefficient on the variable for firm-but-flexible strategies following the violation of a settlement is negative, but it is substantively small and not statistically significant. Thus, firm-but-flexible strategies are slightly more effective in persuading the challenger to yield if they follow the violation of a settlement, but this effect is fairly minimal.

Because the impact of dispute settlements is spread across several variables in my model, I test the overall statistical significance of the influ-

---

[4] One objection would be that challengers respond to the punishment of a violation when the issues at stake are relatively unimportant, but that such understandings become irrelevant when the stakes are high. This problem should be controlled for to a significant degree by my inclusion of the defender's issue at stake in the equation, since challenger and defender stakes are strongly correlated. To be certain, however, I also included the severity of the challenger's issue at stake in my preliminary analyses. Its inclusion did not alter the substantive or statistical significance of the normative variables, so I removed it from the final equation.

ence of settlements by comparing the equation in table 5A to a specification that includes the defender's bargaining strategy but excludes its interaction with previous dispute settlements. A likelihood ratio test revealed that the data that I observe are more likely to have been generated by a process that includes the impact of settlements. The chi-squared value for this test was 11.27 with 3 degrees of freedom ($p < .025$).

The Substantive Effects of International Norms

The substantive effects of dispute settlements on crisis outcomes are also quite large. These effects are summarized in table 5B. In the first section I calculate the changes in the predicted probability of challenger intransigence, compromise, and compliance by varying the presence or absence of a violation for each of the defender's possible bargaining strategies. The second section then reverses this process by varying the defender's bargaining strategy while holding the presence or absence of a settlement violation constant.

Consistent with hypothesis 2, the first section of table 5B demonstrates that when the defender is appeasing, the violation of a previous settlement by the challenger actually increases its insistence on overturning the status quo compared with cases where no previous settlement existed. Specifically, the first row in table 5B states 6that the likelihood of intransigence in response to appeasement increases by 28 percent if the challenger violated a settlement. Conversely, the likelihood of compliance and compromise decrease by 15 percent and 12 percent respectively when the defender is appeasing following a violation. Previous dispute settlements have their most powerful effect on crisis bargaining when the defender uses a bullying strategy. In keeping with hypothesis 3, bullying behavior following the violation of a settlement is 42 percent less likely to elicit intransigence from the challenger than if no settlement has been violated. Conversely, of course, compliance and compromise become more likely responses to bullying behavior when the bullying represents punishment for a violation. Table 5B shows that the probability of each of these outcomes increases by 31 percent and 11 percent respectively. Realist theory cannot explain why the effectiveness of coercive bargaining strategies appears to depend so significantly on the normative context in which such tactics are used.

Finally, as predicted by hypothesis 4, when the defender is firm-but-flexible the presence or absence of a previous settlement has relatively little effect on the challenger's response. In either case the likelihood of compliance or compromise is high. Even so, the fact that the defender is punishing a violation of a previous settlement does have some effect. As table 5B illustrates, when the defender punishes a violation with a firm-

TABLE 5B
Marginal Effects of Normative Variables

Section 1: Effects of Previous Settlements on the Challenger's Response Controlling for the Defender's Bargaining Strategy

Change in Previous Settlement	Change in P(Compliance)	Change in P(Compromise)	Change in P(Intransigence)
If Defender Appeasing: No to Yes	− 15.4%	− 12.3%	+ 27.7%
If Defender Firm-but-Flexible: No to Yes	+ 9.2%	− 3.8%	− 5.4%
If Defender Bullying: No to Yes	+ 31.4%	+ 10.6%	− 42.0%

Section 2: Marginal Effects of the Defender's Bargaining Strategy on the Challenger's Response Controlling for Previous Settlements

Change in Defender Coercion	Change in P(Compliance)	Change in P(Compromise)	Change in P(Intransigence)
If No Previous Settlement Violated			
Appeasing to Firm-but-Flexible	+ 44.0%	− 2.3%	− 41.7%
Firm-but-Flexible to Bullying	− 55.4%	− 5.3%	+ 60.7%
If Previous Settlement Violated			
Appeasing to Firm-but-Flexible	+ 68.7%	+ 6.2%	− 74.8%
Firm-but-Flexible to Bullying	− 33.2%	+ 9.1%	+ 24.1%

Note: Marginal effects were calculated by generating predicted values from the probit model while changing the values of selected variables and holding the others at their means or modes. The predicted values were transformed into probabilities that the outcome would fall into each category by summing the area underneath the cumulative normal distribution between the predicted value and each of the category thresholds.

but-flexible strategy, the probability of challenger compliance increases by 9 percent over cases without the violation of any previous settlement. The probability of compromise and intransigence, on the other hand, go down by 4 percent and 5 percent respectively.

The second section of table 5B also documents the contrasting relationships between the defender's strategy and challenger's response with and without a previous settlement. Here we can see the concave curvilinear relationship develop as expected by hypothesis 1. First, with regard to the crises without a previous settlement, table 5B shows that as the coerciveness of the defender's strategy increases from appeasing to firm-but-flexible, the probability of challenger intransigence drops by 42 percent. The probability of compliance by the challenger, on the other hand, increases by a substantial 44 percent. In fact, the effect of moving from an appeasing to a firm-but-flexible strategy reduces the challenger's insistence on altering the status quo so sharply that it actually reduces the probability of a compromise by 2 percent as the predicted outcomes shift further toward the compliance category. Further increases in the coerciveness of the defender's strategy from firm-but-flexible to bullying, however, quickly reverse this relationship Specifically, this shift in the defender's strategy increases the likelihood of intransigence by a very substantial 61 percent. Conversely, the move from firm-but-flexible to a bullying strategy reduces the predicted probability of challenger compliance and compromise by 55 percent and 5 percent respectively.

When the challenger has violated a previous dispute settlement, however, the relationship between the defender's strategy and the challenger's response is very different. The second section of table 5B shows that as the coerciveness of the defender's strategy increases from appeasing to firm-but-flexible, the probability that the challenger will remain intransigent drops by a striking 75 percent. My normative model expected that this decrease would be sharper after a challenger violation, and indeed this drop is nearly twice as large as when no violation has occurred. Conversely, this shift in defender strategy increases the probability of challenger compliance by 69 percent. This change is more than half again the size of the increase we saw with no previous settlement. The probability of challenger compromise also increases by a modest 6 percent. Finally, contrary to my predictions, I find that continued increases in the coerciveness of the defender's strategy from firm-but-flexible to bullying *do* increase the probability of challenger intransigence somewhat after the violation of a previous settlement. But in this case the increase is only 24 percent—slightly more than one-third the increase that occurs without a violation. Similarly, while this change reduces the probability of compliance by 33 percent, this drop is slightly more than half the size of the decrease when no settlement has been violated. Moreover, the shift from a bullying to a firm-but-flexible strategy actually *increases* the likelihood of compromise by 9 percent. In sum, bullying is not as effective as a firm-but-flexible strategy in lowering challenger resistance after the violation of a settlement. However, bullying is *much* more effective as a response to the violation of a settlement than it is outside of this context. Specifically, the probability of challenger intransigence in response to bullying with no previous settlement is 76 percent. But when bullying represents a punishment for violating a settlement, the probability of challenger intransigence is only 34 percent.

ILLUSTRATING THE IMPACT OF LEGITIMATE DISPUTE SETTLEMENTS

In figure 5A, I illustrate the effects described in tables 5A and 5B by plotting the predicted probabilities of challenger intransigence against the defender's bargaining strategy. In the figure I identify the predicted probabilities by whether or not the challenger violated a settlement. The squares refer to the predictions for situations in which the challenger committed a violation, and the circles refer to the predictions for situations in which no settlement was violated. I have plotted lines that represent the estimated relationships between the defender's strategy and the challenger's response both with and without a previous violation. The dashed line represents the estimated relationship if a violation has occurred, while the dotted line represents the relationship if there was no violation. First, the clearly concave curvilinear form of the dotted line in figure 5A captures the support I found for hypothesis 1. That is, in the absence of a violation of a previous settlement, only firm-but-flexible bargaining strategies will be effective in preventing challenger intransigence. The gap between the dashed and dotted lines on the left-hand side of figure 5A, on the other hand, indicates the support I found for hypothesis 2. Specifically, the dashed line is significantly higher when the defender is appeasing, reflecting a greater probability of challenger intransigence when the appeasement follows a violation. Finally, the strong support I found for hypothesis 3 is reflected in the gap between the dashed and dotted lines on the right-hand side of figure 5A. Here the dashed line is much lower, reflecting the lower likelihood of intransigence as a response to bullying after a settlement has been violated.

Perhaps the clearest way to evaluate the predictions of my model is to compare the relationships described in figures 3A and 5A. The fit between the observed relationships in figure 5A and those predicted in figure 3A is very close. In each case, challengers are more insistent on overturning the status quo in response to appeasing behavior if it follows the violation of a settlement, and they are much less insistent in response to bullying behavior in the same context. In fact, there appears to be only one significant difference between the data and the expectations of my model. Specifically, although it is apparent that bullying is a much more effective strategy when it represents a punishment for the violation of a previous settlement, bullying remains less effective than the firm-but-flex-

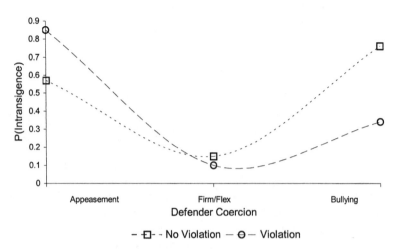

Figure 5A Estimated Relationships between Defender Coercion and Challenger Resistance, Depending on Violation of Previous Settlements

ible strategy even in this context. This finding is reflected in the slight curve that remains in the relationship between the coerciveness of the defender's strategy and the challenger's insistence on overturning the status quo even when a settlement has been violated. Since this finding was unexpected, any attempt to explain it must be recognized as post hoc. Nonetheless, one might postulate that while dispute settlements frequently act as persuasive referents and reputational constraints, these norms are not *always* persuasive. In chapter 7 I turn my attention to the issue of *when* dispute settlements will be effective in constraining crisis behavior.

One final way to illustrate the interactive impact of coercive behavior and legitimate dispute settlements is to review a few brief examples from my data set. Let me begin by illustrating the curvilinear relationship between defender coercion and challenger resistance in the absence of a previous settlement—as predicted by hypothesis 1. In this context, the most common result of appeasement was intransigence on the part of the challenger. In 1968, for example, the Czech leadership published an "Action Program" which called for a moderation of Soviet-style communism, and in June of that year an open letter to the public known as the "Two Thousand Words" called for an acceleration of that program. The Soviet Union perceived this activity as a threat to its influence in Eastern Europe, and Moscow responded—along with other members of the Warsaw Pact—by demanding an abandonment of the Action Program and demanding the resignation of the Czech head of defense because of his criticisms of the Warsaw Pact's structure. The Czech leader, Dubcek, chose to appease the USSR. Specifically, he agreed to fire the head of defense, indicating that military resistance was not an option for Czechoslovakia, and he began negotiating a settlement of the outstanding issues. Rather than exploring these negotiations, however, the Soviet Union took immediate advantage of Dubcek's weak military stance by launching an invasion on August 20. The Soviet forces met little resistance and quickly installed a new staunchly pro-Soviet regime in Prague.

Firm-but-flexible strategies, however, were much more successful, even when no settlement had been violated. In 1961, for example, the Netherlands submitted a proposal to the UN to transfer sovereignty over a former colonial possession known as West Irian directly to the inhabitants of the area. Indonesia, however, also claimed sovereignty over this territory, and so they responded to the Dutch proposal with a carefully calibrated coercive strategy to achieve their goals. On the one hand, Indonesian military forces began to mobilize, and some units began to engage in a low-level infiltration of West Irian. At the same time, however, the Indonesians engaged in UN-sponsored negotiations over the status of the disputed territory. Indonesia's firm-but-flexible stance—backed by the United States and the United Nations—caused a dramatic shift in the Dutch position, for the Netherlands soon agreed to evacuate the area for UN supervision until it could be transferred to Indonesia.

Finally, while modestly coercive tactics like Indonesia's were often successful without the violation of a settlement, bullying strategies most definitely were not. In a crisis during the Korean War, for example, the United States chose to pursue North Korean forces across the thirty-eighth Parallel, creating a crisis for the PRC. The Chinese delivered numerous warnings to the United States throughout September and early October of 1950, making it clear that they would respond to a US invasion of North Korea with force. President Truman and General MacArthur, however, essentially ignored the Chinese warnings and refused to reconsider the escalation of their military goals from the defense of South Korea to the destruction of the North. Instead, American forces pressed as quickly as possible toward the Yalu River. The Chinese response, of course, was a massive intervention in the Korean War, which thwarted US hopes of victory and stalemated the conflict for another three years.

These three crises typify behavior in crises when no settlement has been violated. The markedly different relationship between defender coercion and challenger resistance following the violation of a settlement can be illustrated by examining three other crises from my data set.[5] As

---

[5] My discussion of these cases is drawn from the crisis summaries provided by the ICB data set in Brecher, Wilkenfeld, and Moser (1988); and Brecher and Wilkenfeld (1997).

was the case without a previous settlement, appeasement was not an effective strategy. The classic example of the failure of appeasement, of course, is the outcome of the Munich crisis of 1938. In this case, Germany had pledged only months earlier that it had no aggressive intentions against Czechoslovakia. Hitler blatantly violated this pledge by demanding that Germany be allowed to annex the Czech Sudetenland because many of its inhabitants were ethnically German. Britain and France refused to support the Czechs, however, leaving them with little choice but to concede to Hitler's demands. These concessions not only shattered the Czech state, but also appeared to encourage further German aggression by signaling to Hitler that the Western Powers would not enforce their agreements.

Firm-but-flexible strategies, on the other hand, were almost always successful responses to the violation of a settlement. In October 1978, for example, Argentina violated an agreement with Chile concerning several islands in the Beagle Channel near the southern tip of South America. The agreement stipulated that the islands would be jointly developed by the two countries, but Argentina violated this accord by mobilizing fifty thousand troops for action in the disputed territory and by engaging in clashes across the Chilean border. Chile's response was twofold. On the one hand, Chile mobilized forty-five thousand troops of its own, and canceled naval maneuvers with the United States so as to be prepared for an Argentine invasion. At the same time, however, Chile also proposed renewed mediation of the dispute by a friendly government, and they called on the Organization of American States (OAS) to intervene in the dispute. As it turned out, the pope offered to act as mediator, and his offer was accepted by both parties. In the end, the renewed mediated settlement established Chilean sovereignty over the islands and granted Chile maritime rights to the islands' Pacific waters. Argentina was given control of the Atlantic waters.

The effects of dispute settlements were most prominent, however, when the defender used a bullying strategy. In this case, much higher levels of coercion are often successful in bringing compliance. In 1944, for example, the USSR violated the Tripartite Treaty of Alliance by demanding additional oil concessions in northern Iran. The Soviet government used its military forces to support uprisings in Iran, but the Iranian government flatly rejected Soviet demands and remained unwilling to negotiate on the issue. In fact, the Iranian parliament backed up this tough stance by passing a law making it illegal to negotiate oil concessions with any foreign power. The United States, however, did not support the Iranian position, leaving the Soviets with an overwhelming military preponderance in the area. Despite this massive advantage, the Soviets chose to respond to the tough Iranian bargaining tactics by conceding and allowing the issue to drop. This behavior is difficult to understand from a traditional realist perspective. But my argument about dispute settlements can help to explain it. The Tripartite Treaty communicated to the Soviets that the Iranians did not intend to withdraw all Soviet access to oil or to demand renumeration for previous concessions. In addition, this agreement redefined the Soviet demands as illegitimate. This understanding appears to have been powerful enough—along with some coaxing from the Iranians—to persuade the Soviets to back down.

The influence that dispute settlements have on the perception of coercive behavior can be vividly illustrated by comparing the two cases of bullying discussed earlier. In the Korean War, the United States refused to recognize that its rush to the Yalu River might reasonably be perceived as threatening by the PRC. In fact, however, the Chinese did perceive US behavior as threatening and were concerned about what limits—if any—there might be to US war aims. As a result, despite the fact that the United States represented an extremely formidable and clearly committed military foe, the Chinese chose to launch a massive intervention into the Korean conflict and extended the war for another three years. The Soviet response to Iran's inflexible bargaining stance during their 1944 crisis, however, was sharply different. In that case, the presence of the Tripartite Treaty appeared to alter Soviet interpretations of Iranian behavior. The fact that Iran had agreed to the Tripartite Treaty communicated to the Soviets that Iranian aims in the crisis were limited and defensive. Thus despite a *massive* military advantage in the area, the USSR chose to back down and to reestablish its adherence to the treaty. Rational coercion theory has a very difficult time explaining the Chinese willingness to take on the powerful United States in combination with the USSR's compliance with the demands of a weak minor power. Accounting for the normative role of dispute settlements, however, makes this combination of outcomes less puzzling. I will extend this kind of analysis in the following chapter by comparing Soviet behavior in the Cuban missile crisis with its actions in a subsequent crisis over the basing of missiles in Cuba.

EVALUATING THE REALIST PARADIGM

While the data solidly support my normative bargaining model, the results for the realist control variables are mixed at best. First, consistent with Leng (1993) and Huth (1988), the defender's bargaining strategy does have the curvilinear effect predicted by the realist model, but coercion theory is unable to account for the influence of dispute settlements on the effects of coercion. Second, the balance of military capabilities does have the predicted negative coefficient. The coefficient is substantively large, but it does not achieve conventional levels of statistical sig-

TABLE 5C
Marginal Effects of Selected Realist Variables

Change in Independent Variable	Change in P(Compliance)	Change in P(Compromise)	Change in P(Intransigence)
Balance of Military Capabilities			
1/3 ratio–1/1 ratio	+7.4%	+0.1%	−7.5%
1/1 ratio–3/1 ratio	+7.9%	−0.9%	−7.0%
Defender Previous Capitulation			
No to Yes	−16.0%	−1.7%	+17.7%

Note: Marginal effects were calculated by generating predicted values from the probit model while changing the values of selected variables and holding the others at their means or modes. The predicted values were transformed into probabilities that the outcome would fall into each category by summing the area underneath the cumulative normal distribution between the predicted value and each of the category thresholds.

nificance.[6] The substantive impact of the balance of military capabilities is depicted in table 5C. Here we see that a shift in relative capabilities from a 3 to 1 defender advantage to an even 1 to 1 ratio increases the probability of challenger intransigence by 7.5 percent. A further increase from a 1 to 1 ratio to a 3 to 1 challenger advantage increases the probability of intransigence by another 7 percent. The coefficient on the interaction between the balance of military capabilities and the defender's bullying strategy is also negative, but it is substantively quite small and it does not approach statistical significance. Thus demonstrations of resolve do not appear to be important in creating a coercive impact for the balance of military capabilities.

The defender's capitulation in a previous dispute *does* have an impact on the challenger's subsequent response, though like the balance of forces this coefficient does not achieve statistical significance (p < .125).[7] Still, the coefficient for previous capitulation is much larger than for any of the previous three variables, and it is in the expected positive direction. Substantively, the impact of this variable is similar to that of the balance of military capabilities. If the defender capitulated in the previous crisis, the probability of challenger intransigence increases by 18 percent.

None of the other variables in the realist model perform strongly. The defender's involvement in other militarized disputes, for example, has no

[6] If the nonsignificant interaction term with the defender's use of a bullying strategy is dropped, the statistical significance of this coefficient improves to $p < 0.09$.

[7] Notably, if the dispute settlement variables are dropped from the equation, the coefficient for this variable increases substantially and becomes significant at the 0.05 level.

effect on the challenger's behavior. Not only does its coefficient fail to approach statistical significance, but it is substantively extremely small. Similarly, neither the number of previous crises nor the change in the balance of military capabilities has any independent influence on the challenger's response. The coefficient for the number of previous disputes is extremely near zero and does not approach statistical significance, while the coefficient for the change in the balance of forces is actually in the wrong direction—though it is not statistically significant.

My findings concerning the influence of previous crises are somewhat puzzling, given the powerful support that Huth (1996) finds for the effect of previous crises on the escalation of territorial disputes. However, a closer examination of Huth's argument and my data set can clarify the reasons for these differences. Huth argues that previous disputes create domestic pressures against conciliation. In testing his argument, however, he does not control for the bargaining strategies used by the states in the dispute. A quick look at my data set reveals that the coerciveness of the defender's strategy is positively correlated with the number of previous crises, although this correlation does not quite achieve statistical significance.[8] Thus I would suggest that the link between previous crises and the escalation of a current dispute may be an indirect one. A history of conflict can lead to the escalation of crises *if* this history persuades leaders to rely on bullying strategies when such strategies are counterproductive (i.e., when no settlement has been violated). This explanation is also consistent with Leng's (1983) findings concerning states learning realpolitik lessons about coercive strategies from repeated international conflict.

The effects of the final two variables in the coercion model, however, are the most puzzling. Both the defender's possession of a nuclear first-strike advantage and the defender's interests at stake in the dispute appear to cause a sharp increase in the challenger's insistence on overturning the status quo. I had no theoretical expectations that could explain these results, and so any conclusions in concerning these variables must once again be post hoc. Nonetheless, I examined the cases that appeared to be generating the positive coefficients to search for some tentative explanations.

First, with regard to the defender's possession of a first strike, I should note that its bivariate correlation with the challenger's response is near zero.[9] It is only when the other variables in the coercion model are included in the analysis that it appears to have a positive effect. Moreover, the cases in which the defender has a first-strike advantage appear to fall

---

[8] Specifically, the correlation coefficient is 0.14 ($p < 0.07$).

[9] The bivariate correlation coefficient is -0.03, and it is not statistically differentiable from 0.

into two groups. First, there are a number of crises in which both the challenging and defending states are Great Powers.[10] These cases include clashes between the United States and the PRC over Korea and Taiwan, US-Soviet crises over Cuba and Eastern Europe, and Sino-Soviet border clashes. In these cases the defending United States and the USSR did appear—either tacitly or explicitly—to hold the threat of nuclear weapons over their opponents. Certainly the USSR and the PRC as the respective challengers in these crises considered the potential use of nuclear weapons by their adversaries. For these cases, the defender's possession of a nuclear first-strike capability *does* make the challenger more likely to yield. In none of the cases between Great Powers in which the defender held a first-strike advantage did the challenger remain intransigent.

There is, however, a second set of crises in which the defender possessed a nuclear first strike and the challenger was a minor power that did not possess nuclear weapons. These cases include a series of crises between the United States and North Vietnam, as well as several British and French attempts to defend former colonies. In these situations the possibility of a nuclear first strike was never seriously considered or threatened by the defender, and the challengers did not take the possibility of such use seriously.[11] Moreover, in most of these cases the smaller challenger remained intransigent despite the strenuous (non-nuclear) coercive attempts of the defender. Thus as previous work has found, the possession of a strong nuclear capability can serve as a powerful coercive tool against fellow Great Power adversaries (Huth, Gelpi, and Bennett 1993). Against smaller powers, however, nuclear threats may work, but they are almost never used.[12]

One might argue that nuclear threats are not made against small powers because such nuclear defenders are likely to be more powerful than the small power challengers on the conventional level as well. Such nuclear threats would be unnecessary if the defender can easily prevail without them. In the vast majority of such encounters in my data set, however, the small power remains intransigent while the more powerful defender does not use its nuclear resource. Deterrence and coercion the-

[10] My use of the term "Great Power" follows from Huth, Gelpi, and Bennett (1993); and Levy (1983).

[11] One instance where a state with a nuclear first strike was successful in coercing a minor power is a series of clashes between Britain and Guatemala over Belize. I would argue, however, that the British success was a result of their use of a firm-but-flexible strategy. No nuclear threats were made against Guatemala.

[12] This failure to attempt nuclear coercion cannot be attributed to the fact that the defenders could prevail at the conventional level, since many of them lost the encounters in which they chose not to make nuclear threats. One possible explanation of this nuclear non-use relates to the influence of international norms. See Tannenwald (1999); Price and Tannenwald in Katzenstein (1996); and Paul (1995).

ory have a very difficult time explaining the failure to use this potentially powerful coercive tool, but an approach that incorporates the influence of norms can make sense of this rather puzzling behavior. In particular, some scholars have recently argued that nuclear weapons have not been used since World War II because of the evolution of an international norm against their use.[13] While often tacit, this norm has also been forwarded explicitly in the form of "no first use" treaties that were considered by the United States and the Soviet Union. This nuclear norm particularly prohibits the use of nuclear weapons against defenseless non-nuclear states. Thus when it considers using nuclear weapons in a crisis with a minor power, a Great Power defender must consider costs to using these weapons which coercion theory does not incorporate into its analysis. For example, even by threatening a nuclear first strike against a defenseless state, the defender would be committing an act that is widely recognized as illegitimate. As a result, even if the nuclear threat were successful, the defender would risk provoking enemies not directly involved in the current dispute and would risk losing the support of allies because of its reckless behavior. All of these considerations make the use of nuclear threats against minor powers a much less attractive source of leverage than coercion theory would predict.

The process that is generating the estimated positive effect for the severity of the defender's issue at stake, on the other hand, seems somewhat different. In this case the crucial factor appears to be the selection process by which crises become a part of my data set. As I discussed earlier, any nonrandom process for selecting cases will necessarily affect the coefficients that an analysis generates, and restricts the population of cases to which any results can be generalized (Achen 1986). My set of reinitiated crises are clearly not a randomly selected set of international events. Many challengers may well be deterred from initiating a crisis over an issue that is extremely important to the defender. In addition, they may be even more hesitant to reinitiate a crisis if the defender has already demonstrated that it is highly motivated to defend its interests in a previous crisis over this issue. If a challenger chooses to reinitiate a crisis even when the defender has important assets at stake, then the challenging state must have its own reasons for being very highly motivated to prevail. As a result, when we examine behavior after this selection process, the effect of the defender's issue at stake on the challenger's behavior may be reduced.[14] In fact, such selection processes can have such a

---

[13] See Price and Tannenwald in Katzenstein (1996); and Tannenwald (1999).

[14] These selection effects probably also contribute to the positive coefficient for the defender's possession of a first strike and the insignificant result for the defender's involvement in other disputes. The selection effects seem particularly clear and pronounced, however, on the issues at stake variable.

pronounced effect on the effects of some variables that their coefficients actually reverse sign (Gartner and Siverson 1996; Fearon 1994a).

The data I have collected on the defender's issue at stake and challenger resistance fit this pattern precisely. Remember that the defender stakes variable is coded on a six-point scale ranging from low-level economic or social threats up to the continued existence of the defender's state. Cross-tabulating this variable with the challenger's level of resistance reveals that for the lowest four categories in defender stakes, the probability of challenger intransigence remains constant at approximately 40 percent. In the fifth category—grave damage—the likelihood of intransigence increases to 67 percent, and when the existence of the defending state is at stake, the challenger remains intransigent 82 percent of the time. If we examine the cases in these two highest categories, we can begin to see a pattern emerging. Regardless of the defenders' actions, the challengers had already decided that they would not give in on the issue at hand. As one might expect, many of the cases in the fifth and sixth categories end in wars, since the challengers generally remain intransigent and the defenders' extremely important interests are at stake. Even for those cases that did not end in wars, however, it is fairly clear that the challengers were willing to go to war if the defender did not capitulate. For example, this set of cases includes a series of crises between Germany and its neighbors leading up to the outbreak of World War II. In the Anschluss, the Munich crisis, disputes over Danzig, Memel, and so on, Hitler was clearly aware before initiating these crises that he would be threatening the existence of neighboring states. Even with that knowledge he chose to precipitate these crises because he had decided that he would prefer war to withdrawing his ambitious territorial claims. This type of highly motivated challenger is exactly what one might expect a self-selection process to generate for reinitiated crises in which the defender's interests at stake are high.

As I emphasized in chapter 4, however, the presence of this nonrandom selection process and the effect it has on the estimated coefficients does not imply that the results are "wrong" or that the coefficients are "biased." The effects estimated by my analysis are correct for the population of cases for which they were estimated: *reinitiated crises*. Once a dispute is reinitiated, the presence or absence of a previous settlement in combination with the bargaining strategy used by the defender will have a much more important effect on the resolution of the crisis than will the other core realist variables that I examined. These findings do *not* necessarily imply, however, that variables from realist theory do not have an effect on whether or not a crisis is ever initiated, or is reinitiated. But while my population of cases may limit the generalizability of my results with regard to the realist variables, it also acts to provide a particularly tough test for my normative variables. In particular, since I analyze crises that were initiated, resolved, and then reinitiated, the challenging states in my data set are likely to be very highly motivated to overturn the status quo. It is particularly impressive that international norms can have such a powerful impact on these strongly motivated challenging states.[15]

CONCLUSIONS

I began my analysis with a discussion of international norms, signaling, and the role of dispute settlements in crisis bargaining. Then I presented the realist alternative to my normative model, which is skeptical of the impact of norms and dispute settlements on international conflict behavior. After having tested each of these frameworks, I find that my norm-based argument concerning the role of disputes settlements received strong and consistent empirical support even when tested against the realist alternative. Contrary to the expectations of realist theory, dispute settlements do appear to construct behavioral norms that have a powerful effect on the way states interpret and respond to coercive behavior. In fact, in the reinitiated crises I examined, these norms had a more powerful effect on the way that states respond to coercive behavior than did traditional realist variables such as the balance of military capabilities or bargaining behavior in previous disputes.

Dispute settlements do appear to be able to introduce some definitions of legitimate and illegitimate behavior even into relationships between states that are in many ways highly adversarial. The US-Soviet relationship, for example, was for many years among the most adversarial on the globe. Despite their sharp conflicts of interest, however, my analysis documents how the conclusion of settlements to particular disputed issues— such as the basing of nuclear weapons in Cuba—helped the superpowers to build islands of cooperation in their relationship which were later able to grow. These settlements stabilized cooperation because the punish-

---

[15] It is possible that states that have agreed to a previous settlement are more "reasonable" or willing to negotiate than are other states. Thus they might be less likely to remain intransigent in subsequent crises. However, this latter argument cannot account for the fact that challengers are *more* likely to remain intransigent if the defender responds to the violation of a settlement with an appeasement strategy. Moreover, my reputational argument suggests that states will suffer additional costs by violating a previous settlement than if no settlement existed. Thus there are also reasons to believe that challengers who choose to violate settlements will be *especially* motivated to overturn the status quo. I also attempted to address this issue by developing a selection model (Achen 1986). None of the variables in my analyses—including legitimate dispute settlements—were strong predictors of reinitiation. As a result, I remain confident that my estimated effects of previous settlements represent the influence of norms on behavior, and are not simply the result of a self-selection process.

ment of a violation—even through the use of bullying behavior—generally resulted in compliance with the terms of the settlement or at least in the conclusion of another compromise settlement. The likelihood of a challenger complying with bullying demands when no settlement has been violated, on the other hand, is quite low. Thus dispute settlements solidify cooperation so that a single hostile "defection" need not poison what had been—at least in certain aspects—a cooperative relationship. This capacity of dispute settlements to reestablish cooperation, however, does come at some cost. In particular, if a state signs a settlement agreement, it must be willing to pay the price of punishing violations. For if a state responds to the violation of an agreement by appeasing its adversary and offering concessions, it will face even greater resistance than if there had been no settlement to begin with.

The realist theory of coercion in crisis bargaining did not receive such strong or consistent support in my analysis. Defender coercion does have the curvilinear effect predicted by Leng and Huth when no dispute settlement has been violated, but their approach is unable to explain the substantial difference in challengers' responses to coercive behavior after they violated a dispute settlement. Second, the balance of military capabilities has an important effect on the challenger's behavior when the defender is appeasing, but this difference virtually disappears when the defender adopts a bullying strategy. This finding suggests that military capacity may be a strong coercive tool, but that its most effective use through coercive *behavior* depends critically on the way that states interpret that coercion. Military prowess cannot alter the challenger's interpretation of the intent behind the defender's response in the way that the standards of behavior constructed by a dispute settlement can. The other variables suggested by the realist coercion model do not have their predicted effects on the challenger's crisis behavior. The defender's possession of a nuclear first strike, for example, appeared to have an effect on the actions of Great Power defenders, but nuclear threats were not generally even made against minor power challengers. Defenders failed to use this potential source of leverage even when they were otherwise unsuccessful in coercing small power challengers. While coercion theory finds such behavior inexplicable, a consideration of the influence of international norms and standards of legitimate behavior once again makes this result less puzzling. My analyses suggest that coercion theory's exclusive focus on the capability to inflict damage and the willingness to use it misrepresents some important aspects of crisis behavior.

We must be careful, however, in interpreting this test of coercion theory, since the analysis was performed on a self-selected sample of crises. Indeed, crises themselves represent a self-selected sample of international disagreements. Thus it is possible that coercion theory has great explanatory power when examining state behavior before norm-based standards of behavior have been constructed. The outcome of the first crisis over an issue, for example, might be determined by traditional variables within coercion theory because no notion of "legitimate" behavior exists. Once such crises are settled, however, the meaning that these settlements give to coercive behavior has a larger impact on subsequent crisis outcomes than do traditional sources of coercive power.

In the following chapter I will continue my empirical analysis by selecting several cases from my data set for more detailed investigation. I hope that these case studies help both to illustrate the effects found in my statistical model and to demonstrate that the causal arguments presented in chapter 3 and the empirical patterns I discovered in this chapter continue to make sense when the crises are examined in greater detail.

CHAPTER 6

Cienfuegos and the Six-Day War: Contrasting Normative Narratives

In the previous chapter I presented statistical tests of the hypotheses derived from a realist and an institutionalist approach to crisis bargaining. Overall, my central argument concerning the role of norms created by dispute settlements received solid and consistent support. The realist hypotheses, on the other hand, received more mixed support. Drawing on these results, in this chapter I will dissect two of the crises from my data set in greater detail. I use the first of these two cases as a concrete illustration of my statistical findings and as a test of whether the measurements and causal arguments presented previously continue to make sense when the crises are examined more closely. I use the second case study to begin a discussion of why norms sometimes fail.

Before addressing that issue, however, I will discuss the 1970 Cienfuegos submarine base crisis between the United States and the Soviet Union, in which US bullying behavior brought quick and quiet compliance from their Soviet rivals. In my examination I hope to determine whether or not the US-Soviet settlement following the Cuban missile crisis altered Soviet interpretations of US coercive behavior and facilitated the reestablishment of US-Soviet cooperation after Cienfuegos. In particular, I examine whether the Kennedy-Khrushchev understanding that resolved the Cuban missile crisis influenced both the United States and the Soviet Union to make concessions when their actions were in violation of that understanding. Briefly, my case study indicates that the Kennedy-Khrushchev understanding *did* exert a powerful influence on the propensity of the US and Soviet governments to make concessions both during and after the Cienfuegos crisis in the manner hypothesized by my institutionalist theory of norms. Moreover, I find that this behavior cannot adequately be explained by any of the prominent realist theories of crisis bargaining.

Next, I turn my attention to an exploration of a failed attempt to enforce a settlement: the Six-Day War of 1967. In this case, Israeli punishment of an Egyptian violation of the settlement following the Suez War did not result in Egyptian compliance. From this example I will attempt to draw some tentative generalizations about other reasons why norms may occasionally fail to alter states' behavior in subsequent crises.

This analysis of the Six-Day War will serve as my springboard for a broader investigation of the success and failure of international norms in chapter 7.

The Power of Legitimacy in the Cold War over Cuba

Perhaps the most intense crisis of the Cold War—the Cuban missile crisis—was brought to an end through an understanding between John Kennedy and Nikita Khrushchev. As I shall demonstrate later, the Kennedy-Khrushchev understanding did represent a legitimate dispute settlement in the sense that I have used that term in this work. Although this understanding brought an end to the Cuban missile crisis, it did not bring an end to the superpower clashes over Cuba. In particular, the Soviet Union repeatedly attempted to overturn the status quo in Cuba, and each time they did so they were met with a sharp response by the United States. When the Soviet actions do *not* represent a violation of the Kennedy-Khrushchev understanding, I expect the Soviet leadership to remain intransigent in its challenge to the status quo despite the American attempts at coercion. Similarly, prior to the establishment of the Kennedy-Khrushchev understanding I expect the USSR to respond to American coercion over Cuba with belligerence. As I discussed earlier, international anarchy and the inherent difficulties of estimating the intentions of other states encourages leaders to avoid making any concessions that might be viewed as a sign of weakness. Under these circumstances, I expect the USSR to respond to American coercion with belligerence and intransigence out of fear that making concessions will encourage further American aggression.

> HYPOTHESIS 1.   *When Soviet attempts to overturn the status quo in Cuba* do not violate *the Kennedy-Khrushchev understanding—either because their actions took place prior to the conclusion of a settlement or because their actions did not violate the understanding—the USSR will* remain intransigent *in response to American coercion.*

When Soviet actions in Cuba *do* violate the Kennedy-Khrushchev understanding, however, I expect the USSR to concede to US demands to reestablish the previous status quo. I base this expectation on the two complementary roles of norms as reputational constraints and normative referents. First, let us consider the influence of normative referents in altering Soviet behavior. As I discussed in chapter 3, in the absence of a previous settlement, highly coercive bullying tactics will generate fears of future demands for concessions, which will cause the USSR to become intransigent in its bargaining stance. If the Soviet Union is in violation of a dispute settlement, however, bullying tactics should elicit a very different response. American consent to the Kennedy-Khrushchev understand-ing should persuade the USSR that its demands with regard to Cuba are limited. Thus the USSR will not fear that the US actions represent the beginning of an endless series of demands for concessions over Cuba. As the Soviet Union searches for possible interpretations of American coer-cion before making a response, the normative dimension to the relation-ship created by the dispute settlement will cause the Soviet leadership to reframe its own violation as an "illegitimate act." The American coercion, on the other hand, becomes a "legitimate" defense of the settlement and a *punishment* rather than an act of aggression. Thus when the United States makes a highly coercive response to the violation of the Kennedy-Khrushchev understanding, the Soviet leaders will retain their belief that the United States is not aggressive, but they will have learned that it remains vigilant with regard to its rights in Cuba. Consequently, they will comply with American demands and yield in their challenge to the settle-ment.

The reputational effects of dispute settlements should have an identical influence on subsequent crisis bargaining. First, coercive behavior by the United States in response to the violation of the Kennedy-Khrushchev understanding will inflict substantial reputational costs on the USSR if it remains intransigent. The United States, its allies, and other countries around the world will view the Soviet Union as extremely untrustworthy under these circumstances because it will have demonstrated that it can-not be held to its commitments even by the threat or use of force. Con-ceding to the United States, on the other hand, holds out the promise of rehabilitating the Soviet Union's reputation for upholding its word. While some reputational damage may be inevitable, by reestablishing compliance with the norm, the Soviet leadership can demonstrate that it is not unalterably aggressive and can be held to its word by a vigilant defender. Moreover, this line of argument would suggest that conceding to the United States is likely to do less damage to the USSR's reputation for toughness than it might in other contexts. In particular, the presence of the dispute settlement makes it easier for the Soviet leadership to save face by framing its concession as compliance with the principles of the agreement rather than capitulation to the United States per se.

HYPOTHESIS 2. *When Soviet attempts to overturn the status quo in Cuba* do violate *the settlement of the Cuban missile crisis, the USSR will restore compliance with the settlement in response to American coercion.*

Finally, in addition to changing the predicted behavior of the Soviet Union, the presence of the norms embodied in the Kennedy-Khrushchev understanding should leave traces on the evolution of the subsequent disputes themselves. In particular, threats and concessions by both parties should be framed in terms of the stipulation of the understanding. Once again this expectation derives the role of norms as reputational constraints and normative referents. By framing concessions in terms of the previous settlement, for example, the Soviet leadership can both minimize damage to its reputation for toughness and emphasize that it *will* comply with its international commitments. Moreover, by explicitly calling attention to the settlement as a normative referent, the Soviet Union can communicate to the United States the *reason* that it is conceding to its demands and in so doing can identify the limits of its willingness to make concessions. In fact, even if the Soviet leadership is remaining intransigent, it should *still* frame its intransigence in terms of the settlement to persuade the United States of the legitimacy of its position and the limitations of its expansionist ambitions. The American leadership, on the other hand, should explicitly frame its demands in terms of the Kennedy-Khrushchev understanding because doing so will endow their threats with the added power of legitimacy. Any concessions that the United States makes should also be framed in terms of this understanding both to limit damage to the American reputation for toughness and to indicate to the USSR the limits of its concessions.

HYPOTHESIS 3.   *In any disputes over Cuba subsequent to the Kennedy-Khrushchev understanding, both the United States and the Soviet Union will explicitly frame their threats and concessions in terms of that understanding.*

The Cienfuegos crisis and the subsequent disputes over the Soviet naval presence in Cuba provide an ideal test of these hypotheses because several factors make these interactions *hard cases* for normative and institutional theories to explain.[1] First, these disputes are related to central national security issues. In fact, these disputes are related to perhaps the most central security issue of the Cold War: the ability to launch and defend against a nuclear attack. The basing of Soviet strategic nuclear forces in Cuba had substantial implications both for the vulnerability of Soviet nuclear forces to an American strike and for the vulnerability of the American population to Soviet retaliation. Thus the very core security interests of the two most powerful states in the world were engaged in these disputes over Cuba. Second, the norms involved in the Kennedy-Khrushchev understanding were very weakly institutionalized. The agree-

---

[1] For a discussion of "hard cases" and the construction of research designs for qualitative research, see King, Keohane, and Verba (1994); and Stinchcombe (1987).

ment was not codified in any treaty, nor were any institutions constructed to monitor compliance or to resolve subsequent disputes.[2] All of these mechanisms strengthen the ability of norms to inflict reputational costs on violators and to act as clear and interpretable normative referents. Thus my theory would predict that the Kennedy-Khrushchev understanding is *less* likely to influence state behavior than are more clearly documented, codified, monitored, and institutionalized norms. As a result, any evidence suggesting that the Kennedy-Khrushchev understanding *did* influence US and Soviet behavior with regard to Cuba represents particularly strong confirmation of the utility of normative and institutional approaches to security affairs.

Constructing the Kennedy-Khrushchev Understanding

The Soviet-American Cienfuegos crisis can be traced back to the 1962 Cuban missile crisis. This dispute was resolved through an understanding between Soviet chairman Nikita Khrushchev and US president John F. Kennedy whereby the Soviet Union agreed not to base "offensive" missiles in Cuba in exchange for a US pledge not to invade Cuba. The history of the Cuban missile crisis has been discussed extensively elsewhere, so I will not review the entire crisis in detail. For my purposes, I will review two important aspects of the crisis: (1) the conclusion of the Kennedy-Khrushchev understanding and whether or not this accord constituted what I have defined as a legitimate settlement, and (2) Khrushchev's response to American coercion prior to the conclusion of the settlement.

The Cuban missile crisis began on October 16, 1962, when the CIA presented President Kennedy with their evidence that the Soviet Union was constructing bases for medium- and intermediate-range ballistic missiles in Cuba. After the Executive Committee of the National Security Council (Ex Comm) debated a variety of responses ranging from doing nothing to launching an immediate surprise invasion of Cuba, Kennedy decided on a naval blockade of Cuba to give Khrushchev time to back down rather than risk immediate military confrontation. The Soviet leadership, however, reacted very sharply. Interestingly, their first reaction was to insist that they had every right to defend Cuba by basing missiles there and that American coercion was illegitimate. On October 23, in response to Kennedy's proclamation of the naval "quarantine," Khrushchev stated that

[2] Soviet ambassador Anatoly Dobrynin (1995, 90) argues that the Kennedy administration did not want to formalize the agreement because of fears that Robert Kennedy's offer to make a tacit trade of missiles in Turkey for missiles in Cuba would damage the younger Kennedy's prospects in a possible future run for the presidency.

[t]he United States has taken the path of grossly violating the United Nations Charter, the path of violating the norms of freedom of navigation on the high seas. . . . The United Nations Charter and international norms give no right to any state to institute in international waters the inspection of vessels bound for the shores of the republic of Cuba. And naturally, we cannot recognize the right of the United States to establish control over armaments which are necessary for the Republic of Cuba to strengthen its defense capability.[3]

Khrushchev echoed these statements the following day and drew particular attention to what he viewed as the illegality and illegitimacy of the American demands. He also emphasized the legitimacy and fairness of his own position. In criticizing Kennedy's demands, Khrushchev argued that

if it were a matter of quarantine, as you mention in your letter, then, as is customary in international practice, it can be established only as by states agreeing between themselves, and not by some third party. . . . International law exists, generally accepted standards of conduct exist. We firmly adhere to the principles of international law and strictly observe the standards regulating navigation on the open sea, in international waters. . . . You want to force us to renounce the rights enjoyed by every sovereign state; you are attempting to legislate questions of international law; you are violating the generally accepted standards of this law.[4]

In addition, Khruschev argued for the basic fairness of the Soviet stance. "No, Mr. President," the Soviet leader wrote, "I cannot agree to this, and I think deep inside you will admit that I am right. I am convinced that if you were in my place you would do the same."

After defining American coercion as illegitimate and unfair, Khrushchev responded to Kennedy's demands by threatening the United States with nuclear retaliation for any attack on Soviet forces. In the same October 24 message, Khrushchev states, "This, if you will, is the madness of degenerating imperialism. Unfortunately, people of all nations, not least the American people themselves, could suffer heavily from such madness as this, since with the appearance of modern types of weapons, the

[3] "Messages Exchanged by President Kennedy and Chairman Khrushchev during the Cuban Missile Crisis of October 1962," *Department of State Bulletin* 69, no. 1795 (1973), 636–37. It is worth noting that these communications were private letters between Kennedy and Khrushchev. Thus his rhetoric here cannot be construed as an effort to sway the opinions of foreign leaders, publics, or other potential audiences. Khrushchev is constructing an argument in an attempt to persuade Kennedy to relent.

[4] Text of Khrushchev's October 24 message to Kennedy is drawn from Koenker and Bachman (1997, 717–18).

U.S.A. has lost its former inaccessibility." Finally, he concludes the statement by emphasizing that if the United States interfered with Soviet vessels, "[w]e will then be forced on our part to take those measures that we
deem necessary and sufficient to defend our rights. For this we have all
that is necessary."

Given my argument about the impact of legitimacy, one might have
thought that Khrushchev's appeals to international law should have per-
suaded Kennedy to relent. Recall, however, that my discussion in chapter
2 emphasized the importance of the *individual consent* of states' specific
rules as critical links causing agreements to influence behavior. Kennedy
may have been in violation of customary norms of international navigation, but he was not in violation of any specific commitment made by the
United States regarding Cuba. Thus the Kennedy administration correctly did not view itself as being in violation of any legitimate agreements it had made with the Soviet Union.

It is also worth noting that Kennedy viewed Soviet behavior as a "violation" of sorts because he felt their actions were inconsistent with their
previous statements regarding Cuba. In a private meeting late on October 23 with Ambassador Dobrynin, Robert Kennedy bitterly complained,

> You, for example, particularly told me about the defensive goals be-
> hind the supply of Soviet arms, in particular missiles, at the time of
> our meeting at the beginning of September. I understood you as
> saying that what was involved—at this point and in the future—was
> purely the sending of missiles of a comparatively short range for the
> defense of Cuban territory and the approaches to the island and not
> the sending of missiles that could strike all of the continental United
> States.[5]

Kennedy also complained about a TASS (Soviet news agency) statement of September 12 regarding the "defensive intentions" of the Soviet
Union regarding Cuba. Kennedy's statement superbly summarizes the
misunderstanding that lay at the core of the Cuban missile crisis. The
Soviet Union had repeatedly made reference to their *intentions*, but
the United States had drawn inferences about the *capability* of the weapons the USSR would transfer. This misunderstanding was a direct result
of the failure to specify the term "defensive" in a set of behavioral prescriptions. Thus neither the United States nor the Soviet Union was in
violation of any legitimate agreement regarding Cuba during the Cuban
missile crisis. This lack of a common framework for interpreting coercive

---

[5] Quotation taken from the Archives of the Russian Foreign Ministry as translated in
Fursenko and Naftali (1997, 252).

behavior appears to have contributed substantially to the dangerous escalation of the crisis.

It is unanimously agreed that the Cuban missile crisis brought the United States and the Soviet Union as close as they ever came to a nuclear war. It is difficult to gauge precisely what the probability of nuclear war was during the peak of the confrontation, but the fact that Kennedy later placed the odds that the crisis could have ended in war as "somewhere between one out of three and even" suggests that the use of nuclear weapons was an outcome that was considered seriously by both sides (Sorenson 1965, 705).

As the two states approached the brink, however, they began to negotiate a peaceful settlement to the dispute. On October 26 the Soviets made the opening offer in a rather unorthodox manner. On that day Soviet embassy councillor Alexander Fomin scheduled a lunch meeting with ABC news correspondent John Scali. At the meeting Fomin asked Scali to relay an offer to Dean Rusk: the Soviets would dismantle and withdraw the missiles under UN supervision in exchange for lifting the blockade and a public pledge by the United States not to invade Cuba. Several hours later, the Soviets repeated their offer through more conventional channels. Khrushchev cabled a very long and personal letter to Kennedy that ended with a direct offer of a quid pro quo. "This is my proposal," the Soviet leader wrote. "No more weapons in Cuba and those within Cuba withdrawn or destroyed, and you reciprocate by withdrawing your blockade and also agree not to invade Cuba." (Kennedy 1968, 66) Before the United States could compose a response, however, a second cable—much more formal in tone—arrived from the Kremlin the following morning which added further conditions to the agreement. This time Khrushchev wrote, "I make this proposal: we agree to remove from Cuba those weapons which you regard as offensive weapons. We agree to do this and to state this commitment in the United Nations. Your representatives will make a statement to the effect that the United States, on its part, bearing in mind the anxiety and concern of the Soviet state, will evacuate its analogous weapons from Turkey."[6]

---

[6] "Messages Exchanged by President Kennedy and Chairman Khrushchev," 646. Many have speculated that the first cable took a softer line because it was written by Khrushchev himself, while the second letter represented the views of the entire Politburo and the Foreign Ministry. From more recent discussions with Soviet officials close to the decision-making process at the time, however, the reality seems to have been quite different. Raymond Garthoff cites a "fully informed and senior Soviet participant," who states that the first letter was written in such a hurried, informal style and included further concessions because the Soviets believed that a US invasion of Cuba was imminent. By the morning of the twenty-seventh, the Soviets had received better intelligence suggesting that the US invasion was still some days off and that there was more time to negotiate a better deal. See Garthoff (1988, 74). This explanation is also consistent with Dobrynin (1995, 86).

The United States offered a dual response to these various Soviet offers. First, Kennedy ignored the second more formal cable from the Kremlin, choosing instead to respond favorably to the more generous offer of the cable from the twenty-sixth.[7] Specifically, the president cabled the Soviets that he had given US representatives at the UN permission to work out

> a more permanent solution to the Cuban problem along the lines suggested in your letter of October 26th. As I read your letter, the key elements of your proposals—which seem generally acceptable as I understand them are as follows: 1) You agree to remove these weapons systems from Cuba under appropriate United Nations observation and supervision; and undertake, with suitable safeguards, to halt the further introduction of such weapons systems into Cuba. 2) We, on our part, would agree—upon the establishment of adequate arrangements through the United Nations to ensure the carrying out and continuation of these commitments—(a) to remove promptly the quarantine measures now in effect and (b) to give assurances against the invasion of Cuba. (Kennedy 1968, 86–87)[8]

At the same time, Attorney General Robert Kennedy met with Soviet ambassador Dobrynin to say that the United States could make no explicit quid pro quo of missiles in Turkey for missiles in Cuba. Nonetheless, he assured Dobrynin that "the President had been anxious to remove those missiles from Turkey and Italy for a long period of time. He had ordered their removal some time ago, and it was our judgment that, within a short time after the crisis was over, those missiles would be gone."[9]

On October 28 Khrushchev responded by accepting the US counter-offer, and in doing so he made oblique reference to the tacit understanding concerning the Turkish missiles. "Thus in view of the assurances you have given and our instructions of dismantling, there is every condition for eliminating this conflict," Khrushchev wrote to Kennedy. "I note with satisfaction that you have responded to the desire I expressed with regard to the aforementioned dangerous situation as well as with regard to providing conditions for a more thoughtful appraisal of the international

---

[7] Interestingly, Dobrynin claims in his memoirs that Dean Rusk confided in him years later that the Kennedy administration would have been willing to consider an explicit exchange of missiles in Cuba for missiles in Turkey with under UN auspices (Dobrynin 1995, 90–91). Kennedy's ultimate willingness to make this concession, however, was never tested.

[8] "Message to Chairman Khrushchev Calling for Removal of Soviet Missiles from Cuba, October 27, 1962," *Public Papers of the Presidents* (Washington, D.C.: USGPO, 1963), 814.

[9] See also Rusk (1990). This account is consistent with the Soviet perspective on this exchange (Dobrynin 1995, 87–89).

situation."[10] The "aforementioned dangerous situation" appeared to be a reference to the missiles in Turkey, since Khrushchev had already finished discussing Kennedy's response to the situation in Cuba. Ambassador Dobrynin's memoirs confirm this interpretation of the message (Dobrynin 1995, 90). Kennedy then sealed the deal later on the twenty-eighth by writing to Khrushchev, "I consider my letter to you of October 27th and your reply of today as firm undertakings on the part of both governments which should be promptly carried out."[11]

Despite Kennedy's exhortation, the settlement came under challenge almost immediately. During his televised address to the nation on October 22, President Kennedy referred to the presence of "jet bombers capable of conveying nuclear weapons" in addition to the medium- and intermediate-range missiles. On October 23 Kennedy released a presidential proclamation on the quarantine of Cuba declaring that "the following are to be prohibited materiel: surface-to-surface missiles; bomber aircraft; air-to-surface rockets and guided missiles; warheads for any of the above weapons; mechanical or electronic equipment to support or operate the above items."[12] A slightly elaborated version of this list of banned items for the quarantine became the American definition of "offensive" weapons with regard to Cuba.

During the crisis, however, negotiations focused almost entirely on the missiles. After October 28, the United States reminded the USSR that their understanding of offensive weapons was not restricted to surface-to-surface missiles. Specifically, a letter from Adlai Stevenson to Deputy Prime Minister Anastas Mikoyan on November 2, 1962, identified a list of items that the United States considered offensive in relation to the Kennedy-Khrushchev understanding. The list defined offensive weapons as follows:

1. Surface-to-surface missiles, including those designed for use at sea and including propellants and chemical compounds capable of being used to power missiles
2. Bomber aircraft
3. Bombs, air-to-surface rockets, and guided missiles
4. Warheads for any of the above weapons
5. Mechanical or electronic equipment to support or operate the above items such as communications, supply, and missile launching equipment including KOMAR class motor torpedo boats[13]

[10] "Messages Exchanged by President Kennedy and Chairman Khrushchev," 651.

[11] Messages Exchanged by President Kennedy and Chairman Khrushchev," 654.

[12] "Proclamation 3504: Interdiction of the Delivery of Offensive Weapons to Cuba, October 23, 1962," *Public Papers of the Presidents*, 810.

[13] "United States–Soviet Understandings Concerning the Presence of Offensive Weapons in Cuba," November 19, 1978, *National Security Archive*, Document 0281 (http://www.

Mikoyan accepted the list from Stevenson, and the Soviet leadership offered no objection, suggesting that they accepted this definition. Finally, in follow-up negotiations between John McCloy and Vasily Kuznetsov, the United States and USSR addressed the issue of Soviet bases—particularly submarine bases—in Cuba. During the Cienfuegos crisis Kissinger commented to Nixon that "John McCloy had raised the issue with Kuznetsov on November 5, 1962, stating that the United States objected to the establishment of *any* Soviet military base in Cuba. Kuznetsov said he understood [emphasis original]." (Kissinger 1982, 633)[14]

This definition was clear and well understood, but it did not sit well with Castro. Of particular concern were the IL-28 bombers that the Soviet Union had sent to Cuba and had promised to the Cuban military. Castro's objection to the withdrawal of the IL-28s threatened to scuttle the agreement just as it had succeeded in resolving the conflict.

Interestingly, however, the Soviets placed sufficient value on the Kennedy-Khrushchev understanding that they remained firm in their decision to withdraw the aircraft despite the displeasure of their ally. Perhaps even more important, we can observe the impact of the legitimacy of the settlement through the kinds of arguments that Soviet leaders made to Castro about why they needed to comply with the agreement with the Americans regarding the IL-28s.

On November 12 Mikoyan and Ambassador Alexeev met with Castro to discuss the removal of the IL-28s, and their arguments reflect a remarkable—if grudging—acceptance of the legitimacy of the American position. Moreover, their arguments also reflect the reputational effects of legitimate settlements anticipated by my argument in chapter 3. Specifically, Mikoyan argued to Castro that

> [t]he Americans believe that [the understanding] applied to the IL-28 bombers. Kennedy discussed bombers in his message on October 22. He also mentioned the bombers in his proclamation. They believe we have not fully met our obligations because of the IL-28 bombers. Taking a formal, legalistic stance, they have stated that we have failed to meet our obligations, and because of this, they con-

---

gwu.edu/~nsarchiv). Stevenson's authorship is not challenged. This list was not available in declassified documents until 1978. In a previous release of this document, Document 0280, the list was blacked out.

[14] When he stated that the negotiations fizzled out, it seems likely that Kissinger was referring to the fact that they did not result in the signing of any formal agreement. Nonetheless, these exchanges undoubtedly represent an agreement that was clearly understood by both parties.

sider it their prerogative to repudiate their obligations of lifting the quarantine and providing guarantees.[15]

Mikoyan then assured Castro that the USSR had not yet agreed to remove the bombers, but he continued to argue that the removal of the bombers would be in Cuba's best interest as a method of obtaining an American guarantee against the invasion of Cuba.

> Of course, one might ask what the price of the American guarantees would be. Obviously, they can't be trusted all the way. Imperialism and Socialism are irreconcilable enemies. However, we cannot completely mistrust any promises given by the representatives of bourgeois countries. There are certain international procedures, legal standards, laws, and international public opinion. All of these factors force the imperialists to keep their word. (Koenker and Bachman 1997, 722)

Castro asked for further clarification of the Soviet position, and Mikoyan responded,

> If we decide to remove these bombers with their crews and equipment and thus fulfill our promise to remove all weapons the Americans classify as offensive weapons from Cuba, we will force the Americans to fulfill their obligations and normalize the situation in the Caribbean. As the saying goes, eating whets the appetite. And, of course, we must put an end to these ravenous appetites. But it would be difficult to argue about the IL-28. After all, it is a bomber, albeit only in formal terms. (Koenker and Bachman 1997, 723)[16]

Later Mikoyan added,

> If [Kennedy] is able to get his demands met, then he will be forced to keep his promises, i.e. provide substantial guarantees that the United States will not attack Cuba and lift the blockade. If Kennedy's demand is not met then the United States will maintain its blockade and continue to maintain it while accusing us of failing to keep our promises. And in this case the U.N. would not support us. (Koenker and Bachman 1997, 725)

[15] Quotations from this conversation between Mikoyan and Castro are from the Archives of the President of the Russian Federation as translated in Koenker and Bachman (1997, 722).

[16] It is not clear what Mikoyan means here by "albeit only in formal terms." The IL-28 was unquestionably a bomber in every sense. This language may reflect Mikoyan's discomfort in asking Castro to yield to additional demands of the United States immediately in the wake of the defeat over the missiles.

Castro eventually agreed to the withdrawal of the IL-28 bombers, but he refused to allow on site inspection of the withdrawal in Cuba. As I will discuss later, this alteration in implementing the withdrawal was acceptable to the United States. A telegram from Mikoyan to Khrushchev and the Politburo immediately following the meeting with Castro demonstrates that the views expressed to Castro reflected those of Khrushchev and the entire Soviet leadership. "I met Fidel Castro and carried out the instructions (your No. 1013, concerning everything connected with the IL-28)," wrote Mikoyan, "discussing nearly all the arguments summarized in Comrade Khrushchev's letter to me." (Koenker and Bachman 1997, 727)

With the issue of the IL-28s resolved, on November 20 Kennedy announced that "I have this afternoon instructed the Secretary of Defense to lift our naval quarantine." Kennedy also noted Castro's denial of on-site inspections, and responded that "this Government has no choice but to pursue its own means of checking on military activities on Cuba." Later in the same speech he dropped the requirement of UN supervision as a condition for continuing the agreement, saying, "As for our part, if all offensive weapons are removed from Cuba and kept out of the hemisphere in the future, under adequate verification and safeguards . . . there will be peace in the Caribbean."[17] The Soviet Union made no objection to the close American naval and aerial surveillance of the removal of both the missiles and the bombers, despite the fact that these activities would, in all likelihood, have been considered acts of war by the USSR before the conclusion of the settlement.[18] As a result, it seems reasonable to infer that the Soviet leadership consented to this alteration in the agreement.

The Kennedy-Khrushchev understanding that resolved the Cuban missile crisis clearly constitutes what I have previously defined as a legitimate settlement. Some might object to this label because the terms of the settlement favored the United States and were "forced" on the Soviet Union. It is certainly true that the Kennedy-Khrushchev understanding was hardly what the Soviets were hoping to achieve at the outset of the crisis. Moreover, they certainly accepted the settlement while under some coercive pressure. But no choice by any state is entirely free from external pressures, so complete "freedom to choose" cannot be viewed as the proper standard for assessing the legitimacy of an agreement. As I discussed earlier, my criteria for determining the legitimacy of a settlement are: (1) is the final settlement responsive to the wishes of both parties as

[17] "President's News Conference of November 20, 1962," *Public Papers of the Presidents* (Washington, D.C.: U.S. Government Printing Office), 830–31.

[18] See Harlan Cleveland, "Memorandum to for the NSC Executive Committee, November 12, 1962," *Department of State*, Document 02256.

they express them during the bargaining process? and (2) does the settlement define a set of acts as illegitimate? The US-Soviet understanding concerning Cuba clearly meets these criteria.

First, let us consider the responsiveness of the settlement to the wishes of both parties. The Soviets made an opening bid in Khrushchev's letter and through Fomin's meeting with Scali. Then, before the United States could respond, they upped the ante somewhat by demanding the removal of American missiles in Turkey. The US response struck a middle ground between these two demands, refusing an explicit exchange of missiles, but assuring the Soviets that the Turkish missiles would go. Furthermore, when Castro blocked UN supervision of the dismantling of the missiles, both sides were flexible enough to allow for other (US) methods of verification. Thus while the settlement was not what the Soviets had hoped for, it was largely constructed at their suggestion, and the United States did show some responsiveness to their increased demands concerning Turkey, and to Castro's blockage of UN supervision. Second, the Cuban understanding identified a set of behaviors as illegitimate for both superpowers. Specifically, the Soviet Union was to refrain from basing "offensive" (i.e., surface-to-surface) missiles in Cuba, while the United States was to refrain from invading Cuba and prevent other Western states from doing so as well.

Nonetheless, a number of scholars have dismissed the importance of the Kennedy-Khrushchev understanding and have even denied the existence of any commonly recognized obligations. These objections have focused on two issues: (1) whether the conditions underpinning the understanding were ever implemented, and (2) whether the understanding actually provided specific norms about proscribed behavior. Raymond Garthoff, for example, has suggested that because Fidel Castro blocked UN inspection, the understanding was void and not considered binding by either side. (Garthoff 1983, 1985)[19] As I discussed earlier, however, Kennedy dropped the requirement of UN supervision in his statement of November 20, requiring only that "adequate" US supervision continue. In fact, by the end of 1962 the United States declared itself satisfied that the USSR had withdrawn all missiles from Cuba, and Garthoff concedes that, in a meeting with Mikoyan on October 29, 1962, Kennedy reaffirmed that if the Soviets would continue to abide by their correspondence, so would the United States. Garthoff is correct in noting that the issue of surveillance was sharply contested throughout November of

---

[19] In addition, during the Cienfuegos crisis, Senator Fullbright also stated that it was a "questionable proposition" whether the United States could deny the Soviets their "right" to construct a base in Cuba (*New York Times*, October 1, 1970, 1). At the time Senator Fullbright was speaking, however, the specific terms of the Kennedy-Khrushchev understandings were still classified.

1962. The diplomatic record of these exchanges, however, indicates that the two countries *did* reach a mutually endorsed understanding that allowed the United States to substitute national technical means of surveillance for UN on-site inspection of the Soviet withdrawal. On November 23, following discussions with Soviet representative Vasily Kuznetsov, John McCloy drafted a statement that reiterated the US noninvasion pledge and which emphasized that

> [t]his statement is made on the understanding that by reason of the refusal of Cuba to permit arrangements contemplated to assure the carrying out and continuation of the commitments in regard to the maintenance and introduction of such weapons systems in Cuba, the United States will, until such time as such arrangements can be effected, continue to employ such other means of observation and verification as may be necessary.[20]

This position was bolstered further on November 25 when CIA Director John McCone wrote to National Security Adviser McGeorge Bundy stating, "I believe the proposed declaration satisfactorily meets the condition of continuing surveillance of Cuba in the absence of latter agreement on UN inspection."[21] Then on November 26, in a statement to the UN Security Council—never publicly delivered—Adlai Stevenson echoed McCloy's words and added that

> [a]n inspection procedure was arranged in cooperation with the USSR under which United States naval vessels have received substantial verification that Soviet vessels leaving Cuba carried out the number of missiles which the USSR certified to the United States as having been in Cuba. The Soviet Union has also agreed to a similar form of verification of the impending withdrawal of all IL-28 bomber aircraft introduced into Cuba.[22]

In January 1963, Stevenson and Kuznetsov sent a joint letter to UN Secretary General U Thant proposing that the conflict in Cuba be taken off the agenda for the Security Council, indicating joint consent to the terms of the settlement (Dobrynin 1995, 91).

Finally, in 1964 a US State Department spokesperson made public the substitution of US surveillance for UN measures as an explicit part of the agreement.

[20] "McCloy Draft, 11/23/62, 3:30 P.M.," *National Security Archive*, Document 2572.
[21] "Memorandum for Mr. Bundy, 11/25/62, 10:45 P.M.," *National Security Archive*, Document 2586.
[22] "Draft United States Declaration in the Security Council," *National Security Archive*, Document 2590.

I would recall that the overflights are a substitute for the on-site inspection agreed to by the Soviets in 1962 but which Fidel Castro refused to permit. . . . I would remind you of the various statements made by the late President Kennedy and Secretary Rusk during the past fifteen months on this subject making it unmistakably clear that we regard the overflights as a necessity to avoid the deception that was practiced against us in 1962. (Bender 1975, 58)

As a result, the US surveillance of Cuba continued unmolested even after the emplacement of Soviet surface-to-air missile (SAM) batteries. Thus there seems to be no question but that the United States and the USSR considered their understanding concerning Cuba to be binding on both parties.

Second, other scholars, such as Lynne Bender, have dismissed the importance of the Kennedy-Khrushchev understanding on Cuba by suggesting that it is too vague and diffuse to define any specific behaviors as proscribed. "The nub of the problem," Bender claims, "is defining exactly what is an 'offensive weapons system.' The definition changes over time, usually through a unilateral declaration by the United States in response to some Soviet initiative." (Bender 1975, 61)[23] Upon careful consideration, however, this charge proves to be flatly wrong, especially with regard to submarines that were the crucial issue in the Cienfuegos crisis eight years later. In fact, the superpowers did discuss the precise definition of an "offensive weapons system," and they explicitly concluded that a surface-to-surface missile capability—including a sea-based capability—fell within this category. Moreover, as we shall see next, this definition was not infinitely malleable.

One indirect piece of evidence suggesting that the American definition of "offensive" weapons remained, in fact, limited is that the United States made no objection to the placement of Soviet SAM batteries in Cuba, so long as they did not attempt to interfere with American surveillance of Soviet military capabilities on the island. However, there is also more direct evidence of a stable, commonly understood definition of offensive weaponry. As I discussed earlier, on October 23, the day after his television address, Kennedy released a presidential proclamation on the quarantine of Cuba that clearly specified the items subject to blockade. Moreover the United States clarified this definition on November 2, and the Soviets accepted this definition without objection. Finally, the November 12 negotiations between Mikoyan and Castro demonstrate that the Soviet leadership had a very clear understanding of which weapons systems were prohibited and which systems were not.

[23] George H. Quester (1971) expresses a similar skepticism concerning the sufficient specificity of the understanding.

Thus despite Garthoff and Bender's objections, it seems clear that the resolution of the Cuban missile crisis represented a legitimate settlement of this disputed issue. The understanding was responsive in some way to the wishes of both superpowers, both parties took the required actions to bring the agreement into effect, each state continued to consider its terms binding, and the agreement specifically defined standards of behavior for both the United States and the Soviet Union. It was in this context in which the USSR began construction on a submarine base in Cuba during the fall of 1970.

Soviet Submarines in Cienfuegos

After the conclusion of the Cuban missile crisis, the Soviet navy made no visits to Cuban ports for almost seven years. Nonetheless, the arrival of a Soviet flotilla in Cuba during July 1969 attracted little attention in the United States. Instead, what triggered US suspicions about Soviet activities in the Caribbean was a suggestion by the Soviet chargé d'affaires, Yuri Vorontsov, that the superpowers reaffirm the Kennedy-Khrushchev understanding. Feeling that this request came out of the blue, Kissinger states that he discussed the question with the president before responding (Kissinger 1982, 632–33). After researching the understanding and discussing it with Nixon, Kissinger replied that "the understandings of 1962 were still in full force," but he noted that Soviet naval activity in the Caribbean threatened to press the limits of this understanding and asked that "the greatest restraint [be] exercised with regard to Soviet Naval operations in the Caribbean." (Kissinger 1982, 637–38)

On August 26, a U-2 flight photographed construction activity on a small island in Cienfuegos harbor on the southern coast of Cuba. The construction did not appear unusual until the United States noted the arrival of a Soviet naval flotilla in Cienfuegos on September 9. The flotilla included a ship designed for submarine maintenance and two barges used for the storage of nuclear waste materials from submarines. At this point Nixon ordered daily U-2 flights, which began on September 14, but much to the Nixon administration's surprise and dismay, the U-2 flights received heavy harassment from MiG fighters unlike any it had experienced in recent years (Kissinger 1982, 637–38). As a result, on September 16 Kissinger issued his first oblique warning to the USSR, stating that the operation or servicing of Soviet missile-carrying submarines from bases in Cuba would have "grave consequences." That same day the United States finally gained photographic confirmation that the Soviets were building a base at Cienfuegos. Specifically, the U-2 data showed five key clues: (1) a submarine tender was "moored in permanent fashion to four buoys"; (2) the two barges had been moved into position alongside the tender, making it ready to serve submarines; (3) antisubmarine nets guarded the entrance to Cienfuegos harbor; (4) a short distance away, work had begun on a major communications facility; and (5) a soccer field had been constructed.[24] Faced with this information, Nixon, Kissinger, and the Washington Special Actions Group (WSAG) met to discuss US options. Nixon was reluctant to face the Soviets down over this issue immediately, both because he did not wish to cancel a planned diplomatic visit to Europe, and because he worried that the precipitation of a crisis over Cuba shortly before the looming mid-term elections would appear to be a crass electioneering ploy.[25] Thus over Kissinger's strong objections, Nixon decided to remain quiet about Soviet activity in the Caribbean until after the elections.

Nonetheless, the story was leaked to the press despite Nixon's demand of silence. A spokesperson at the Pentagon did not understand that he was not to reveal information concerning Soviet activity in Cuba, and so he answered all questions from the press on the subject as fully as he could at one of his morning briefings. The result was that C. L. Sulzberger of the *New York Times* broke the story to the public on September 25, in a story entitled "Ugly Clouds in the South." Once the secret was out, the Nixon administration had no choice but to respond or be perceived as appeasing the Soviets. Nixon chose to stand firm. Consequently, on the afternoon of the twenty-fifth Kissinger held a briefing at the White House in which he explicitly drew attention to the fact that the Soviets were in violation of the 1962 understanding. Insisting that he be quoted as "a White House source," Kissinger stated, "The Soviet Union can be under no doubt that we would view the establishment of a strategic base in the Caribbean with the utmost seriousness."[26] Kissinger continued by quoting President Kennedy's statement on November 20 that if the Soviets kept offensive weapons out of Cuba, there would be peace in the Caribbean. "The operative part, of course," Kissinger continued, "is 'if all offensive weapons are removed from Cuba and kept out of the hemisphere in the future.' This, of course, remains the policy of this government."[27]

Two hours later, Kissinger met with Ambassador Dobrynin and was

[24] Kissinger (1982, 638) says that the soccer field proved to him that the base was designed for Soviet use. Apparently he was unaware of the popularity of soccer in Cuba. Garthoff (1985) attributes the soccer insight to the CIA. At any rate, while US leaders were right about the presence of a Soviet base, they may have been right for the wrong reasons.

[25] In fact, several commentators—such as Senator William Fullbright and the editors of the *London Times*—did attribute such motives to Nixon when the crisis broke, despite his desire to delay it.

[26] *New York Times*, September 26, 1970, 1.

[27] *New York Times*, September 26, 1970, 1.

more blunt and unyielding than he had been in his press briefing. According to Kissinger's recollection of the meeting, he stated that the United States "considered the construction at Cienfuegos to be unmistakably a submarine base. Moscow should be under no illusion; we would view continued construction with the utmost gravity. The base could not remain. We would not shrink from other measures, including public steps, if forced to it." Richard Nixon recalled that Dobrynin's face turned "ashen" when faced with the US discovery and its absolute insistence on the dismantling of the base. The president stated that Dobrynin at first tried to minimize the importance of the issue, but Kissinger continued to insist that the base be eliminated. Finally, the Soviet ambassador specifically asked if the Nixon administration was alleging a violation of the 1962 understanding. Kissinger stated that it was, and Dobrynin responded that he would inform the Kremlin immediately (Nixon 1978). Finally, to emphasize the seriousness of the ultimatum, Nixon ordered that a US destroyer take up a position outside Cienfuegos harbor. Shortly after this meeting Nixon left on his scheduled trip for Europe, and the administration used this distraction as a short breathing space to allow the Soviets to comply quietly.

While Nixon was out of the country, the Soviet press agency, TASS, released a statement accusing the United States of creating a "war psychosis," but it is interesting to note that they did not specifically deny the US charge of building a base in Cuba.[28] It is also interesting to note that the general reaction among much of the press and diplomatic corps—who were not aware of Kissinger and Dobrynin's private confrontation nor of the specificity of the terms of the Kennedy-Khrushchev understanding—was that Nixon and Kissinger were being too confrontational with the Soviets. Senator Frank Church, for example, called Kissinger's public statements "inflammatory," and many diplomats felt the United States had "overreacted."[29] Nonetheless, by the time Nixon returned to the White House on October 5, the Soviets appeared ready to comply with US demands. Dobrynin requested an urgent meeting with Kissinger for the following day, at which he delivered Kissinger a note containing the Kremlin's response, which read:

> The Soviet side has not done and is not doing in Cuba now—that includes the area of the Cienfuegos port—anything of the kind that would contradict that mentioned understanding. . . . In any case, we would like to reaffirm once again that the Soviet Union strictly adheres to its part of the understanding on the Cuban question and

---

[28] *New York Times*, October 1, 1970, 1.

[29] Comments from Western diplomats in *New York Times*, October 1, 1970, 1. Senator Church's comments can be found in the *New York Times*, October 4, 1970, 23.

will continue to adhere to it in the future on the assumption that the American side, as President Nixon has reaffirmed, will also strictly observe its part of the understanding. (Kissinger 1982, 649)

In addition, Kissinger states that Dobrynin verbally clarified this concession by saying that "while he could not make an agreement that Soviet submarines would never call at Cuban ports, he was on the part of his government prepared to affirm that ballistic missile submarines would not call there in an operational capacity." Kissinger accepted the Soviet note, and October 9 he responded to the joint chiefs of staff with some "clarifications" of what constituted a "base" in Cuba, which he had worked out with his liaison:

> The US government understands that the USSR will not establish, utilize, or permit the *establishment of any facility in Cuba* that can be employed to support or repair Soviet naval ships capable of carrying offensive weapons; i.e. submarines or surface ships armed with nuclear capable surface-to-surface missiles [emphasis added]. (Kissinger 1982, 650)

The Soviet ambassador accepted this note, which Kissinger seemed to view as an expansion of the original agreement. As we have seen, however, naval bases and a sea-based surface-to-surface missile capability had already been explicitly included in the understanding since the follow-up negotiations of 1962. Finally, Dobrynin told Kissinger that TASS would be publishing a formal reaffirmation of the 1962 understanding.[30]

The following day it became clear that the Soviets intended to carry out their promised compliance with the stipulations of the Kennedy-Khrushchev agreement. The submarine tender, which had been "moored in a permanent fashion," left Cienfuegos harbor along with a tugboat. Construction on all port facilities had already ceased several days earlier. Then, as promised, TASS released a statement on October 13 which reiterated Dobrynin's private guarantees. While the statement in effect acknowledged compliance with US demands concerning a base in Cuba, it also refined the terms of the agreement by reemphasizing Dobrynin's distinction between a Soviet base and Soviet calls at foreign ports:

> If Soviet ships and vessels enter ports of foreign states, including the ports of the Republic of Cuba, on official visits and business calls, they do so with the permission of the governments of the states concerned. It is obvious that such calls are an inalienable right of

[30] Interestingly, Dobrynin's memoirs entirely omit discussion of this episode. His lack of attention to the confrontation in light of the available documentary evidence surrounding these incidents may suggest the Soviet diplomat omitted the episode because the violation of the Kennedy-Khrushchev agreement does not reflect well on him or his superiors.

sovereign states, universally recognized and confirmed by many centuries of international practice. (*Keesing's Contemporary Archives*
1971, 24,412)

The United States raised no objection to the TASS statement, and the
Soviets were correct in noting that port calls were not covered by the
1962 understanding. So Dobrynin brought the Cienfuegos crisis to a
close on October 23 by relaying to Kissinger a final statement on the
issue by the Soviets. "We do not have a submarine base in Cuba," the
Soviet ambassador repeated, "nor are we building a military naval facility.
We do not intend to have a military naval facility, and we will abide
strictly by our understandings of 1962. We are also making the exchanges from August onward part of the understandings of 1962."
(Kissinger 1982, 650)

Continuing Disputes over Cuba

This statement brought an end to the crisis over a submarine base at
Cienfuegos, but it did not stop the US-Soviet games of naval cat-and-
mouse in the Caribbean. Although the submarine tender left the developing base at Cienfuegos, it turned in to the port of Mariel, on Cuba's
northern coast, where the Soviet missiles had been shipped eight years
earlier. Then on October 31, the tender left Mariel only to return to
Cienfuegos on November 7. Kissinger states that he "protested angrily"
to Dobrynin about the Soviet naval moves, but on November 24 Yuri
Vorontsov replied that the submarine tender *would* tend to submarines,
but *not* while docked at Cuban ports (Kissinger 1982, 651). Then on
December 6 another three-ship squadron arrived in Cuba for a seven-
teen-day visit. Frustrated with the persistence of Soviet naval activity in
the Caribbean, Kissinger delivered a warning to Dobrynin very similar to
the one concerning the Cienfuegos base, stating that "servicing submarines in or from Cuban ports would lead to the most grave situation
between the United States and the Soviet Union." (Kissinger 1982, 651)
It is important to note that in addition to delivering a threat, Kissinger
was also attempting to unilaterally expand the domain of the 1962 agreement. The US-Soviet discussions had made no mention of servicing submarines *from* bases in Cuba. They had only discussed facilities and weapons *in* Cuba. Thus because of the Soviet right to port calls in consenting
states, they were well within their rights to have submarine tenders call at
Cuban ports and then service submarines while at sea. Kissinger reiterated his bid to broaden the understanding by releasing a statement to the
press the following day which warned the Soviets against servicing sub-

marines from Cuban ports.[31] Then in a nationally televised interview on January 4, 1971, Nixon once again put forward the expanded US version of the 1962 understanding. "Now in the event that nuclear submarines were serviced either in Cuba or from Cuba," the president stated, "that would be a violation of the understanding." (*Keesing's Contemporary Archives* 1971, 24,412)

Nonetheless, Soviet ships continued what Secretary of Defense Melvin Laird referred to as their pattern of "harbor hopping." During the first two months of 1971 Kissinger states that he delivered three separate protests to Dobrynin concerning Soviet naval activities around Cuba. In addition, US forces harassed Soviet submarines in the Caribbean, forcing them to surface and tailing them closely. The Soviets responded by firing flares at US ships and taking high-speed evasive maneuvers, but the port calls did not stop (Garthoff 1983, 59). Soviet ships left the Caribbean on January 3, but on February 10 another flotilla returned, this time including a submarine tender and a nuclear-powered attack submarine (Blechman and Levinson 1975, 32). Following the return of the Soviet sub, Nixon finally conceded their right to port calls in Cuba. On February 17, in response to a question concerning the Soviet naval presence in Cuba, the president stated:

> Now as far as this submarine is concerned, the question is a rather technical one, whether it is there for a port call or it is there for servicing. We are watching it very closely. The Soviet Union is aware of the fact that we think there is an understanding and we will, of course, bring the matter to their attention if we find that the understanding is violated.[32]

Following this statement, the Nixon administration allowed the issue to drop despite its extreme irritation over the continuing port calls. Once again in May a flotilla, including a nuclear-powered submarine that did not carry nuclear weapons, visited Cuba for a "brief training mission." Then in April 1972 a non-nuclear missile sub visited Bahia de Nipe, and at least three more visits occurred over the next two years (Blechman and Levinson 1975, 32–33). In sum, the Soviets completely rejected Nixon

[31] See the *New York Times*, December 24, 1970, 13. Perhaps not surprisingly, while Dobrynin omits the Cienfuegos episode from his memoirs, he does make oblique references to these harbor-hopping incidents. He writes, "All subsequent US administrations confirmed, in one way or another, their willingness to abide by the 1962 accords. On the other hand, the Americans repeatedly presented us with various claims attempting to interpret the accords more broadly, that is, in their own interest." (Dobrynin 1995, 91)

[32] Richard Nixon, "The President's News Conference of February 17, 1971, *Public Papers of the Presidents* (Washington, D.C.: U.S. Government Printing Office), 163.

and Kissinger's unilateral efforts to expand the 1962 understanding, ignored US protests of activities that did not violate the understanding, and demonstrated their defiance by pressing their naval activity in the Caribbean to the very limits of the Kennedy-Khrushchev understanding. The Soviets refused to expand their concessions beyond the requirements of the bilateral understanding, and the United States was reluctant to challenge the Soviet right to port calls explicitly because "formally proscribing port-calls would have had widespread ramifications for the movement of the US Navy and our principle of the freedom of the seas." (Kissinger 1982, 652)

The Kennedy-Khrushchev Understanding and Soviet Behavior in Cuba

The US-Soviet dispute over the submarine base at Cienfuegos demonstrates the potential power of dispute settlements as tools for reestablishing cooperative relations. The substantial effect that a previous settlement can have on bargaining behavior is illustrated in the very different Soviet responses to US coercive behavior in the Cuban missile crisis, the Cienfuegos dispute, and the subsequent naval posturing. The diplomatic positions taken by the United States in the three contexts were virtually identical. In each case the United States insisted that the Soviet presence in and around Cuba be eliminated. In each case the United States essentially issued an ultimatum demanding Soviet compliance, and in neither case did the United States actively offer any concessions or alternative solutions to the dispute.[33] It is undoubtedly true that US military moves were most sharply escalatory during the Cuban missile crisis. Nonetheless, Kissinger did make semiveiled threats to use force if necessary, and the United States made some military moves in the Caribbean by tailing and harassing Soviet vessels and placing a ship off Cienfuegos harbor. Thus while Kennedy was more belligerent than Nixon and Kissinger, the American coercive strategy in all of these cases can reasonably be described as "bullying."

Despite the similar substance of the US positions in 1962 and the 1970s, Soviet behavior varied greatly across these encounters. First, let us consider Khrushchev's actions in the Cuban missile crisis. It is true, of course, that the USSR eventually acquiesced to American demands. This capitulation represents important evidence in support of the realist focus on relative power in explaining crisis behavior. Richard Betts, for exam-

---

[33] In the 1962 case the United States did agree to a relatively small tacit concession concerning missiles in Turkey, but they did not *propose* any concessions or exchanges. They only demanded Soviet compliance and, in the end, accepted Soviet proposals.

ple, concludes that Soviet compliance at the end of the Cuban missile crisis is best explained by American nuclear superiority in 1962 (Betts 1987). However, important aspects of Soviet behavior concerning Cuba cannot be explained by realist theory. In particular, realism has great difficulty in explaining the substantial *differences* between Soviet actions in the Cuban missile crisis and the subsequent encounter over Cienfuegos.

Although they eventually conceded to Kennedy's demands, Soviet resistance in the Cuban missile crisis was undoubtedly high. As I discussed earlier, the Cuban missile crisis represents by consensus the closest humanity has ever come to a nuclear war. The high level of Soviet resistance in 1962 is also demonstrated by examining the specific Soviet actions at the outset of the crisis. Khrushchev's initial response to the US quarantine was an angry assertion that the USSR had every right to place missiles in Cuba and that US coercion was both aggressive and illegitimate. In addition, he escalated the crisis militarily by threatening nuclear war. Moreover, inside Cuba the Soviet response during the early part of the Cuban missile crisis was to *accelerate* their construction of the missiles.

Compare Khrushchev's angry threats and frantic missile construction, on the other hand, to the Soviet response to American demands in the Cienfuegos crisis. No Soviet official made any claim that the USSR had any right to base ballistic missile submarines in Cuba. Instead the Soviet leadership explicitly framed their response in terms of the existing norm by inquiring if the United States was alleging a violation of the Kennedy-Khrushchev understanding. The Soviets quickly ceased all construction on the base and made no counterthreat to use force to defend themselves or their base. Neither the participants in the crisis nor subsequent scholars believed that there was any significant risk of nuclear war. After the United States presented the USSR with its evidence of a Soviet violation of the 1962 understanding and threatened to punish the violation, the Soviets promptly complied with the agreement. In fact, the Soviets complied so quickly with American demands that the dispute over Cienfuegos did not even derail US-Soviet negotiations over convening a Nixon-Brezhnev summit. The issue quickly passed, and the superpowers continued their progress toward détente.

However, after reestablishing compliance with the Kennedy-Khrushchev understanding, Soviet compliance quickly changed to intransigence when the United States attempted to expand the terms of the understanding unilaterally. Despite continued US irritation with the Soviet exploitation of port calls, the Soviets flouted US objections by sending more submarines. In this case it was the United States which was forced to concede by allowing the Soviets to continue to engage in military behavior *not* covered by the understanding.

What can account for this difference in Soviet behavior across these contexts? The statements by the participants in the crises suggest that the 1962 understanding played a significant role in shaping Soviet perceptions of US coercive behavior as well as both states' perceptions of the legitimacy of their own behavior. In 1970, for example, the United States clearly attempted to legitimize its coercive demands by explicitly and repeatedly referring to the Kennedy-Khrushchev agreement both in public and in private. During the Cuban missile crisis, however, the United States made no attempt to justify its behavior in terms of mutually agreed upon principles.

Similarly, comparing the statements made by the Soviet leadership in response to American demands in 1962 and 1970 demonstrates the impact of the Kennedy-Khrushchev understanding. Khrushchev accused the United States of "banditry," asserted that the USSR had every right to place missiles in Cuba, and threatened to use nuclear weapons to defend that right. Eight years later, Brezhnev's immediate response was to inquire diplomatically as to whether Nixon was asserting that they were in violation of the 1962 understanding. When the Nixon administration stated that it was claiming that a violation had occurred, the Soviets did not challenge the legitimacy of the 1962 understanding, they did not deny that they were in violation of the settlement, and only after all construction on the base had stopped and the submarine tender had left Cienfuegos did they proclaim that they were not in violation.

Statements made by Soviet leaders while negotiating the withdrawal of the IL-28 bombers with Castro also demonstrate the normative impact of the Kennedy-Khrushchev understanding. Both Mikoyan and Castro were clearly irritated by the United States forcing the issue of the IL-28s. Nonetheless, Mikoyan's arguments about why they should comply reflect a number of my arguments about the impact of legitimate dispute settlements.

First, Mikoyan's arguments acknowledge that the US demand for withdrawal of the bombers is legitimate and offers this as a reason for compliance. Mikoyan begins his statement to Castro with an assertion that the USSR does not believe it is obligated to withdraw the bombers. It seems likely, however, that he opened his comments in this way because he was caught in a somewhat embarrassing situation. The USSR had already agreed to withdraw the IL-28s, but as Garthoff (1980, 433) notes, these bombers were supposed to have been turned over to the Cuban government. Thus to admit that the United States was correct would be to admit that they had negotiated away Cuban military assets without Cuba's knowledge or consent. Mikoyan appears to have wanted to give Castro the impression that he had a say in the decision to withdraw the IL-28s.

At any rate, Mikoyan's *real* position becomes clear after this single brief demurral of Soviet obligations. The Soviet diplomat's very next statement is to admit that "Kennedy discussed bombers in his message of October 22. He also mentioned the bombers in his proclamation." Mikoyan also accuses Kennedy of being "formal" and "legalistic," but once again this characterization actually *acknowledges* the legitimacy—at least on technical grounds—of the US position. Finally, Mikoyan pleads with Castro by saying, "It would be difficult to argue about the IL-28. After all, it is a bomber. . . ." In fact, all of Mikoyan's remaining statements— over what was a lengthy two-hour discussion—essentially acknowledge that the United States has a legitimate basis for its claims.

Second, Mikoyan also used the settlement to portray both US demands and Soviet concessions as limited. With regard to US motives, he repeatedly noted that if the USSR complied, relations in the Caribbean would be normalized. Moreover, he uses the status of the bombers in the settlement negotiations to assure Castro that Kennedy will not object to the MiGs, saying, "Kennedy knows these planes are in Cuba. But he has not said a word about them." (Koenker and Bachman 1997, 723) With regard to the limitations of Soviet concessions, Mikoyan acknowledged Castro's concerns about appeasing the United States, saying, "As the saying goes, eating whets the appetite." But he immediately followed that acknowledgment with a statement that the Soviet Union could not make a *legitimate* argument about the IL-28s, saying, "[I]t would be difficult to argue about the IL-28. After all, it is a bomber, albeit only in formal terms." (Koenker and Bachman 1997, 723) He then reassured Castro, "[w]ith respect to any other military assets, we will firmly and categorically reject any American demands. If we were to remove the bombers from Cuba, this would ensure ourselves of UN support." (Koenker and Bachman 1997, 723)

Third, Mikoyan argued that Soviet compliance with the agreement would constrain future US behavior because of American concern over its reputation for trustworthiness. For example, Mikoyan argued that Soviet compliance with the settlement would cause the United States to be constrained by "international procedures, legal standards, laws, and international public opinion." When Castro asked again how he could be sure that Kennedy would not raise further demands at a later date, Mikoyan's reply was that Soviet compliance with the settlement would leave Kennedy "forced to keep his promises."

Fourth, Mikoyan acknowledges that continued failure to comply with the terms of the agreement would harm the Soviet Union's reputation— both with the United States and with other countries—for keeping its word. In particular, he stated that failure to comply would cause the

United States to continue "accusing us of failing to keep our promises," and he noted that other states in the UN would support the American position rather than the Soviet one.

Finally, the importance of the previous settlement can be seen in the Soviet response to American coercive behavior when Nixon and Kissinger attempted to unilaterally expand the terms of the 1962 understanding. As I discussed previously, although the Soviets immediately complied with the terms of the Kennedy-Khrushchev understanding, they explicitly took note that the agreement did not restrict the Soviet right to port calls. Thus they conceded that they were not allowed to construct a base or to service submarines in Cuban ports, but they reminded the United States that their submarine tenders were allowed to call at Cuban ports, and that there was no restriction on servicing Soviet subs in international waters. Fearing that the Soviets had found a loophole through which they could recoup some of the strategic losses they suffered by dismantling the base, the Nixon administration decided that it would *unilaterally* expand the terms of the agreement to close the loophole. Both Nixon and Kissinger publicly claimed that servicing submarines "from" Cuban ports constituted a violation, despite the fact that the terms of the 1962 understanding set no such condition. Kissinger backed up this claim with protests, threats of "grave consequences," and naval harassment of Soviet ships, much as he had done regarding the Cienfuegos base. This time, however, the Soviets would hear none of it. The Soviets repeatedly ignored the US demands over a period of months, and appeared unwilling to discuss their naval activities in Cuba any further with the United States. The difference between this level of intransigence and their prior compliance in the Cienfuegos crisis is particularly striking because the only substantial difference between the two encounters is whether or not Soviet actions represented a violation of the Kennedy-Khrushchev understanding. Even Kissinger seems to have viewed American coercive behavior after Cienfuegos as less legitimate, since he allowed the issue to drop despite Soviet intransigence.

Thus I find strong support for all three of the hypotheses derived from my theory of norms and crisis bargaining. My quantitative research on this topic documented a general pattern of responses to the violation of norms that is consistent with this theory. This case study of US-Soviet interactions over Cuba, however, has demonstrated that the causal process posited by my theory is, in fact, influencing state responses to the violation of norms. Consistent with hypothesis 1, the Soviets viewed American coercive behavior as *illegitimate* when they were *not* in violation of a previous dispute settlement. Moreover, this perception of US behavior led the USSR to *escalate* its hostile activity rather than concede to US demands. Khrushchev declared US actions to be illegal and threatened nuclear war before the settlement existed. And when the settlement was not being violated, Brezhnev simply responded to Nixon and Kissinger's heavy-handed attempts to alter the understanding by sending more subs for port calls without comment. Consistent with hypothesis 2, on the other hand, when the USSR *was* in violation of a previous dispute settlement—both regarding the withdrawal of the IL-28 bombers and during the Cienfuegos crisis—they *did* view the American coercive response as legitimate. My discussion documented Soviet perceptions of the legitimacy of American coercive demands through private statements by Soviet diplomats during the withdrawal of the IL-28 bombers. These perceptions also appear to be reflected in the Soviet leadership's decision to comply with US demands quickly and quietly during the Cienfuegos crisis. Finally, consistent with hypothesis 3, the Kennedy-Khrushchev understanding left observable traces on the foreign policy process. In *all* of the exchanges over Cuba after 1962, both sides describe and justify their own behavior and the behavior of their opponent in terms of the stipulations of the Kennedy-Khrushchev accord.

TESTING REALIST EXPLANATIONS OF CIENFUEGOS

While the evidence supporting my hypotheses appears to be substantial, I must also consider the prominent realist explanations of US-Soviet relations in the Caribbean before drawing any final conclusions.

Perhaps the most obvious realist explanation of Soviet compliance in Cienfuegos is the massive local military advantage enjoyed by the United States. While this argument may be plausible on its face, Richard Betts suggests that the local military balance does not even provide a good explanation of behavior in the Cuban missile crisis. "If the imbalance of conventional forces in the Caribbean was the determinant of the outcome in Cuba, as is often asserted," Betts writes, "there is no good explanation for why the Soviets did not counter the US naval blockade with a blockade of Berlin, where the conventional balance was reversed."[34]

If the balance of conventional forces does not give us a good explanation of Soviet behavior in the Cuban missile crisis, it certainly cannot

---

[34] Betts (1987, 115). One might object to Betts's point because the presence of many tactical warheads in Europe meant that the blockade of Berlin raised the specter of nuclear war even more directly than did a clash over Cuba. Two responses can be made to this point. First, Khrushchev had demonstrated only the previous year that he was willing to risk a conflict with the United States in Berlin. Second, even if one concedes that the fear of nuclear war prevented the USSR from expanding the dispute in Cuba to include Berlin in 1962, there is little reason to believe that this fear motivated them in 1970. As I will discuss later, the improvement in Soviet nuclear capabilities in the intervening period suggests that the United States could not use nuclear threats to intimidate the Kremlin from taking action in Eastern Europe by 1970.

explain why the Soviets were *less* resistant to US coercion in the Cienfuegos crisis than they were in 1962. During the intervening eight years, Soviet military capability made some strong improvements relative to that of the United States. This is especially true with regard to the Soviet ability to *project* its capabilities to areas far from Soviet borders. This increased power projection ability was driven by the development of an increasingly effective blue-water navy during the 1960s and 1970s as well as dramatic improvements in Soviet airlift capabilities.[35]

As Soviet projection capabilities improved, the USSR became more willing to employ its military forces at greater distances from its borders. Following the conclusion of World War II, the USSR restricted its military activities to intervention in communist states on its borders. In fact, at the time of the Cuban missile crisis the Kremlin had neither used its military forces nor lent military support outside of North Korea and Eastern Europe. The first employment of Soviet troops in combat outside this restricted zone was in the Yemen civil war from 1965 to 1969.[36] Just prior to the outbreak of the Cienfuegos crisis, Soviet military involvement in distant conflicts increased once again with their substantial combat support of Egypt in the War of Attrition. During the 1970s, moreover, the Soviets progressively extended their military reach. In 1975 the Soviets injected their military forces, along with Cuban troops, into the Angolan civil war, and in 1977 they used a similar strategy to support Ethiopia in its war with Somalia. In addition to increasing the size of the military forces they deployed and the distances to which they projected them, the USSR also became increasingly willing to oppose American client states in the Third World during 1960s and 1970s. As a result we can be confident that this steady *increase* in Soviet military power and their ability to project it suggests that the local military balance of forces cannot explain the *decrease* in Soviet resistance between the Cuban missile crisis and the Cienfuegos crisis. Moreover, American conventional superiority cannot *begin* to explain the shift in Soviet behavior between the Cienfuegos crisis and the continuing naval engagements that followed it.

A second prominent realist explanation for Soviet behavior regarding Cuba has been American strategic nuclear superiority. As I discussed earlier, Betts contends that US nuclear predominance was an important cause of Soviet compliance in the Cuban missile crisis. By the early 1970s, however, American nuclear hegemony—which allowed the United States

[35] For a detailed discussion of the improvement in Soviet power projection, see chapter 2 in Porter (1984).

[36] For a list of all Soviet military involvements in the Third World, see Porter (1984, 6). For a chronology of the extension of Soviet attempts to project military power, see Porter (1984, 241–43).

to use nuclear weapons as coercive tools—had largely evaporated. In 1962 the House Armed Services Committee determined that the United States possessed 420 intercontinental ballistic missiles (ICBMs) and sub-marine-launched ballistic missiles (SLBMs). In addition, the United States possessed 630 long-range bombers. The USSR, on the other hand, had only 75 ICBMs, 200 long-range bombers, and only a very few SLBM launchers in 1962.[37] By the time of the Cienfuegos crisis, the nuclear balance had changed dramatically. The United States had increased its number of strategic launchers—including ICBMs, SLBMs, and bombers—to 2,213 in 1970. But the Soviet Union had increased its strategic stockpile to 1,720 launchers—including 280 SLBMs (Institute for Strategic Studies 1970). Nixon and Kissinger were faced with a Soviet Union that was roughly their nuclear equal. Betts observes the difference that this change made in Soviet behavior in his analysis of the October War of 1973. In that case, he describes the proposition that US nuclear forces were responsible for the Soviet reluctance to intervene directly in the conflict as "doubtful." (Betts 1987, 129) Once again, we can be confident that a relative *improvement* in the Soviet nuclear balance cannot account for the fact that Soviet behavior was *less* belligerent in the Cienfuegos crisis. And as was the case with the conventional balance of forces, American nuclear capabilities cannot explain the change in Soviet behavior between the Cienfuegos crisis and the disputes over port calls that followed.

Since neither the conventional nor the nuclear military balance can explain Soviet behavior in the Cienfuegos crisis, a realist might argue that the Soviets complied more quickly and quietly in the Cienfuegos crisis because the submarine base was not as important to Soviet strategic interests in 1970 as the Cuban missiles were in 1962. My response to this argument is twofold. First, some evidence suggests that the medium- and intermediate-range missiles in Cuba during 1962 did not have as dramatic an effect on the nuclear balance as some have claimed. During the Ex Comm meetings, for example, Secretary McNamara stated at one point that the missiles did not affect the military balance. Others, however, such as General Maxwell Taylor, felt that the Soviet missiles were critically important and should have been destroyed immediately (Kennedy 1968). A more recent and dispassionate analysis suggests that the Soviet missiles in Cuba increased their first-strike capability by approximately 40 percent and that their use in an all-out first strike would have reduced available retaliatory US nuclear forces by approximately 30 percent, leaving 15 percent of the total US force available for retaliation

[37] See *The Changing Strategic Military Balance: USA vs. USSR* (1967). The Institute for Strategic Studies (1970) also presents figures that are very similar to these estimates.

(Betts 1987, 116). Thus the Soviet missiles did have some effect on the nuclear balance, but they did not represent a quantum leap in Soviet capabilities. The Soviet Union would not have gained anything like a first-strike capability, and while US superiority might have been weakened, Washington would have retained the ability to destroy the vast majority of Soviet launchers if they chose to execute a first strike.

Second, we must not overlook the potential military impact of a Soviet submarine base in Cuba in 1970. As I discussed previously, during the late 1960s and early 1970s the USSR was substantially increasing its SLBM force. One of the principal logistical problems facing the Soviet Union was the substantial amount of time that submarines had to spend in transit to and from their positions at sea for maintenance, shore leave, and so on. Military analysts at the time stated that "by using Cienfuegos to allow submarine crews periodic time ashore . . . the Soviet Union can save 12 days in the normal 17 day round-trip its nuclear submarines would have to make from their stations at sea 1,500 miles off the United States east coast, to their home port near Murmansk."[38] Blechman and Levinson agree with this assessment and also point out that a Cuban submarine base would have reduced the strategic vulnerability of the Soviet submarine force by reducing the necessity for them to move through the passage between Greenland, Iceland, and the United Kingdom to reach their bases on the Kola Peninsula. Passing through this narrow gap exposes submarines and makes them more vulnerable to detection and tracking by US forces. These twin advantages of increased alert status and reduced vulnerability to tracking could have been advantageous in various scenarios of military conflict with the United States (Blechman and Levinson 1975, 34). Finally, Defense Secretary Laird estimated that the facilities at Cienfuegos would have increased the number of Soviet SLBMs on station and targeted at the United States at any one time by between 33 percent and 40 percent (Blechman and Levinson 1975, 496–97). Given the number of Soviet SLBMs at the time, this estimate indicates that the number of missiles at stake in 1962 and 1970 were nearly equal.[39] That is, in purely military terms, the gravity of the issues at stake for the Soviet Union in Cuba during 1962 and 1970 were not all that different. A number of American policy makers in 1970 shared this estimation of the gravity of the threat posed by a submarine base at Cienfuegos. In fact, Alexander Haig, then working on the National Security Council, argued that "the base at Cienfuegos was a far more serious threat than the missile bases that had precipitated the Cuban Missile Crisis." (Haig 1992, 251–52) The port calls that the Soviets substituted for the Cienfuegos

[38] United States "naval sources" quoted in the *New York Times*, December 24, 1970, 13.
[39] See The Institute for Strategic Studies (1970).

base mitigated some of the effect of this setback, but without permanent basing facilities in Cuba, Soviet submarine crews were unable to make substantial repairs or to get shore leave without returning to the USSR. Thus the submarine tenders were not a strategically effective substitute.[40]

One final realist explanation of Soviet compliance over Cienfuegos is that the United States had *already* demonstrated its willingness to use force over the issue of missiles in Cuba. Thus the Soviets may have had greater respect for American resolve in 1970 because of their previous experience. On its face this argument has a ring of plausibility. The previous demonstration of US resolve, however, cannot explain significant aspects of the Cienfuegos interaction. In particular, this argument cannot account for the fact that the Soviets refused to comply with US demands that Soviet submarine tenders not call at Cuban ports. Kissinger made threats of "grave consequences" much as he did over the construction of the base at Cienfuegos. Moreover, as I mentioned earlier, the port calls were *not* a strategically effective substitute for the base at Cienfuegos. Thus the only reason for the Soviets to remain intransigent in this final encounter was to demonstrate that *they* would not be bullied by the United States over Cuba and to demonstrate that they would stand firm in defense of their rights under the Kennedy-Khrushchev understanding. If the USSR was so intimidated by American resolve in the crisis over Cienfuegos, why was the Kremlin willing to stand firm in defense of its reputation concerning the right to port calls?

In sum, my argument concerning legitimate dispute settlements and their role as reputational constraints and normative referents is the most plausible explanation of US and Soviet behavior regarding Cuba. The resolution of the Cuban missile crisis in 1962 established standards of behavior with regard to Cuba for both of the superpowers. When the Soviets violated these standards—regarding the IL-28s and in the Cienfuegos crisis—the United States explicitly phrased its protest in terms of the previous agreement and the USSR quickly complied with US demands. Moreover, in declaring their compliance, the Soviet Union consistently and specifically referred to its obligations under the 1962 understanding. Finally, when the United States attempted to press further concessions on the USSR by unilaterally expanding the terms of the agreement, the USSR stubbornly refused to accept the American terms. None of the alternative arguments I have considered—including the balance of nuclear and conventional forces, the interests at stake in the crises, and previous American bargaining behavior—can explain this pattern of outcomes.

---

[40] See the comments of Secretary Laird in the *New York Times*, December 3, 1970, 2; and Kissinger (1982, 652).

Thus Cienfuegos stands as an excellent example of the powerful impact that international norms can have on crisis behavior. More specifically, my analysis of the Cienfuegos crisis provides further support for my institutionalist approach to the study of international norms. In previous quantitative research I documented a pattern of behavior that was consistent with this approach (Gelpi 1997). Through this case study I have demonstrated that the causal mechanisms that were posited to be central in that more general study can be more directly observed when instances of norm violation are examined in detail.

On the other hand, my findings represent a challenge to realist scholars who argue that peace can only be maintained by military force and deterrent threats. Undoubtedly, power and threats *do* play an important role in determining behavior in international crises. For example, American nuclear superiority seems to have contributed to Khrushchev's decision to back down in the Cuban missile crisis after he escalated the confrontation to the brink of nuclear war. Moreover, it seems likely that the USSR would not have made the concessions in the Cienfuegos crisis had the United States not made firm demands that they do so. But a strictly realist view overlooks at least two important aspects of crisis bargaining. First, it neglects the fact that threats can be interpreted in a variety of ways. As a result, policy makers' normative referents—which shape the meaning of coercive behavior—have as important an influence on the outcome of international crises as do relative power and bargaining strategies. Second, in emphasizing the importance of a reputation for toughness, the realist paradigm ignores the value that states place on a reputation for trustworthiness. It is both by altering these referents and by engaging state reputations that international norms have a powerful influence on state responses to coercive behavior.

THE SIX-DAY WAR AND THE FAILURE OF THE SUEZ SETTLEMENT

Far from representing an isolated case, Cienfuegos is one of many crises in which a dispute settlement contributed to a reestablishment of cooperation on the basis of the previous agreement. As table 6A indicates, my data set contains twenty-eight reinitiated crises in which no violation occurred and the defender utilized a bullying strategy. In twenty-four of these crises the challenger remained intransigent. Of the twenty-nine cases in which defenders used a bullying strategy to *punish a violation*, on the other hand, the challenger either complied or compromised in sixteen times. In addition to Cienfuegos, this set of cases includes crises between the Soviet Union and Iran over oil concessions in northern Iran during 1944, a series of crises between Turkey and Greece over the status

TABLE 6A

Challenger Responses to Bullying, with and without the Violation of a
Previous Dispute Settlement

Challenger's Response	No Settlement Violated	Previous Settlement Violated	Total
Compliance	4	11	15
	14%	38%	26%
Compromise	0	5	5
	0%	17%	9%
Intransigence	24	13	37
	86%	45%	65%
Total	28	29	57

Note: Pearon Chi-Squared (2d.f.) = 11.52, $p < 0.00$.

of Cyprus, the so-called Christmas bombing campaign during the Vietnam conflict, and a number of other disputes. Thus dispute settlements do appear to be effective across the entire temporal coverage of the data set, and they are effective among a great variety of conflicting states.

Nonetheless, I also observed thirteen reinitiated crises in which the punishment of a violation did not result in challenger compliance or compromise. One such case is the Six-Day War, which followed an Egyptian violation of the United Nations Emergency Force (UNEF) settlement that brought an end to the Suez War. Through the analysis of this case study I hope to investigate some of the possible reasons that dispute settlements may fail to alter the challenger's response to coercive behavior in these cases. The results of the investigation will serve as the foundation for my more systematic examination in chapter 7 of when dispute settlements will succeed or fail.

SETTLING THE SUEZ CRISIS

The Suez crisis began when Egypt's president Gamal Abdel Nasser nationalized the internationally run Suez Canal on July 26, 1956, in response to the British and American withdrawal of $75 million in aid for the construction of the Aswan Dam. After the United States and United Kingdom, the World Bank promptly withdrew the $200 million it had offered, leaving Egypt with virtually no funding for this critical development project. Both Britain and France were immediately livid at Nasser's fait accompli. British prime minister Anthony Eden began calling up military reserves and talking about the need to use force to "bring Nasser to his senses," while the French were so outraged as to compare Nasser's actions to Hitler's reoccupation of the Rhineland.[41] London and Paris were so exercised about the nationalization because of their fears about what Nasser's actions would do for his image in the Arab world. Specifically, Nasser's popularity as an Arab nationalist presented potentially serious problems for British relations with more conservative states such as Jordan, Saudi Arabia, and Iraq. The French, on the other hand, were concerned about the influence Nasser might have on the rebel forces in Algeria which were already driving France to a civil war (Nutting 1967).

The problem facing Eden and his French counterpart, Guy Mollet, was that Nasser had given them no pretext for using force. Although Nasser had nationalized the canal, he had not used force, had made relatively generous offers of compensation to the shareholders, and had even allowed British and French ships to pass through the canal free of charge when they refused to remit payment to the Egyptian-owned canal company. Thus the Western Powers turned to Israel to give them a pretext for military intervention. Israel had only a marginal interest in the canal, but it had other grievances against Egypt. In particular, Israel hoped to open the Straits of Tiran—which Egypt had closed since Israel's independence in 1948—to give them access to the Red Sea and to gain control of the Gaza Strip, which had become a constant source of terrorist harassment for them. At France's suggestion, the three states met and concocted a plan that could achieve all of their goals.[42] The upshot of these negotiations was that Israel would launch a surprise attack against Egyptian positions in Gaza and the Sinai, pressing as quickly as possible toward both the Suez Canal and Egyptian positions at Sharm el Sheik, which controlled the Straits of Tiran. After the attack had begun, Eden and Mollet would intervene as "peacemakers," demanding that both Egyptian and Israeli forces withdraw from the immediate canal zone so that British and French troops could move in to assure the "safety" of the canal and to protect the peace. Since the Israelis had little interest in the canal zone per se, they would quickly comply. After the Egyptians refused to evacuate their own territory, the British and French would attack and occupy the canal, leaving Nasser defeated, the canal in British and French hands, and Israel in control of Gaza, the Straits of Tiran, and much of the Sinai.

On October 29 the conspirators began executing their plan, and by the time that Paris and London issued their ultimatum, Israel was already

---

[41] See Nutting (1967, 48–49) for a discussion of the British and French initial response.
[42] For a detailed description of the conspiracy leading up to the launching of the Suez War, see Dyan (1976) and Nutting (1967).

closing on the canal.[43] After facing severe international criticism for their transparent ploy—especially from the United States and the Arab states— Eden and Mollet balked at sending their troops. British and French paratroopers did not land near the canal until November 6, the day after Egyptian-Israeli fighting had stopped of its own accord.[44] By that time Egypt had blocked the Suez Canal, Saudi Arabia had embargoed the sale of oil to Britain and France, and Syria had destroyed the oil pipeline running across its territory. Thus Britain and France were forced to import oil from sources in North and South America, which wanted payment in US dollars rather than pounds or francs, but they lacked the financial resources to make the necessary exchanges. The United States, for its part, demanded the immediate withdrawal of Franco-British forces as a precondition for even discussing the extension of dollar credits. By the end of November, gasoline rationing had begun in both Britain and France, persuading Mollet and Eden to capitulate, and their troops began to withdraw from the canal zone in abject defeat by the beginning of December.

Israeli troops, however, remained in control of almost the entire Sinai, and it was the resolution of this aspect of the dispute which is most relevant to the Six-Day War. The settlement of the situation in the Sinai began on November 2, when the Canadian foreign minister proposed the formation of UNEF. This force would move into the Sinai to "secure and supervise the cessation of hostilities in accordance with all terms of General Assembly Resolution 997 (ES-I) of 2 November 1956."[45] Resolution 997, in turn, called on all parties to move their forces behind the 1949 armistice line and to end all raids across that line. On November 5 both Israel and Egypt accepted an unconditional cease-fire, and Egypt accepted the presence of UNEF on its soil. On that same date, the General Assembly also adopted a resolution officially forming the UNEF. It was only after the fighting had stopped, however, that the real bargaining about the shape of the subsequent settlement began.

The key issues at stake in the negotiations were relatively straightforward. For its part, Egypt was concerned with the kinds of restraints that might be placed on it in terms of its right to expel the UNEF forces if they so desired. Egyptian leaders wanted to know how long UNEF would stay and under what conditions they would leave. Israel was interested in these very same issues, but from the opposing perspective. The

---

[43] For a detailed description of the course of battlefield operations in the Sinai during the 1956 war, see Dyan (1976, 235–59).

[44] For a detailed discussion of the international response to British, French, and Israeli actions, see Nutting (1967) and Mezerik (1969).

[45] UN resolution 1000 (ES-I) of November 5, 1956, quoted in Mezerik (1969, 87).

Israelis wanted guarantees that UNEF would remain in the Sinai until a general resolution to the Arab-Israeli problem had been found. In addition, they were particularly concerned that UNEF forces take up positions in Gaza and Sharm el Sheik to prevent terrorist raids and ensure that the Straits of Tiran remained open.

From the very outset of the negotiations, Israel refused to consider the placement of any UNEF units on its territory, and at first they even refused to evacuate the Sinai so that the UNEF could take up positions in Egypt. Egypt, for its part, immediately asserted its right to expel UNEF at their discretion. On November 10, the chief Egyptian delegate to the UN, Ambassador Omar Loutfi, stated in an aide-mémoire that "[i]t being agreed that the consent of Egypt is indispensable for entry and presence of the UN forces in any part of its territory, if such consent no longer persists, these forces shall withdraw."[46] UN General Secretary Dag Hammarskjöld, however, felt that some constraints on Egyptian prerogatives were necessary to give some teeth to the settlement. Specifically, he wanted to gain Egyptian agreement that UNEF would not be withdrawn until its "tasks had been completed" (i.e., all border and territorial issues between Egypt and Israel had been permanently settled). Hammarskjöld's original statement concerning the withdrawal of UNEF was that "[i]n case of different views as to when the crisis does not any longer warrant the presence of the troops, the matter would have to be negotiated by the parties."[47] After Loutfi's objection, however, the general secretary altered his stance somewhat, suggesting on November 12 that "[i]f a difference should develop, whether or not the reasons for the arrangement are still valid, the matter should be brought up for negotiations with the United Nations."[48]

This formulation was more acceptable to Egypt, since it required discussion with the UN—where some states would be sympathetic to the Egyptian cause—rather than negotiating with Israel directly. Nonetheless, the proposal did not address all of Cairo's concerns, and so on November 13 Egyptian foreign minister Mahmud Fawzi privately threatened to scuttle the entire UNEF arrangement and suspended Egyptian agreement to the placement of UNEF until all disputes were ironed out.

[46] Private Memorandum of Secretary Dag Hammarskjöld, August 5, 1957, quoted in Draper (1968, 142). This lengthy memorandum represents the best and most complete record of the very private negotiations between Egypt and the UN concerning the UNEF forces. As a result, much of my own recounting of the negotiations is drawn from this memorandum.

[47] Private Memorandum of Secretary Dag Hammarskjöld, August 5, 1957, quoted in Draper (1968, 142).

[48] Private Memorandum of Secretary Dag Hammarskjöld, August 5, 1957, quoted in Draper (1968, 143).

Hammarskjöld did not back down, however, and in a personal message to Fawzi, he stated that the expulsion of UNEF before its tasks were completed "although within the rights of the Egyptian government, would go against its acceptance of the basic resolution of the General Assembly."[49] In other words, removing the troops before the UN determined that the Egyptian-Israeli problem was settled was within their rights as a sovereign state, but doing so would represent a violation of their agreement with the UN. Furthermore, the general secretary insisted that if Egypt did not relent, he would be forced to refer their disagreement over UNEF to the General Assembly "putting it to their judgement as to what could or could not be considered and understanding." The general secretary continued:

> This situation would be a most embarrassing one for all, but I would fear the political repercussions, as obviously very few would find it reasonable that recognition of your freedom of action should mean that you, after having permitted the force to come, might ask it to withdraw at a time when the very reasons which had previously prompted you to accept were still obviously valid.[50]

Faced with the clear prospect of defeat in the General Assembly, the collapse of the peace process, the possibility of prolonged Israeli occupation of the Sinai, and continued Egyptian vulnerability to Israeli forces, Egypt conceded and allowed the first UNEF troops to land in the canal zone on November 15.

To seal the agreement and to ensure that there was a common understanding about the terms for withdrawal of UNEF, Hammarskjöld worked on the text of an agreement between Egypt and the UN which he could discuss directly with Nasser. In this document, the general secretary stated that "Egypt would declare to the United Nations that it would exert its sovereign rights with regard to the troops on the basis of a good faith interpretation of the tasks of the force. The United Nations should make a reciprocal commitment not to withdraw the force as long as the task was not completed." He continued by clarifying that

> [t]he procedure in case of a request from Egypt for the withdrawal of UNEF would be as follows. The matter would be at once brought before the General Assembly. If the General Assembly found that the task was completed, everything would be all right. If they found that the task was not completed and Egypt, all the same,

---

[49] Private Memorandum of Secretary Dag Hammarskjöld, August 5, 1957, quoted in Draper (1968, 144).

[50] Private Memorandum of Secretary Dag Hammarskjöld, August 5, 1957, quoted in Draper (1968, 144–45).

maintained its stand and enforced the withdrawal, Egypt would break its agreement with the United Nations.[51]

Egypt balked once again, however, when Hammarskjöld met with Nasser on November 17 to finalize the agreement. After reminding Nasser three times that the general secretary's alternative to this arrangement was to call for the dissolution of UNEF, Hammarskjöld gained Nasser's consent to the understanding. On November 24 the United Nations sealed the agreement passing a resolution that designated its consent to the accord Hammarskjöld had constructed.[52]

After forging an agreement with the Egyptians, the United Nations—and other parties such as the United States—turned their attention to constructing a settlement with Israel. On November 21, Israel signaled that it was willing to consider negotiated settlements of the issue by announcing that it had withdrawn from its "most advanced" positions in the Sinai. Despite Hammarskjöld's insistence that the Israelis withdraw from Sinai unconditionally, however, they still refused to withdraw their forces from Gaza or positions necessary for defending the Straits of Tiran. The Israelis requested assurances that the Straits of Tiran would remain open and that Egyptian-supported terrorism from Gaza would cease. This might be accomplished, they suggested, by (1) a joint administration of Gaza by Israeli authorities and UNEF forces in Gaza and (2) stationing UNEF soldiers at Sharm el Sheik as well as along the international border in the Sinai. This problem was finally resolved by American pressure on Israel to comply with UN resolutions. In an aide-mémoire from John Foster Dulles to Israeli ambassador Abba Eban, the United States stated that Israeli administration of Gaza was unacceptable, but that UNEF forces could be placed in Gaza and Sharm el Sheik. The UN also forwarded the conditions that Egypt had accepted for the withdrawal of UNEF to the Israeli government as further reassurance. Finally, Dulles pledged the United States to maintain freedom of navigation through the Straits of Tiran, saying that "the United States believes that the Gulf comprehends international waters and that no nation has the right to prevent free and innocent passage in the Gulf and through the Straits giving access thereto."[53] Other major powers, such as Britain and France, echoed the US statement concerning freedom of navigation. The Israeli government found this combination of gestures acceptable, and on March 1, 1957, Israeli foreign minister Golda Meir announced to the

---

[51] Private Memorandum of Secretary Dag Hammarskjöld, August 5, 1957, quoted in Draper (1968, 146).

[52] See United Nation Resolution 1121 (XI) of November 24, 1956.

[53] Aide-mémoire handed to Israeli ambassador Abba Eban by Secretary of State John Foster Dulles on February 11, 1957.

UN General Assembly that her nation would withdraw completely from Sinai and Gaza. In doing so, however, Meir explicitly noted several conditions for Israel's acceptance of the settlement. First, she stated that interference with Israeli ships in the Gulf of Aqaba would be "regarded by Israel as an attack entitling her to exercise her inherent right of self-defense under article 51 of the Charter." Second, she insisted that "the takeover of Gaza from the military and civilian control of Israel will be exclusively by the United Nations Emergency Force." And third, she insisted that these arrangements would continue "for a transitory period from the takeover until there is a peace settlement, to be sought as rapidly as possible."[54]

Thus like the Kennedy-Khrushchev understanding, the resolution of the Suez crisis between Israel and Egypt represented a semiformal agreement and a legitimate settlement as I have used the term in this work. First, the agreement was legitimate because it was responsive to the wishes of both states. For its part, Egypt acceded to the placement of UN troops on its soil, but it was able to gain an Israeli evacuation of the Sinai. In addition, the agreement required Egypt to receive consent from the UN General Assembly rather than directly from Israel to remove UNEF. Israel, on the other hand, gave up military and administrative control of Sinai and the Gaza Strip. At the same time, however, Israel was able to prevent Egyptian occupation and administration of the Gaza Strip, they were able to open up the Straits of Tiran, and they received a guarantee by the United States, Britain, and France that the straits would remain open. Second, the UNEF agreement represented a legitimate settlement because it specified behaviors that would constitute a violation of the understanding. Specifically, Egypt was not to expel UNEF until it could make a "good faith" assessment that its tasks were complete (i.e., the Egypt-Israel dispute had been permanently settled). An Egyptian request for removal of the troops would be referred to the General Assembly for a vote. If the General Assembly voted that UNEF's tasks were not complete, then an Egyptian insistence that they be withdrawn would constitute a violation. Both Egypt and Israel, of course, also agreed to respect the integrity of their international border as well as the armistice line around Gaza.

COLLAPSE OF UNEF AND THE SIX-DAY WAR

The Suez settlement was fairly successful in reducing Egyptian-Israeli conflict for almost a decade. From 1957 until 1966, terrorist raids into

---

[54] Excerpts from remarks made by the Israeli foreign minister to the United Nations General Assembly, March 1, 1957. Quoted in Mezerik (1969, 90–91).

Israel were greatly reduced, as were Israeli reprisals on Arab territory. In addition, Israeli shipping passed through the Straits of Tiran unharassed. Beginning in late 1966, however, conflict increased between Israel and its other Arab neighbors, Jordan and Syria, and these disputes eventually spilled over to Egypt. During this period the government of Jordan made a concerted effort to restrict terrorist activities on its soil, but with only mixed success. On November 13, 1966, in response to one of the terrorist raids that Jordan was unable to prevent, Israel conducted a major reprisal on the Jordanian village of El Samu. Eighteen Jordanians were killed and fifty-four wounded, and at least 125 structures were destroyed. The Jordanians responded to their setback by blasting Nasser and Egypt for hiding behind UNEF and failing to come to their aid. Although Egypt acted as though it was not bothered by this criticism, later events suggested that they were more disturbed than they had allowed. Then, on April 7, 1967, Syrian and Israeli jets engaged in intense dogfighting over their common border. The Israeli Defense Force (IDF) soundly defeated their opponents—downing six Syrian fighters in the process—and emphasized their victory by repeatedly flying low over the roofs of Damascus while the Syrian government was helpless to stop them. Egypt's forces, however, remained motionless in the Sinai, despite the fact that Nasser had signed a defense pact with Syria only five months earlier. Instead, Cairo simply released a statement insisting that their defense pact did not require Egypt to respond to a "merely local incident."[55]

Into this tense atmosphere, the Soviet Union cast a spark which sharply changed Nasser's attitude. On May 13 the USSR delivered a warning to Egypt that as many as thirteen brigades of the IDF were massing on the Syrian border and that they intended to invade Syria on May 17. In retrospect, the report of troop concentrations appears to have been untrue, since the United Nations Truce Supervision Organization (UNTSO) searched the area and found no such concentrations. Moreover, we must remember that the reported thirteen brigades represented more than half of Israel's fully mobilized military capacity. It would be exceedingly difficult to hide such a group in a small area like Galilee (Parker 1993, 12–14). It remains unclear whether the Soviets believed the report, but they remained adamant about Israel's intention to invade Syria even after they were given the opportunity to observe the border area themselves. What is clear, however, is that Egypt took the Soviet warning seriously, and continued to believe the Soviets even after Western nations tried to reassure them. The Egyptian faith in the warning is understandable, however, both because an Israeli attack on Syria was

---

[55] Egyptian prime minister Sidqi Suleiman quoted in Michael Bar-Zohar (1970, 10).

plausible, and because the Soviets had generally been responsible and trustworthy allies to Egypt.[56]

At almost the same time that the Soviets were delivering their warning, IDF Chief of Staff Yitzhak Rabin was quoted by Arab sources as threatening to topple the Syrian government. Later on in the crisis when he closed the Straits of Tiran, Nasser cited this statement as a principal provocation of Egyptian action, but no independent record of any such statement by Rabin exists. On May 11 Rabin did make a statement differentiating between Israeli reprisal raids on Jordan and Lebanon—states that did not support the terrorists—and the Israeli responses to Syrian support of terrorist raids. What Rabin said, however, was that "our aims in regard to Syria are different from our aims in respect to Jordan and Lebanon." (Bar-Zohar 1970, 12) While perhaps somewhat ominous in tone, this statement is not a threat to overthrow the Syrian government. One possible source of the misunderstanding is a misquote by a United Press International (UPI) reporter, who quoted an unnamed "high Israeli source" as saying that "Israel would take limited military action designed to topple the Damascus army regime if Syrian terrorists continued sabotage raids inside Israel."[57] Again, there is no corroborative record of any such statement by an Israeli official. Regardless of the specific content of Israeli statements, however, Egyptian leaders were correct in their perception that Israel was beginning to talk tougher toward Syria, and combined with the Soviet intelligence concerning troop concentrations, Cairo felt compelled to respond.

On May 14 Egypt declared a state of emergency and ordered troops to begin taking up positions in the Sinai. The mobilization was a highly public affair, as Nasser closed all highways to civilian traffic and military trucks rolled through the streets of Cairo all night long. In fact, Nasser made such a show that many of the Egyptian onlookers apparently thought that they were witnessing a military parade of some sort. Even with the troops deployed in Sinai, however, Nasser still could not credibly deter an Israeli invasion of Syria because of the presence of the UNEF forces in Gaza and on the Egyptian-Israeli border. Thus the Egyptian president sought to escape this problem by requesting a partial withdrawal of UNEF from the international border to positions in Gaza and Sharm el Sheik.

On May 16 a letter was delivered to the commander of the UNEF

[56] See Parker (1993) for a detailed discussion of where the report of troop concentrations came from, why the Soviets passed it to Cairo, and why they continued to insist that Israel intended to attack Syria.

[57] Parker (1993, 15). Parker also discusses various other interpretations of the mysterious Rabin statement and reviews its effect on the Egyptian response.

troops, General Rikhye, from General Fawzi, and since its delivery this note has raised significant questions about the intent behind the Egyptian demands. The text of the letter—translated from Arabic into English—stated that "our troops are already concentrated in Sinai along our eastern border. For the sake of the complete security of all UN troops which install OP's [observation posts] along our borders, I request that you give orders to withdraw all these troops immediately." (Bar-Zohar 1970, 32) The precise meaning behind this request is unclear. Specifically, was Egypt demanding a total withdrawal of UNEF, or were they asking for troops along the Sinai international border to be moved to Sharm el Sheik or to posts along the armistice line in Gaza? Interestingly, however, the English text of the letter is not the one that Nasser ordered sent to the UNEF commander. After viewing the previous translation of the note, Nasser demanded two significant wording changes: (1) that the phrase *all these troops* be changed to simply *these troops;* and (2) that the word *withdraw* be changed to *redeploy* (Parker 1993, 65–67). Thus it seems clear in retrospect that Nasser intended to ask for a partial withdrawal of UNEF. The Egyptian president's subsequent statements also substantiate this view. In a 1970 interview with Robert Stephens, for example, Nasser recalled that

> [i]t was not in our plan to close the Gulf of Aqaba at that time. When we moved our troops into Sinai we sent to U Thant asking him to withdraw UNEF from Rafah to Eilat [the length of the international border] and to keep UNEF in Gaza and Sharm el Sheik. We decided on this step in order not to face complications about the Gulf of Aqaba.[58]

During the 1967 crisis, however, the Egyptian chief of staff, General Amr, never made the changes Nasser requested, and delivered the ambiguous note on General Fawzi's behalf instead.

General Rikhye forwarded Amr's message to U Thant, since a request for the withdrawal of UNEF was to be sent directly to the general secretary rather than the commander on the ground. Thant responded both by asking Egypt for clarification about its intent and by issuing a threat. He replied that "if [the request] meant the temporary withdrawal of UNEF troops from the line or part of it, it would be unacceptable because the purpose of the UN force in Gaza and Sinai is to prevent a recurrence of fighting, and it cannot be asked to stand aside in order to

---

[58] Stephens (1971, 474). This statement suggests that Nasser's original intent may have been to bend the UNEF settlement rather than to break it. Although the UNEF settlement ultimately failed, Nasser's desire to avoid a flagrant violation suggests that the settlement did have an impact on Egyptian behavior—even in this rather extreme circumstance.

enable the two sides to resume fighting."[59] Thant went on to insist that UNEF either be left in place or that Egypt clearly demand its complete withdrawal. He appears to have chosen this all-or-nothing strategy on the advice of UN Undersecretary General Ralph Bunche, who told Thant to insist on total withdrawal because "[a]s Nasser does not want them withdrawn, he will have to go into reverse." (Bar-Zohar 1970, 33)

The Egyptian response was quite the opposite of the one Bunche expected. Thant's ultimatum left Nasser with a choice between scrapping the Suez settlement and appearing to capitulate before the UN and the Western powers. The latter course would have utterly defeated Nasser's original goal in beginning the dispute, which was to demonstrate Egyptian support and solidarity with Syria and Jordan. Thus he chose the former option, and on May 18 Egypt asked U Thant to remove UNEF entirely from Egyptian soil. Strangely, Thant then immediately shifted from playing tough with Nasser to capitulating to his demands. Upon receiving the request for a withdrawal of UNEF, Thant had several options. Principally, he could have formally contended that the "tasks" of UNEF had not been achieved and could have referred the issue to the General Assembly as to whether UNEF would withdraw. Instead, Thant simply capitulated and ordered UNEF's withdrawal. In subsequent writings, Thant gave a number of reasons for his quick about-face.[60] First, he stated that he referred the issue to the UNEF advisory committee that chose not to force a vote in the General Assembly. This does not explain, however, why Thant himself did not force a vote, since doing so would have been his prerogative. It is true, as he suggests, that the Yugoslav and Indian contingents of UNEF were likely to withdraw in solidarity with Egypt, but other troops could have remained and perhaps have been reinforced by troops from other nations. Second, Thant stated that UNEF was not militarily viable and would have been defeated in combat with Egypt. This is true, of course, but it misses the entire point of UNEF. These troops were never expected to be a militarily viable opponent to the Egyptian military or the IDF. The troops were only in place to provide a salient trip wire that would designate the clear violation of the Suez settlement, identify the party violating the settlement, and draw other nations directly into the dispute through the UN. But Thant withdrew the wire after Egypt had only stubbed its toe on it. Finally, in a very strange turn, Thant attempted to claim that he had no authority to keep

[59] Report of General Secretary U Thant on the Withdrawal of the United Nations Emergency Force, May 18, 1967. Quoted in Draper (1968, 152).

[60] For the full text of Thant's discussion, see the Report of the General Secretary on the Withdrawal of the United Nations Emergency Force, June 26, 1967. Reprinted in Draper (1968). Thant wrote this document as a rebuttal to the many critics of his policy who had sprung up as the situation spiraled into war.

UNEF in Egypt. He complained that "[t]here is no official United Nations document on the basis of which any case could be made that there was any limitation on the authority of the Government of Egypt to . . . obtain at any time the removal of UNEF from its territory."[61] This statement is flatly untrue, and U Thant knew it. Hammarskjöld had clearly established a procedure for the removal of UNEF, with the consent of both Israel and Egypt, and Hammarskjöld's understanding was explicitly acknowledged by the General Assembly as the proper understanding of the UNEF agreement on November 24, 1956.[62] Thus rather than any of Thant's many excuses, perhaps the best explanation for his abrupt change of heart is that he lost his stomach for confrontation with Egypt and its supporters.

In contrast with the actions of the UN, however, Israel's response to the Egyptian mobilization was both swift and firm. On May 15 the IDF was placed on alert in response to the Egyptian state of emergency. The following day, Israel began a limited mobilization of reserves, and Yitzhak Rabin began moving Israeli-armored divisions south toward Sinai. Then, on May 17, after Nasser's request for the withdrawal of UNEF, Israeli representative to the UN, Gideon Rafael, approached U Thant directly and demanded that the UN not capitulate to Nasser's request. In addition, Rafael specifically brought the text of the understanding between Hammarskjöld and Nasser to the general secretary's attention (Bar-Zohar 1970). After Thant had capitulated the following day, Foreign Minister Eban spoke with the UN representatives of France, Britain, and the United States, emphasizing that Egypt was in violation of its agreement concerning UNEF and urging the Great Powers to take action. In the Security Council meeting at which Thant announced his decision to withdraw UNEF, Rafael and the US representative openly pleaded with Thant not to withdraw or at least to leave troops in Sharm el Sheik (Bar-Zohar 1970, 32–43). Thant refused. Then, as UN diplomacy failed, Israel moved its defense readiness to the level of a general mobilization, and moved its forces into offensive positions in the Sinai, ready to strike.[63]

The 1967 crisis reached its second turning point on May 23, when

[61] Report of the General Secretary on the Withdrawal of the United Nations Emergency Force, June 26, 1967. Quoted in Draper (1968, 191).

[62] See United Nations Resolution 1121 (XI) of November 24, 1956.

[63] Some analysts have described Israel's response during this early part of the crisis as "appeasement" because the Israeli government did not immediately respond with force. Israel's actions and the substance of their demands, however, demonstrate that their policy bore no resemblance to one of appeasement. Israel matched each escalatory military move and steadfastly insisted in the UN and elsewhere that Egypt must remove its forces and reestablish UNEF. In fact, while they were not irresponsibly aggressive, they made no conciliatory gestures of any kind in terms of concessions or offers of compromise.

Nasser announced that Egypt had closed the Straits of Tiran and block-aded the Gulf of Aqaba. In a speech at an Egyptian air force headquarters in Sinai, Nasser stated, "The armed forces yesterday occupied Sharm el Sheik. It is an affirmation of our rights and our sovereignty over the Gulf of Aqaba. The Gulf constitutes Egyptian territorial waters. Under no cir-cumstances will we allow the Israeli flag to pass through the Gulf of Aqaba." (*Keesing's Research Report* 1968, 18) Israel had previously stated that it would consider the closure of the straits casus belli, and their closure also represented another violation of the conditions under which Israel agreed to the Suez settlement. Consequently, Nasser must have known that his action would press the dispute quickly to the brink of war. Just as he did so, however, Nasser's bargaining behavior began to change. On the one hand, the Egyptian president's public rhetoric re-mained heated and virulently anti-Israeli throughout the remainder of the crisis. Three days later, on May 26, for example, Nasser stated that if war came, "it will be total and the objective will be the destruction of Israel. We feel confident that we can win a war with Israel, with God's help."[64] Two days later he declared that Arabs would never accept coexis-tence with Israel. On the other hand, Egypt pointedly refrained from taking any further escalatory military action. Moreover, in private the Egyptian government let it be known that their tough statements were "mere words designed for public consumption,"[65] and they demonstrated a willingness to make some concessions to avoid war. Specifically, Nasser met with U Thant on May 24, and although the Egyptian president remained unwilling to open the Gulf of Aqaba entirely or to allow UNEF on Egyptian territory, he did make several other conciliatory gestures. First, Nasser assured the general secretary that Egypt would not begin any military conflict. Furthermore, the Egyptian president stated that he would accept UN mediation of the dispute with Israel. To ease tensions during the mediation he offered to open the straits to ships bound for Israel provided that the ships themselves were not Israeli and that they carried no strategic materials. Finally, he suggested that Israel bring the dispute to a close by inviting UNEF onto its territory (Bar-Zohar 1970, 102; Lacoutre 1973, 303–4). These "concessions" were relatively lim-ited, since none of the suggestions directly contradicted current Egyptian policies. Nonetheless, when combined with the lack of further military escalation, these proposals do suggest that Egypt was beginning to look for a nonviolent way out of the crisis without losing Sinai, Gaza, and the prestige that their victory brought them in the Arab world.

[64] Quoted in the *New York Times*, May 27, 1967.
[65] Egyptian minister of information Mohammed Fayek's statement in an interview with a French correspondent in Egypt. Quoted in Lacoutre (1973, 305).

Nasser's snubbing of Israel and the UN undoubtedly bolstered his image and popularity across North Africa and the Middle East. Other Arab governments quickly rallied to support Egypt by mobilizing their own military forces, and some even took the unusual step of sending small military units to serve directly under Egyptian command. Jordan, for example, reached full mobilization on May 24, and at the same time Amman gave permission for the placement of Saudi and Iraqi troops on Jordanian territory. Syria, for its part, began to mobilize on May 18. Sudan also joined the Egyptian bandwagon and reached general mobilization on May 28. Similarly, Algeria sent some military units to Egypt's aid the following day, and on May 30 Morocco announced that it would place some units at Egypt's disposal. None of these latter moves had any real impact on the military situation in Sinai, but for Nasser they were welcome because of the support they represented for him in other Arab nations. Riding this wave of popularity, on May 30 Nasser also signed a defense pact with King Hussein of Jordan. Under the conditions of the agreement Nasser was to take direct control of Jordanian military forces in case of a conflict. Such a granting of power to a foreign leader would be extraordinary under any circumstances, but the Jordanian concessions were particularly so because of the poisonous state of relations that had existed between Cairo and Amman before the outbreak of the crisis.[66] Jordan's yielding of sovereignty over their own armed forces indicates that Nasser had returned to his position as the undisputed leader of the Pan-Arab movement. His popularity could hardly have been higher.

Faced with the closing of the straits, however, Israel was unimpressed with Nasser's conciliatory gestures to U Thant, and reacted even more sharply than they had in the early stages of the crisis. On May 23 Israel increased its state of military readiness from general to total mobilization for war. Weapons and equipment were stockpiled for battle in a furious airlift. In addition, that evening in a speech before Parliament, Israeli prime minister Levi Eshkol insisted that Egypt's actions "violated international regulations in a flagrant manner." (Lacoutre 1973, 304) Moreover, he made an unconditional demand that "the great powers respect without delay the right of free passage to our southern port, a legal right for all states without exception."[67] Meanwhile, Foreign Minister Eban

[66] Bar-Zohar (1970, 153) notes that only two days earlier, Radio Cairo had referred to Hussein as a "Hashemite whore," and the head of the Palestine Liberation Organization (PLO), Ahmed Shukairy, had been plotting the ouster of Hussein. After the signing of the treaty, however, Hussein and Shukairy were greeted upon their return to Jordan by jubilation in the streets and pictures of Nasser on houses and stores across the city.

[67] Quoted in Bar-Zohar (1970, 87). There has been a persistent perception by observers of this crisis—especially those on the Israeli side—that Eshkol's behavior during the crisis was weak and indecisive. A review of his statements and actions during May and June 1967

reminded the French and British governments of Golda Meir's statement that Israel would invoke its right to self-defense if the straits were blocked. Finally, on the evening of May 23, the Israeli cabinet met and decided to launch a preemptive strike if Egypt did not open the straits in forty-eight hours. D-Day was set for May 25. Only hours before the attack was to begin, however, US undersecretary of state Eugene Rostow asked for a delay of ten days to two weeks for any Israeli military action while the United States attempted to find a nonviolent solution. In fact, Britain, France, and the United States all attempted to stall Israeli military action, but they were not all equally supportive of Israel on the diplomatic front. Contrary to its behavior in 1956, the French government almost totally abandoned its support for Israel in 1967. In addition to pleading with Israel not to attack, French president Charles de Gaulle began pulling back on promised shipments of weapons to Israel. Finally, on June 2, shortly before hostilities broke out, France totally abandoned its ally by announcing publicly that "France is pledged in no way to any of the nations involved." (Bar-Zohar 1970, 179) Britain was much more supportive of Israel than was France, but Prime Minister Wilson was extremely reluctant to take action without American support. Thus international support for Israel depended critically on the position of the United States. After asking Israel for a delay, the Johnson administration made a concerted effort to find a diplomatic solution that would open the Gulf of Aqaba. The most prominent idea was an international flotilla of ships which was to accompany an Israeli vessel through the straits, forcing Nasser to fire on US and other vessels or back down from his blockade. This so-called Red Sea Regatta made little progress with US allies, however, and by May 30—after the signing of the Nasser-Hussein defense pact—Rostow admitted to Israeli ambassadorial minister Ephraim Evron that the international flotilla was dead in the water (Bar-Zohar 1970, 157). Faced with the failure of the Red Sea Regatta, the Johnson administration became paralyzed. The direct use of American military force was out of the question for Johnson, because of congressional restraints resulting from US involvement in Vietnam. On May 31 Secretary of State Dean Rusk reassured senators in a hearing on the crisis that "[t]he United States is not contemplating any unilateral moves in the Middle East, but only within the framework of the United Nations and with other countries." (Bar-Zohar 1970, 161) Losing patience with the futility of US

---

clearly reveals, however, that this perception is incorrect. Michael Brecher, for example, writes, "Notwithstanding the widespread belief in Eshkol's hesitancy during the 1967 crisis, his advocacy of Israeli objectives was the model of clarity." (Brecher 1980, 97) At every turn Eshkol mobilized Israeli forces in response to Egyptian actions, and his diplomatic position was an unyielding demand for a return to the status quo ante. In addition, in meetings with the Israeli cabinet he clearly showed that he was willing to use force.

efforts, Eban stated that Israel was willing to accept a solution that guaranteed freedom of passage through the Gulf of Aqaba, but that such a diplomatic solution would have to be found within "days or weeks, not month or years." Otherwise Israel would take unilateral action to break the blockade.[68]

The dispute took its final turn toward war on May 31 and June 1. Through the evolution of the crisis, Levi Eshkol—who had been acting as both prime minister and defense minister—came to be perceived as insufficiently tough in defending Israel's security. This image developed despite the fact that Eshkol made no diplomatic concessions and responded quickly to each Egyptian military move in the Sinai. Apparently, the simple fact that he withheld the Israeli attack for several days at the request of the United States was enough to brand him as weak. At any rate, an increasing number of parliamentarians, both within and outside the cabinet, began to lobby for Moshe Dyan to take over the defense portfolio. Dyan was widely viewed as a hawk and was a particularly popular figure as the nation moved to war because of his important role in the Israeli victory of 1956. This move was finally made on June 1, as the former IDF chief of staff, Dyan, took over the defense ministry in a "government of national unity." Eshkol, for his part, was able to retain his position as prime minister. Since the Israeli government had already decided to use force and had suggested that time was running out, it seems unlikely that this governmental shake-up had much effect on Israeli policy. Nonetheless, Dyan's presence did create a perception of implacability both at home and abroad, for after hearing that Dyan had been named minister of defense, Nasser stated that he felt war had become a certainty. In addition, while neither Israel's operational plans nor their diplomatic demands changed, Dyan's rhetoric did bring a tone of near arrogance to Israeli statements concerning the crisis. On June 3, for example, the defense minister stated that Israel did not even want direct Western military help in the event of a war with Egypt because he did "not want British or American boys to get killed" defending Israel.[69]

Despite the continued tough talk from Israel, Egypt did not yield in its blockade of the straits. Nasser continued to stall for time and appeared to be looking for a way to avoid military hostilities, but he was unwilling to take any steps that could be construed by other Arabs as capitulating to Israel, the United States, or the United Nations. Some minor concessions were forthcoming, however. For example, in a private conversation with U Thant, the Egyptian president reportedly proposed sending the issue of sovereignty over the Gulf of Aqaba to the International Court of

---

[68] *Keesing's Contemporary Archives* (1968, 22–23).
[69] *Keesing's Contemporary Archives* (1968, 25).

Justice (ICJ).[70] However, one of Nasser's biographers, Robert Stephens, concluded that Nasser would likely have tried to broaden the discussion of the gulf into other areas of the Arab-Israeli conflict. At the same time Nasser was also careful to avoid any further military provocation of Israel. The orders from the Egyptian high command to the troops in Sinai on June 2 were as follows: "Don't give the Israelis an excuse to attack! Gain time! That is an order." (Bar-Zohar 1970, 176) On that same day, in response to a private query from British minister of Parliament Christopher Mayhew, Nasser stated, "We do not intend to attack Israel." (Lacoutre 1973, 308) Nonetheless, Nasser kept up his publicly aggressive front and refused to comply with the terms of the Suez settlement. As late as June 4, Nasser stated, that Egypt would never accept that the Gulf of Aqaba was international waters and that Egypt would consider any such statement "a preliminary act of war."[71]

Israel began its attack on the morning of June 5 with a series of bombing sorties against Egyptian air force bases, which lasted throughout the day.[72] The entire Egyptian air force was effectively destroyed by these raids within a matter of hours. Israel then warned Syria and Jordan not to attack, but Egypt's allies would not sit still. Both Syrian and Jordanian fighters took to the air, and Syrian jets made some minor bombing attacks on positions in northern Israel, while the Jordanian military fired a number of shells onto Israeli territory. Before much damage could be done, however, the IDF successfully eliminated the Syrian and Jordanian air forces. The establishment of Israeli air superiority also effectively eliminated any significant military threat to Israel on its northern and eastern borders during the conflict. At the same time, the major Israeli armored offensive moved into the northern and central Sinai, quickly routing the exposed Egyptian positions and sending the Arab forces into full retreat. The IDF pressed all the way to the Suez Canal and also moved south to occupy Sharm el Sheik. With Egypt quickly defeated, Israel concluded its offensive operations by turning on Jordanian and Syrian positions in the West Bank and the Golan Heights. Once again, Israeli operations met with quick success against the outgunned and outmaneuvered Arab forces.

Despite the extremely swift and decisive Israeli successes on the battlefield, Egypt did not comply with Israeli demands until its forces were utterly defeated. On the evening of the first day of battle, Nasser and Amr had agreed that a total withdrawal from Sinai was necessary and that

---

[70] Robert Stephens reports Nasser's offer of an ICJ settlement based on the testimony of one of Nasser's closest advisers, Mohamed Heikal. See Stephens (1971, 496).

[71] *Keesing's Contemporary Archives* (1968, 24).

[72] For a detailed description of the course of battlefield operations, see Dyan (1976, 358–81). See also *Keesing's Contemporary Archives* (1968).

Egyptian forces would attempt to regroup on the west bank of the Suez Canal (Stephens 1971, 497). Their disastrous military position notwithstanding, Egypt continued to state that it would only accept a cease-fire predicated on restoring the situation of June 4. Israel's demands, on the other hand, remained the same as they had been throughout the entire crisis: restore the status quo ante and reinstate UNEF. In a statement to the UN Security Council on June 5, Israeli representative Arthur Goldberg reiterated that "the situation must be restored to what it was before the crisis began—namely freedom of navigation in the Gulf of Aqaba and the restoration of the UN Emergency Force in the Sinai peninsula." (Bar-Zohar 1970, 222) Despite the fact that this deal offered Egypt substantially more than it could possibly achieve through combat, Cairo continued to refuse a cease-fire under those conditions, and even made some obviously baseless claims that Egypt had launched a counteroffensive into Israeli territory. Finally, when Nasser's forces had been entirely defeated and expelled from Sinai, the Egyptian president asked the USSR to obtain an unconditional cease-fire. Kosygin and President Johnson took this proposal to the UN, but when it passed and was accepted by Israel, Egypt reversed itself once again and rejected the cease-fire. Finally, on June 8, Egypt accepted an unconditional cease-fire, bringing their participation in the Six-Day War to a close.

EXPLAINING THE FAILURE OF THE SUEZ SETTLEMENT

According to my institutionalist argument concerning norms and settlements, the Six-Day War should have been prevented by the Suez settlement and the Israeli willingness to enforce it. Egyptian expulsion of the UNEF was not based on a "good faith" interpretation of the tasks of the force that they had agreed to in 1956. Israel also explicitly identified the Egyptian action as a violation of their previous agreement both in the United Nations and in bilateral discussions with other powers. Finally, Israel clearly and sharply punished Egypt's violation. Throughout the crisis Israel steadfastly and intransigently demanded a return to the status quo ante as the condition for resolving the crisis. In addition, the Israeli leadership matched each of Egypt's escalatory military moves during the early part of the crisis, and at its peak they chose to use force unilaterally to resolve the problem. According to the coding rules discussed in chapter 4, the Israeli bargaining strategy in this crisis was "bullying." Israel never suggested any compromises or alternative solutions, never showed any interest in suggestions of compromise by the Egyptians or others, and eventually escalated the military conflict further than the Egyptians had by carrying out their massive attack on June 5.

Despite the violation of the previous settlement and the firm Israeli response, Egypt most decidedly did not comply with Israeli demands. During the prewar bargaining Cairo did make some cosmetic concessions, but Nasser never seriously considered compliance with the 1956 settlement. Even when it was apparent that his forces would be soundly defeated on the battlefield, Nasser refused to comply. It was not until he was utterly decimated on the battlefield, and the west bank of Suez was exposed to Israeli attacks that Nasser finally conceded defeat. The important question that we face, then, is why did the Suez settlement fail to bring about Egyptian compliance with Israeli demands in 1967?

I shall begin answering this question by looking to the assumptions made by my argument about the impact of norms. Perhaps the UNEF settlement was unsuccessful because one or more of those assumptions proved to be invalid in this case. First, my argument assumes that states act as rational decision makers. Thus I will investigate the frequent claims that Nasser's behavior prior to the Six-Day War was "irrational." Second I assume that states share a common understanding of the content of a settlement and thus can agree on what constitutes a violation. Third, I assume that the defender's threat to enforce the settlement is viewed as credible by the challenger. And fourth, my argument focuses on the costs that international audiences can inflict on leaders who violate settlements. It does not, however, account for the influence of domestic audiences on compliance with settlements.

I shall address each of these explanations of the failure of the UNEF settlement and will use the lessons of this investigation to construct a more systematic analysis of the success and failure of dispute settlements in chapter 7.

Nasser's Mistakes or Misperceptions?

Perhaps the most common explanation of Nasser's behavior in May and June of 1967 is that he was suffering from rather severe and systematic misperceptions regarding the likely outcome of a war with Israel. First, a common assertion is that Nasser overestimated the strength of his military forces and that this hubris led to his aggressive behavior (Parker 1993). A careful analysis of Nasser's statements and actions, however, indicates that he suffered from no such delusions. As late as March 1966, Nasser explicitly stated that "any attack on Israel from the south is not possible from a military point of view." Nothing changed in the military situation between 1966 and 1967 that should have convinced Nasser otherwise. His continued belief in the futility of Egypt's military position is reflected in the orders given by the Egyptian high command as the crisis reached its peak: "Don't give the Israelis an excuse to attack!" While telling his military to avoid provocations, Nasser was also attempting to head off military hostilities by stalling the dispute in mediated discussions or possibly the ICJ. If the Egyptian president truly believed his own statements about being ready to fight—with God's help—for the elimination of Israel, he should at least have been planning to take the military initiative. No plans for an Egyptian attack were even in the works.

Undoubtedly, Nasser did not expect his forces to be routed as badly as they were, but his inability to predict the precise course of battle does not constitute a "misperception" of Egyptian strength. Not even the Israelis expected the campaign to be as one-sided as it turned out. Nasser's perception appears to have been that Egypt was in a weak though not crippled military position, and this perception was reasonable given the information available to him at the time. The Egyptian president may have been incorrect in his estimation of how long Egypt could limit the progress of Israeli forces, but making an incorrect guess based on the available information is not the same thing as distorting that information into a "misperception" of Egyptian strength.

A second common "misperception" attributed to Nasser is that he believed that Israel would not fight a war without support from Britain, France, or the United States. It is true that early on in the crisis, Nasser felt that the Israeli response would be muffled by a lack of external support. It is also true that the Egyptian president turned out to be incorrect in his estimation. Two factors, however, militate against calling this error a misperception that drove Nasser's aggressive actions. First, by the time the crisis reached its peak in the last days of May and first days of June, Nasser was under no illusions that Israel would not fight alone. When he decided to blockade the Gulf of Aqaba, for example, Nasser told his advisers that he estimated the chance of war as a result of that move was 50 percent, and by the time Dyan joined the Israeli government he said that war was certain (Stephens 1971, 477). In addition to the fact that Nasser altered his estimate of the chances of unilateral Israeli action as the crisis progressed, we should also take note that Nasser's original belief concerning Israeli reliance on the Western Powers was not unreasonable. The Straits of Tiran had been closed to Israel for over a decade before the Suez crisis, yet Israel took no action to open them until Britain and France supported them. Even Moshe Dyan himself stated that Israel would not have gone to war in 1956 if it had not been supported by the British and French (Dyan 1976, 192). Levi Eshkol may have inadvertently reinforced this perception somewhat in 1967, when his statement on the straits called on the "great powers" to respect the right of free passage. Thus with the United States distracted by Vietnam, and Britain and France unwilling to act without the United States, it was not unreasonable for Nasser to believe that Israel might feel restricted by this lack of support. This is especially so, when one considers that Egypt's relationship with the USSR was likely to draw Moscow into the dispute should the United States become irectly involved.[73] It seems likely that Nasser's initial belief that Israel would be reticent to use force alone contributed to his willingness to initiate a dispute with Israel.[74] Such a belief was reasonable, however, given the information available to Nasser, and should not be considered a "misperception." In addition, it is clear that Israeli actions during the crisis altered Nasser's perception of Israeli resolve, and so his original belief cannot account for the fact that he did not comply with Israeli demands before war broke out on June 5.

In sum, Nasser may have constructed his preferences differently from what we might do in retrospect, and he may taken some fairly large risks in escalating the crisis. There seems little basis, however, for questioning whether Nasser was behaving rationally—at least in the limited sense that I use that term in this work. That is, the evidence suggests that Nasser was gathering the available information regarding the behavior of other actors in the crisis, and he was making reasonable judgments based upon that information.

Clarity and Enforcement of the Suez Settlement

A second possible explanation of the failure of UNEF is that the disputants did not share a common understanding of the meaning of the settlement. The UNEF agreement was complicated by the fact that Israel and Egypt negotiated only indirectly through the United Nations. Thus technically each party had an agreement with the UN rather than a direct bilateral understanding. Nonetheless, the general secretary made sure that Nasser agreed to the stipulation that Egypt not expel UNEF until he could make a "good faith" estimation that the "tasks" of UNEF had been completed (i.e., a permanent settlement of the Egyptian-Israeli dispute about the status of Israel). Israel, for its part, had agreed with the UN that the troops would remain until a permanent settlement was

---

[73] In fact, Nasser explicitly sought and received Soviet reassurances that they would counter any US attempt to intervene in the dispute militarily. See Draper (1968, 79).

[74] This scenario coincides nicely with my argument concerning dispute settlements. Recall that if settlements are effective costly signals, then states that prefer conflict to cooperation should not agree to settlements. This raises the important question, then, of why settlements are ever broken once signed. The answer is that while states that settle may prefer mutual cooperation to conflict, they may also prefer cheating on the settlement (if their partner continues to cooperate) as compared to continued mutual cooperation. Thus states may test their partner to see if the terms of the agreement will be enforced. If they are, the violator should back down; if not, the violator should continue to cheat. Thus Egypt's initial violation of the Suez settlement fits with my theory concerning settlements and norms. The remaining puzzle is why Israeli punishment was ineffective.

found as well. An additional complication was thrown into this process by the fact that U Thant did not go to the General Assembly to get an official declaration that Egypt was in violation of its agreement. Nonetheless, it was clear to all parties involved that Egyptian actions were in violation of the Suez settlement. Egypt did not even attempt to argue that their request for UNEF's withdrawal was based on a "good faith" estimation that its tasks were completed, nor did they attempt to exploit the loophole left by Thant. Nasser made no attempt to claim he was within the bounds of the Suez settlement, and Egyptian representatives did not dispute Israeli claims in the United Nations that a violation had occurred. Instead, Nasser declared not only that the Suez settlement was illegitimate but also that the 1949 armistice with Israel was illegitimate and would be overturned by military force. Thus the complexities of the diplomatic process in 1956 and 1967 cannot explain Egyptian behavior preceding the Six-Day War.

Credible Enforcement of the UNEF Settlement

Hammarskjöld's sleight of hand and Thant's heavy-handedness did not obscure the fundamental meaning of the UNEF settlement. However, Thant's failure to bring the Egyptian demand to the General Assembly may have contributed to Nasser's continued intransigence in another manner. The statistical model that I developed in chapter 4 and tested in chapter 5 included only the bargaining behavior of the challenging and defending states. In a case such as the Six-Day War, however, Egypt is clearly responding not only to the bargaining behavior of the principal defender, Israel, but also to the actions of the United Nations—with whom the settlement was technically made—and major powers such as the United States, Britain, and France. The bargaining behavior of all these other actors toward Egypt would have been coded—according to the procedures in chapter 4—as appeasing. France's policy was unabashedly one of appeasement. The United States and UN began by talking tough, but as Egypt resisted, they both reduced their level of coercion. This weak version of what was termed the "trial and error" strategy has the same predicted effects as appeasement. The fact that other actors were appeasing Egypt makes its intransigence more understandable, especially since at the outset of the crisis Nasser believed that Israeli actions would depend critically on support from the UN and its allies.

This argument suggests that the failure of the Suez settlement is not quite as puzzling for my normative approach as it seemed at the outset. In this case, my statistical model may have predicted Egyptian behavior incorrectly because I could not account for the bargaining behavior of third parties, not because the normative argument is logically flawed. That is, I assumed that bullying sends a clear signal of resolve to enforce the settlement. In this case, however, the bargaining signals sent by Israel's allies sent dissonant messages to Cairo. The weak stance of the UN, France, Britain, and the United States might have encouraged Nasser early on in the crisis, but by the last days of May and the first days of June Israel had demonstrated that it was unquestionably ready to fight on its own to enforce the settlement. When war broke out Nasser knew that Israel was willing to fight, and as we have seen he had no illusions about Israel's relative military position. Although these facts eventually became clear to the Egyptian president, we still cannot explain why he refused to comply with Israel's demands for the reinstatement of the status quo ante.

The Constraints of Domestic Politics

Although there were few formal constraints on his authority, Gamel Abdel Nasser faced substantial domestic challenges to keeping his grip on power. In Nasser's case, the constituency he was most concerned with were radical Arabs both in Egypt and across the Middle East. The Soviet report of troop concentrations and Israel's tough talk made Nasser feel as though he was required to make some kind of response for at least two reasons. First, Nasser had just recently signed a defense pact with Syria. And second, he had already failed to come to the aid of other Arab states on several occasions. In fact, Nasser had remained silent so many times that other Arab leaders were beginning to chide him for being a coward. As I previously discussed, Nasser failed to respond to Israeli raids into Jordan and Syria in 1966 and early 1967. The day after the air battle over Syria, the leading Jordanian newspaper ran a headline demanding, "What has Cairo done in the face of this flagrant air aggression against Damascus?" (Draper 1968, 48) Nasser's inaction was made even more embarrassing by the fact that he had abandoned the Syrians in a similar situation during 1960. In that case Nasser quietly moved troops into Sinai, but the troops were just as quietly withdrawn without any effect on Israeli behavior. One important reason that the Egyptian troop movements were ineffective was the presence of UNEF troops between Egyptian and Israeli forces. Thus in May 1967 Nasser felt that he had to do something more substantial or risk serious damage to his reputation as leader of the Arab world.

Once Nasser initiated the dispute, moreover, the costs of backing down compounded quickly as the crisis continued. From the very outset Egyptian troop movements into Sinai were highly publicized and were clearly designed to make a brave show both to Arabs and Israelis. To give the troop deployments an air of seriousness that they lacked in 1960, however, Nasser had to move UNEF at least partially out of the way so that Egypt could engage Israeli forces directly. Thus the Egyptian took as careful and measured a step as he could toward this end by asking for a temporary *redeployment* of UNEF to Gaza and Sharm el Sheik. Thant's original response to Nasser was at least implicitly coercive—rejecting partial withdrawal or redeployment and forcing Egypt to choose between backing down and leaving itself totally exposed to the IDF. Under ordinary circumstances such a threat might have been effective, but for Nasser in this situation backing down would have meant utter humiliation both at home and abroad. Syria and Jordan had long been urging Egypt to stand up to Israel, and Jordan had specifically demanded that Egypt remove UNEF, "so that the Egyptian army—the largest army in the Arab world—can take part in the battle."[75] To begin mobilizing troops publicly and request the removal of UNEF only to back down before the UN would have cost Nasser a great deal of support across the Arab world. Thus Nasser chose to dissolve UNEF.

Once UNEF became inactive and Egyptian forces took up positions at Sharm el Sheik, however, Arabs immediately began calling for the closure of the Straits of Tiran. Jordanian radio, for example, began to challenge Nasser: "Be a man! You chased out the UN, now close the strait. Blockade Aqaba! Don't let the Zionist ships through! Be a man, Nasser!" (Bar-Zohar 1970, 51) The Egyptian president clearly felt this pressure, for in a meeting on May 22—at which he decided to blockade the Gulf of Aqaba—Nasser stated that closing the straits was "one of the things our Arab brothers had always insisted upon." (Stephens 1971, 477) Moreover, in a subsequent interview Egyptian vice president Zakaria Muhieddin stated that those in the May 22 meeting felt that they had no choice but to close the straits or look foolish before the entire Arab world (Parker 1993, 72).

After removing placing forces in Sinai, removing UNEF, and closing the Straits of Tiran, Nasser had done enough to appease radical Arab opinion. Now other Arab governments were flocking to Nasser's support rather than taunting him and calling him weak. At that point Nasser immediately stopped escalating the dispute and began to stall for time and hope for a peaceful resolution. Even while attempting to avoid a war, however, Nasser was acutely conscious of the domestic and foreign audiences observing his behavior. In private discussions with UN and other diplomatic representatives, Nasser was genial and reassuring, and spoke of possible compromises. In public, however, his rhetoric remained boastful, intransigent, and virulently anti-Israeli. Nasser wanted to avoid

[75] *Washington Post*, January 8, 1967.

war, but he clearly wanted to do so without creating the appearance that he was dealing with or tolerating the Israelis. One more piece of evidence suggesting the crucial impact that constituency pressures had on Nasser's behavior is the extremely public way in which he conducted himself during the crisis. In general, Nasser made few public appearances or speeches, preferring to conduct the business of policy making in private. During the weeks leading up to the Six-Day War, however, Nasser was constantly in the public view, exhorting the Egyptian military and berating Israel (Parker 1993).

Finally, as I mentioned previously, Nasser's attempts to rally the Arab world behind him were quite successful. Foreign governments gave him control of their armed forces, and mass rallies supporting Nasser occurred both within Egypt and abroad. Richard Parker writes that "Nasser's, and Egypt's, prestige had never been higher, and the entire Arab world was rallying around." (Parker 1993, 76) In sum, the evidence supporting the role of constituency pressures in causing Nasser's failure to respond to Israeli punishment of Egypt's violation seems convincing. The dilemma Nasser faced in 1967 was that in addition to bargaining with the UN and Israel, the Egyptian president was also bargaining with leaders in Amman and Damascus as well as with Arab citizens across the Middle East. In his interactions with the UN and the Israelis Nasser's goal was to avoid war, but when appealing to other Arabs Nasser needed to look tough and ready to fight. In the end his pursuit of these two goals proved incompatible. In one prominent distillation of Nasser's calculations, Malcom Kerr stated that

> Nasir had more important things to do than make war on Israel. . . . With much of his army bogged down in Yemen, his treasury empty, and the Anglo-Americans and Arab Monarchs ganging up on him, his first concern was to secure his political base: Egypt, the Soviet partnership, and his leadership of the Arab left. This last was now being threatened. . . . If he tried to deter Israel he risked war; if he left the Syrians unprotected he revealed himself to the Arabs as untrustworthy, irresolute, and incapable of providing protection. (Kerr 1971, 126–27)

Thus in striving for the leadership of the "Arab left," Nasser's position was closer to that of a democratic leader campaigning for popular support than it was to an authoritarian leader who can command obedience. In the end, the pressure to remain in power overwhelmed the pressure from the international community to comply with the UNEF settlement.

In sum, the outbreak of the Six-Day War seems best explained by two factors: (1) the weak enforcement behavior of the United Nations, the United States, Britain, and France; and (2) the constraints placed on

Nasser by the "Arab left." These arguments relate directly to two of the assumptions made by my normative argument. That is, this anomalous case can be explained—at least in part—because the conditions necessary for my argument to hold were not met. In the next chapter, I will take a more systematic look at the assumptions made by my argument. By doing so, I hope to begin a discussion of when dispute settlements will and will not be effective in persuading a violator to comply.

CONCLUSIONS

My analyses of the Cienfuegos crisis and the Six-Day War support and extend the quantitative results I presented in chapter 5. Moreover, I believe that these discussions should add to our confidence in the coefficients and marginal effects discussed in chapter 5. In particular, the case studies serve to reassure us that the coefficients I observed in chapter 5 exist for the *reasons* that I hypothesized they would in chapter 3. Upon reviewing a crisis such as the dispute over Cienfuegos, I can state with confidence that dispute settlements, interacting with the enforcement of those settlements, do act as signals that reshape states' interpretations of coercive behavior. In comparing Soviet behavior in the Cuban missile crisis and the Cienfuegos crisis, it seems apparent both in their words and in their deeds that the presence of the 1962 understanding legitimated Kissinger's coercive behavior in the Soviets' eyes. The agreement eased a common fear among competitive states: "If we don't make a stand here, where will they push us next?" The leaders in the Kremlin understood that they had attempted to overturn an agreed-upon status quo—making US behavior seem defensive rather than as aggressive as it had in 1962.

Far from being an exception, the bargaining pattern of the Cienfuegos crisis appears to be the rule when states act quickly to punish the violation of settlements. Nonetheless, in some cases—such as the Six-Day War—the punishment of settlements was ineffective. However, my discussion of that conflict revealed that the *assumptions* made to construct my argument about the normative impact of settlements may be useful in identifying the *conditions* under which settlements may be effective. It is to this next task that I turn my attention in chapter 7.

CHAPTER 7

The Success and Failure of International Norms

Chapters 5 and 6 addressed the impact that international norms can have on the process of crisis bargaining. The quantitative analysis in chapter 5 outlined the overall pattern of this relationship. It showed how a challenging state alters its response to the defender's bargaining strategy depending on whether or not it is in violation of a previous dispute settlement. In particular, this chapter showed us that challengers are generally much less likely to remain intransigent in the face of bullying behavior on the part of the defender *if* that bullying follows the violation of a settlement. Chapter 6, on the other hand, traced this process in greater detail. Here we learned that my theoretical explanation of the quantitative results was also supported by a closer look at the history of crisis bargaining over Cuba. The documentary evidence from these cases continues to indicate that international norms influence state behavior by acting both as reputational constraints and as normative referents.

Despite the substantial evidence I have uncovered concerning the influence of international norms, however, my analyses also suggest that international norms do not *always* have an impact in international crises. For example, the case study of the Six-Day War demonstrated that the firm punishment of the violation of a settlement provides no guarantee that the violator will comply. In that case, it seemed that domestic constraints on several of the parties—Nasser in particular—combined with some clumsy diplomacy on the part of the UN to prevent Egypt from returning to compliance with the UNEF settlement.

The quantitative analysis in chapter 5 also indicates that dispute settlements are not always effective in bringing about compliance. Specifically, in chapter 3 I predicted that the challenger's response to bullying following the violation of a settlement would not differ from their response to a firm-but-flexible strategy. Consistent with my hypothesis, the difference between these categories was not statistically significant. Nonetheless, when the defender utilized a bullying strategy following the violation of a settlement, the challenger responded with compliance in eleven cases, with a compromise in five cases, and with intransigence in thirteen cases. This differs starkly from the response to bullying when no settlement has been violated (four cases of compliance and twenty-four of intransigence), but there remains substantial variation in the "effectiveness" of these international norms. Specifically, one could think of the "compliance" and "compromise" outcomes as situations in which a norm was "effective" in helping the defender prevent the erosion of the status quo. According to this categorization, international norms are effective in helping defend the status quo against a challenge about 55 percent of the time when the defender uses a bullying strategy.[1]

The central goal of this chapter is to explain variation in the effectiveness of international norms. Specifically, I hope to explain variations in the challenger's resistance when the defender uses a bullying strategy to punish the violation of a legitimate settlement. The chapter proceeds in four sections. First, I will derive a number of hypotheses concerning the effectiveness of international norms. The logic supporting these hypotheses will be drawn from my discussion in chapter 3 as to why international norms might have any impact to begin with. Second, I will discuss the empirical measures I will use to test these auxiliary hypotheses about the effectiveness of norms. Third, I will test my hypotheses against the twenty-nine cases in which a settlement was violated and the defender responded with a bullying strategy. Finally, I will discuss the implications of my findings for the normative and realist approaches to crisis bargaining. That is, I will discuss whether causes of failure for international norms are best explained from a realist or an institutionalist perspective.

HYPOTHESES ON EFFECTIVE DISPUTE SETTLEMENTS

My initial argument predicting compliance or compromise as a response to bullying behavior following the violation of a dispute settlement rested on three critical assumptions. First, I assumed that bullying behavior sent a credible signal to the challenger that the defender was motivated to defend the status quo and would be willing to punish continued violations. Second, I assumed that the presence of the previous settlement would send a credible signal to the challenger that the defender's aims were limited to a reestablishment of the status quo ante. As a result, I also argued that this limitation of the defender's aims would cause the challenger to reframe its interpretation of the defender's coercion as "punishment" rather than aggression. Finally, I assumed that the challenger would prefer to return to the previous settlement (assuming that was a reliable option) rather than continue to suffer the defender's punishment.

[1] This value should not be interpreted as a measure of the effectiveness of norms *in general*. It is important to remember that this result only includes cases in which international norms have been violated *and* the defender responds to the violation with a bullying strategy. Thus the figure of 55 percent selects out only those cases in which international norms are least likely to work. Viewed in this light, a 55 percent success rate seems rather encouraging.

In trying to understand why dispute settlements succeed or fail in establishing effective norms, I will focus on these three assumptions to identify situations in which one or more of them may be unlikely to hold.[2] I begin with the assumption that bullying behavior sends a credible and effective signal of resolve.

Bullying and the Credibility of Resolve

A bullying diplomatic strategy invokes an explicit or implicit threat to use force to resolve the issue if the challenging state does not comply with the defender's demands. When framed as "legitimate punishment" for a violation, such a willingness can persuade a challenger to retreat. However, demonstrating the willingness to use force may have little impact on the challenger's behavior if the defending state does not have the military capacity to make the use of force very costly to the challenger. Consequently, it may be the case that punishing the violation of international norms will only be effective if the state defending the norm has a substantial military capacity to enforce its will.

HYPOTHESIS 1. *The more favorable the balance of conventional military capabilities is toward the defender, the more effective the defender's punishment of a violation should be.*

I should note that the argument that settlements work only when backed by substantial military force is a distinctively realist position. Thus strong support for hypothesis 1 would notably circumscribe the empirical weight of my institutionalist argument concerning the impact of norms.

Domestic Constraints

Military capability is one factor that may contribute to the credibility of a bullying strategy, but other factors surely contribute as well. In particular, domestic political structures have received a great deal of attention as potential sources of credibility (Schelling 1960, 1966; Putnam 1988; Bueno de Mesquita and Lalman 1992; Fearon 1994b; Gaubatz 1996;

---

[2] In this chapter I do not address two potential explanations for the failure of a settlement that I investigated in my study of the Six-Day War: psychological misperceptions and a lack of clarity in the settlement. The case study indicated that these two arguments were not promising avenues of inquiry. In particular, the Six-Day War must be considered an "easy case" for misperception to explain; yet as I discussed in the previous chapter, I found such arguments unpersuasive. The complexity and delicacy of the UNEF settlement also make it an easy case for a lack of clarity to explain the failure. Once again, these arguments failed. Moreover, measuring a lack of clarity in the quantitative study is a rather difficult task. One possible measure of clarity would be to compare the effectiveness of tacit and explicit settlements. Unfortunately, there are not enough cases of tacit settlements to allow such a comparison.

Gelpi and Griesdorf 2001; Gelpi and Grieco 1998; Schultz 1999). According to this approach international crises may be viewed as public contests in which each disputant's performance is evaluated by its domestic audience. Of course, all state leaders have some audience whom they must satisfy to remain in power. However, the institutionalized electoral constraints of democratic political structures make it easier for audiences to remove their leaders for inadequate performance. More important, the transparency of democratic institutions makes it easier for democratic leaders to *communicate* the nature of their constraints to their opponents. It is possible, for example, that authoritarian leaders may be under severe domestic constraints and may face draconian punishment for inadequate performance (Goemans 2000). However, if they are unable to *demonstrate* these constraints to opposing states, they will be unable to use them to increase the credibility of their international bargaining behavior.

Thus when democratic leaders choose to escalate international crises, their threats will be taken as highly credible. The act of threatening force signals the democratic leader's commitment to fight by jeopardizing his or her domestic prestige over the dispute. This argument suggests that democratic states enjoy a substantial advantage over nondemocracies in making their bargaining signals credible. States that enjoy such an advantage in generating credible threats should be able to coerce their opponent into backing down when they show the willingness to use force by implementing a bullying bargaining strategy.

HYPOTHESIS 2. *The more democratic the defender's domestic political system is relative to that of the challenger, the more effective the defender's punishment of a violation should be.*

Legitimacy of the Previous Settlement

The analysis in chapter 5 assumed that all of the legitimate dispute settlements observed in my data set were equally legitimate in the eyes of the disputants. Of course, we know that this is not the case. Certain dispute settlements are taken more seriously than others and carry greater normative influence and reputational impact. In general we would expect that the defender's punishment of important norms should be more effective than punishment of norms that the challenger does not view as significant. A variety of factors may contribute to the perceived normative influence and reputational importance of a particular settlement.

REGIME CHANGE AND THE LEGITIMACY OF DISPUTE SETTLEMENTS

International law dictates that new regimes must undertake all the international obligations of the old regime. Thus in principle one could argue that regime change should be irrelevant with regard to the legitimacy of dispute settlements. In practice, however, this relationship may be more problematic. First, there are strong logical reasons to suspect that new regimes will not view the commitments of the previous regime as holding equal normative status with their own diplomatic initiatives. After all, a substantial regime change almost always indicates a sharp difference in policy preferences between the incoming and outgoing regimes (Siverson and Starr 1994). Moreover, the fact that the new regime overthrew the old one provides at least prima facie evidence that the new government viewed the old one as illegitimate.[3] If the outgoing regime was illegitimate, it is only a small step to declare their international commitments illegitimate as well. One can think of numerous prominent examples— such as the Russian and Chinese revolutions—of new regimes repudiating the commitments of the overthrown leaders and even disputing the legitimate borders of their state.

If the challenger's regime has changed since the conclusion of the previous dispute settlement, then this clearly may have an impact on the effectiveness of the defender's attempts to punish violations of the settlement. My argument suggests that settlements play a critical role in reassuring the challenger that the defender's aims are limited. If the challenger rejects the legitimacy of the previous settlement, then it may not view the reestablishment of that status quo as constituting "limited aims" on the part of the defender. Moreover, if the challenger rejects the legitimacy of the previous settlement, then it will not frame the defender's coercive behavior as "punishment" rather than aggression. Consequently, the use of a bullying strategy by the defender in such crises is likely to generate fears on the part of the challenger that any concessions will lead to more extreme demands from the defender.

Additionally, if the regime in the defending state has changed this also may undermine their effectiveness. In this case the challenging regime may be unsure whether the defender will truly be satisfied with reestablishing the previous settlement or will use the crisis as an opportunity to press for greater demands. Thus once again the settlement may become incapable of sending a credible signal of "limited aims" on the part of the defender.

HYPOTHESIS 3. *If the regime of the challenging or defending state has changed since the conclusion of the previous settlement, then the defender's punishment of a violation should be less effective.*

LONGEVITY OF THE DISPUTE SETTLEMENT

A variety of different arguments can be made about the relationship between the longevity of a dispute settlement and its effectiveness in influ-

---

[3] It is important to note that when I refer to a "regime change," I am referring to a change in the institutions of government, not simply a change in leadership.

encing crisis behavior. First, it is possible that newly formed settlements will be relatively ineffective in aiding the punishment of violations. Soon after a particular settlement is concluded, for example, the wide variety of alternative settlements and demands will be salient to both parties and to their domestic constituents. Moreover, when a settlement is new it is not clear to the parties whether it will be stable and lasting. As a result, the costs of abandoning the settlement in favor of a renewal of the conflict will seem relatively modest.

Over time, however, dispute settlements may come to have a "taken for granted" quality to them as the legitimate status quo regarding that particular issue. The entrenchment of the norms embodied in the settlements may begin to limit the perceived alternatives to their own perpetuation. In some cases norms may become so entrenched that their violation becomes "unthinkable." (Tannewald 1990; Price 1995; Price and Tannewald in Katzenstein 1996) Moreover, as a settlement continues to endure it comes to have value to both parties as a stable and certain settlement of the issue. Consequently, abandoning this stable outcome for an uncertain renewal of the conflict becomes increasingly unattractive.

HYPOTHESIS 4. *The longer the dispute settlement has endured, the more effective the defender's punishment of a violation will be.*

Alternatively, the impact of dispute settlements could weaken over time. It is possible, for example, that dispute settlements are perceived as highly legitimate shortly after they are signed. At that time both parties had recently consented to the settlement. The important achievement of the settlement as well as the costs endured during the dispute may be highly salient to the parties. Moreover, the conclusion of the settlement will be highly salient to *other* state leaders, raising the reputational costs of violating the settlement and of remaining in violation despite the defender's efforts to enforce the settlement.

Over time, however, the salience of the settlement may fade in significance both to the disputants and to other state leaders. New issues will arise that will displace the previously disputed issue as the focus of diplomatic attention. Indeed, states' interests with regard to these new issues may conflict with the terms of the previous settlement and may place pressure on leaders to violate their commitment (Downs 1995). Consequently, the gains to be made by violating a previous settlement may become salient, while the costs suffered in the dispute leading up to the settlement may appear less significant. Moreover, the reduction in the perceived importance of the previous settlement both among mass publics and elites reduces the reputational costs that leaders will suffer if they violate the settlement and if they remain in violation despite the defender's enforcement efforts.

HYPOTHESIS 5. *The longer the dispute settlement has endured, the less effective the defender's punishment of a violation will be.*

Finally, it is possible that both of these arguments are correct, but that the processes that strengthen and entrench norms are more powerful at one point in time, while the forces that undermine their influence are more powerful at another. One combination of these arguments stands out as particularly salient and intuitively plausible. It may be the case that at first, the longevity of dispute settlements increases their influence. The settlements in my data set are often fragile understandings and the parties may not be certain that they are stable and worth an investment of reputation and restraint. As it becomes clear that the settlement is stable, however, states will come to view it as valuable and worth the costs of maintenance. Nonetheless, the value of these settlements is not limitless, and so in the longer term—as new issues arise—state leaders may come to view a particular dispute settlement as less central to its security policy than the new issue at hand. This argument predicts a curvilinear relationship between settlement longevity and the effectiveness of punishment.

HYPOTHESIS 6. *There is a curvilinear relationship between the longevity of a dispute settlement and the effectiveness of the defender's punishment of a violation. At first, increases in longevity will increase the effectiveness of punishment. Later on, however, further increases in longevity will reduce this effectiveness.*

A TREND TOWARD THE EFFECTIVENESS OF SETTLEMENTS?

The end of the Cold War generated talk of a "New World Order" and a new importance for international law and international norms. While it may be difficult to point to anything that resembles a coherent New World Order, international norms and institutions do appear to be gaining in strength. The transformation of the weaker GATT into the WTO, the development of a common European currency, the strengthening of the European Court of Justice, the expansion in the scope and volume of UN peacekeeping missions, and the launching of a world criminal court are only the most prominent examples of this trend. In fact, however, the current trend toward reliance on normative and institutional foreign policy instruments appears to predate the collapse of the Cold War. The literature on the so-called democratic peace, for example, notes that the impact of democracy on international conflict is more prominent and robust during the Cold War than during the nineteenth or early twentieth centuries. (Farber and Gowa 1995).

According to this view, the end of World War II represented a transformation of international politics that was at least as significant as the end of the Cold War. The American decision to assume a global leadership role has undoubtedly had a profound impact on international politics. But it may have had a particular effect on its normative and legal structure. American support for certain legal and institutional forms—such as democracy, the GATT, and the World Bank—allowed these institutions to grow and prosper in the second half of the twentieth century. On the other hand, norms and institutions less favored by the United States—such as formal colonialism—rapidly eroded over this same period. Although there are numerous exceptions to this trend,[4] in general the American lessons drawn from the World War II experience led the United States to favor increased formalization and legalization of world politics along the institutionalist lines consistent with my argument about legitimate settlements.

Of course, this kind of normative change does not take root overnight. Thus if American preferences for the efficacy of legalistic institutions have had an impact on the behavior of other states in international crises, we would expect the efficacy of such institutions to have increased noticeably over the time period covered by my data. In particular, we should expect a noticeable increase in the effectiveness of settlements concluded after World War II, and we would expect that trend to continue throughout the data.

HYPOTHESIS 7. *There is a positive relationship between the year a settlement was concluded and the effectiveness of the defender's punishment of a violation.*

THE PERSISTENCE OF THE CHALLENGER'S REGIME

The final variable I will consider concerning the perceived legitimacy of the settlement is the length of time that the challenging regime has been a member of the international system. As I discussed earlier, there are strong reasons to expect that regime change will also bring a change in leaders' preferences and in the legitimacy that they accord the commitments of the previous elites. These issues led me to posit hypothesis 3. However, previous research also suggests that regime change may affect leaders' perceptions of the legitimacy of the international system in general. For example, research by Zeev Maoz suggests that new regimes may be more likely to initiate the use of military force because they tend to be dissatisfied with the international status quo and view the norms and practices of the international system as illegitimate. Over time, however, he argues that these regimes are socialized into "joining the club of nations." They gradually become more peaceful as they become increas-

---

[4] Perhaps the most egregious exceptions to this pattern have been related to American anticommunist activity. American behavior in Nicaragua, Chile, and Guatemala often flouted international law. However, this fact should leave us relatively optimistic about future trends in the strength of international institutions.

ingly invested in the status quo, until after ten or twenty years they have become a "normal" member of the system (Maoz 1989; Walt 1996; Mansfield and Snyder 1995).

The logic of this argument concerning the initiation of disputes can easily be extended to explain leaders' perceptions of the legitimacy of international agreements. When new regimes come to power, their leaders have little invested in their state's reputation as a member of the international community. In fact, they may often view that community as illegitimate to the extent that its members supported the previous regime and tried to prevent the new leaders from coming to power. Thus in the early days of a new regime, their leaders may give little weight to things like international reputation and may feel relatively unconstrained from violating their agreements. In the wake of the Russian Revolution, for example, Lenin and the Bolshevik leadership made international commitments that they had no intention of upholding in the long term. Over time, however, these regimes come to understand that they need to rely on the international community to achieve a whole variety of goals that they may have given little thought to earlier. Thus over a period of ten or twenty years, leaders may come to understand the importance of developing and maintaining a reputation for trustworthy behavior. If so, then we would expect that mature challenging regimes would be more likely to be influenced by the presence of a previous settlement.

HYPOTHESIS 8. *There is a positive relationship between the persistence of the challenger's regime and the effectiveness of the defender's punishment of a violation.*

Satisfaction with the Previous Settlement

The final assumption that I relied upon to construct my argument about the impact of norms on crisis bargaining was that both disputants prefer to return to a previously agreed settlement rather than fight a war. If this assumption does not hold, then the bargaining situation is no longer a prisoner's dilemma (PD) because at least one of the parties does not prefer compromise (CC) (mutual cooperation) to a fight (DD) (mutual defection). If the bargaining states prefer war to compromise, then all the arguments I made concerning the importance of a reputation for trustworthiness become moot.

In general, the assumption that states have prisoner's dilemma preferences is a relatively plausible one. A very wide variety of situations in international politics—and security affairs in particular—are well represented by the PD. Certainly we can be confident in our assumption that the defending state in the crisis prefers a resumption of the previous settlement to a war. If they did not, then they should have initiated the conflict themselves. For challengers, on the other hand, this assumption may not always be valid.

SUBSTANTIVE OUTCOME OF THE PREVIOUS DISPUTE

Obviously, the challenger's preference for fighting or returning the previous settlement will depend on what that previous settlement meant to the challenger. The more favorable the previous settlement to the goals of the challenger, the more likely it should be that the challenger will prefer a resumption of the settlement to an escalation of the armed conflict. According to this logic, challengers should be less likely to feel constrained by a settlement if that agreement represented a defeat for their interests. If the settlement represented a challenger victory in the previous dispute, on the other hand, it should be more willing to return to the status quo ante.

HYPOTHESIS 9. *There is a positive relationship between the favorableness of the previous settlement to the interests of the challenger and the effectiveness of the defender's punishment of a violation.*

CHALLENGER DEMANDS

Finally, the demands made by the challenger in the current dispute should give us some insight into its preference for fighting relative to a resumption of the previous settlement. For example, if the challenger makes very extreme demands of the defender—such as demanding that it change its domestic regime or that it cease to exist as a state—then the challenger is probably relatively dissatisfied with the status quo (and thus with the terms of the previous settlement). In such cases it seems plausible that the challenger would prefer to fight rather than accept a return to the status quo ante. On the other hand, challengers that demand relatively small changes in the status quo should be easier to persuade to return to the previous settlement.

Fortunately, my analysis has already developed a measure of the demands made by the challenger: the defender's issues at stake. The more substantial the defender's issues at stake, the greater the demands being made by the challenger. Thus I would expect dispute settlements to be more effective in disputes in which the defender is facing relatively modest threats from the challenger.

HYPOTHESIS 10. *There is a negative relationship between the challenger's demands and the effectiveness of the defender's punishment of a violation.*

RESEARCH DESIGN AND MEASUREMENTS

As I discussed earlier, the key to demonstrating the success or failure of international norms focuses on the situation where (1) an international norm has been violated, and (2) that violation has been punished with a bullying strategy. The change in the challenger's response to a bullying strategy represents my central piece of evidence in support of the effectiveness of international norms. Thus the question of the effectiveness of norms revolves around challenger responses to the bullying punishment of a norm violation.

In my data set of 122 reinitiated international crises, I observe 29 instances of a dispute settlement being violated and the defender responding with bullying. Thus I will focus on these 29 cases in addressing the question of when dispute settlements are likely to be effective. Obviously, 29 cases does not represent a large sample for analysis. Consequently, it is important to view my results somewhat tentatively. This work represents one of the first efforts to test the impact of norms systematically, and so clearly this is an issue in need of further research. Nonetheless, it is noteworthy that these data support my expectations about the effectiveness of dispute settlements rather robustly. Thus I feel reasonably confident that these results will be borne out by more extensive research.

Measurements

EFFECTIVENESS OF THE DISPUTE SETTLEMENT

As one would expect, the dependent variable in this analysis is based on the challenger's resistance to the coercion of the defender. In my previous analysis, challenger resistance was ranked on an ordinal scale from low (compliance) to high (intransigence). In this case, however, my research question is framed somewhat differently. Here we are focusing only on cases of norm violation with a bullying response and asking whether the dispute settlement was effective in reducing resistance to that bullying. Thus the smaller the challenger's resistance, the greater the effectiveness of the settlement. For greater ease in interpreting the results, I reverse the coding of the challenger's resistance. Compliance by the challenger is assigned a value of 3, compromise a value of 2, and intransigence a value of 1. By using this coding scheme, variables that yield *positive* coefficients in the analysis will have a *positive* impact on the effectiveness of settlements.

BALANCE OF CONVENTIONAL MILITARY CAPABILITIES

I use the same measure as discussed in chapter 4 and used in the analyses in chapter 5. The measure varies from zero to 1, with zero indicating that the challenger controls 100 percent of the capabilities in the dyad and 1 indicating that the defender controls all of the capabilities. A score of 0.5, of course, indicates that the disputants have equal levels of military capabilities.

RELATIVE DOMESTIC CONSTRAINTS

Data for this variable were drawn from the Polity III data set, collected by Gurr and Jaggers, which has become the standard source for cross-national quantitative measures of domestic political institutions (Gurr and Jaggers 1995). The measure is based upon the institutional features of each regime, and thus it nicely captures the extent of the domestic decision-making constraints under which leaders must operate. Jaggers and Gurr score each state on a democracy scale that ranges from zero to 10, with a zero indicating a strongly authoritarian government and a 10 indicating a solidly democratic regime. To capture the relative domestic constraints of the defender, I subtract the challenger's democracy score from that of the defender. Thus the final variable ranges from −10 to 10. A 10 indicates that the defender has more substantial domestic constraints—and thus should send more credible bargaining signals. A score of −10, on the other hand, indicates that the challenging regime is more constrained.

NUMBER OF REGIME CHANGES

Data for this variable are also drawn from the Polity III data set. I rely on a measure of regime change developed by Edward Mansfield and Jack Snyder for an analysis of regime change and involvement in international conflict (Mansfield and Snyder 1995). Mansfield and Snyder place regimes into one of three categories based on their Polity III democracy scores: autocracies, democracies, and anocracies. Anocracies occupy the middle ground between democracy and autocracy, and they share a mixture of these types of institutions.[5] Following Mansfield and Snyder, I code any shift across the boundary between these categories as representing a change in regime type. Of course, the use of specific boundaries for categories is always arbitrary to some extent. However, using this measure allows me to distinguish substantial shifts in regime type from small fluctuations in Polity scores.[6]

I determined whether each of the disputants had undergone a regime change since the conclusion of the previous settlement. I assigned a value of zero if neither state had undergone a regime change, a value of 1 if one of the disputants had undergone a regime change, and a value of 2 if both regimes had changed.

---

[5] Elsewhere, Snyder (1991) refers to these regimes as "oligarchies." Goemans (2000) also uses the term "oligarchies" to describe these mixed regimes.

[6] Enterline (1996) uses a more continuous measure of regime change. This measure may be appropriate for some circumstances, but for the purposes of the current analysis, I am focusing on large shifts in regime type. These shifts are more appropriately captured by the Mansfield and Snyder (1995) measure.

YEARS SETTLEMENT HAS EXISTED

This variable is simply the number of years that have elapsed between the current crisis and the creation of the dispute settlement. This variable is included along with its square to test hypothesis 5 that time has a curvilinear impact on the effectiveness of settlements.

YEAR SETTLEMENT WAS CONCLUDED

This variable simply records the year in which the previous settlement was concluded.

SUBSTANCE OF PREVIOUS SETTLEMENT

Data for this variable were drawn from the ICB data set discussed earlier. ICB coded the substantive outcomes of crises into four categories from the perspective of each crisis actor: win, compromise, stalemate, and lose. Although these categories may form something like an ordinal scale, it is not always clear whether disputants will prefer a compromise or a stalemate. For example, leaders who are strongly committed to a complete victory may prefer to stalemate and fight again another day rather than make any concessions toward compromise. Leaders who prefer to avoid fighting, on the other hand, might prefer compromise to a stalemate. A victory, however, is an unambiguously positive outcome for any disputant. Thus I create a dummy variable indicating that the challenger was victorious in the dispute that resulted in the previous settlement. If challengers are more likely to be influenced by settlements that are favorable to them, then we would expect a positive coefficient on this variable.

CHALLENGER'S DEMANDS

As I discussed earlier, the variable I use to measure the demands made by the challenger is the defender's issues at stake. The variable is measured in the same manner discussed in chapters 4 and 5.

ANALYSES AND RESULTS

As with the previous analyses, I rely on a multinomial probit estimator because my dependent variable is ordinal with three categories. The results of these analyses are presented in table 7A. In general, these results strongly support my expectations about the effectiveness of dispute settlements. Given the relatively modest number of cases available, the results of these tests are surprisingly clear and robust. Overall, the model fits the data quite well. The model predicts 83 percent of the cases correctly (twenty-four of twenty-nine). The null model would only predict 45 percent of the cases correctly (thirteen of twenty-nine). Thus my analyses of

TABLE 7A
Probit Analysis Predicting Challenger Resistance When Norm Is
Violated and Punished

Explanatory Variables	Coefficient	Standard Error	Significance Level
Credibility of Defender Threat			
Balance of Military Capabilities	0.75	1.66	—
Defender Domestic Constraints	0.17	0.08	< 0.05
Legitimacy of Dispute Settlement			
Number of Regime Changes	−1.51	0.75	< 0.025[a]
Years Settlement Existed	0.59	0.29	< 0.05[b]
Years of Existence Squared	−0.03	0.02	< 0.12[b]
Year Settlement Created	0.04	0.02	< 0.06[a]
Persistence of Challenger Regime	−0.62	0.42	< 0.15
Challenger Satisfaction with Settlement			
Settlement Was Challenger Victory	−0.30	0.32	—
Defender Issue at Stake	−1.24	0.08	< 0.00
First Threshold	0.54	1.82	Ancillary
Second Threshold	1.67	1.82	Parameters

Note: Number of observations = 29; number of observations correctly predicted = 24; percent correctly predicted = 83%; proportional reduction in error = 69%; initial log likelihood = −29.88; log likelihood at convergence = −15.15.
  [a] = One-tailed test for significance. All other tests are two-tailed.
  [b] = Joint significance level for years settlement has existed is 0.05.

the effectiveness of dispute settlements provides a 69 percent reduction in error over the null model.

Even more important, we can clearly see that each of the three assumptions I made in developing my argument about the impact of legitimate dispute settlements has an important effect on the efficacy of these agreements. Let us begin with the credibility of the defender's coercive threat. The balance of conventional military capabilities has its expected negative impact on challenger resistance ($b = −0.75$). That is, the greater the proportion of military capabilities controlled by the defender, the greater the probability that the challenger will comply with its demands. However, this variable does not approach statistical significance. Given the relatively small number of cases in the analysis, one might automatically attribute this statistical insignificance to a problem of multicolinearity. In fact, however, the auxiliary r-square for this variable is only 0.26—a modest level of colinearity even for such a small number of cases. Moreover, other variables in the analysis that do achieve statistical significance manage to do so despite somewhat higher levels of multicolinearity. A bivariate analysis revealed no significant effect for military capabilities, and the standard errors in this analysis were only modestly narrower than those reported in table 7A.

Thus military capabilities do not appear to have any substantial impact on the effectiveness of dispute settlements. This result may not be too surprising, since military capabilities had only a modest impact on my previous analysis. The irrelevance of military capabilities might be viewed as substantial vindication for the institutionalist perspective and its focus on the legitimacy of dispute settlements. At the same time, as I discussed in chapter 5, it is important to remember that selection effects may also help to explain why military capabilities have little impact on dispute behavior as a conflict continues to escalate over time.

But while military capabilities did not appear to contribute to the credibility of the defender's threats of punishment, domestic decision-making constraints appear to have a powerful effect. The coefficient for the defender's domestic constraints is positive and statistically significant ($b = 0.17$, $p < 0.05$), indicating that the more constrained the defender is relative to the challenger, the more credible and effective the defender's threats of punishment become. In addition to being statistically significant, the impact of domestic constraints on the credibility of bargaining signals is also substantively large. The marginal impact of this variable on the effectiveness of dispute settlements is displayed in table 7B. Clearly, democratic defenders faced with an authoritarian challenger have little difficulty in making dispute settlements effective. When the challenger's domestic constraints score a 10, the probability that the challenger will comply is more than 95 percent. As the challenger's domestic constraints increase relative to the defender's, however, the effectiveness of punishment declines. A decrease in the defender's domestic constraints to a score of 5 decreases the probability of compliance by 15 percent, and a further decrease in the defender's constraints to a score of zero reduces this probability by an additional 30 percent. Thus if two disputants have equal levels of domestic constraints (and thus equal ability to send credible signals), then the probability that the challenger will comply with the defender's demands to resume the settlement is just over 51 percent. Further decreases in the defender's domestic constraints relative to those of the challenger lead to further erosion in the effectiveness of punishment. Thus when a democratic challenger faces punishment for violating a settlement with an authoritarian defender, the probability that it will comply is only 5 percent. The probability it will compromise with the defender is approximately 25 percent, leaving a 70 percent chance that the democratic challenger will remain intransigent in the face of punishment.

TABLE 7B
Marginal Effects of Defender Domestic Constraints

Change in Independent Variable	Change in P(Compliance)	Change in P(Compromise)	Change in P(Intransigence)
Defender Domestic Constraints			
10 to 5	− 14.7%	+ 12.7%	+ 2.0%
5 to 0	− 30.1%	+ 19.9%	+ 10.2%
0 to − 5	− 30.8%	+ 4.9%	+ 25.9%
− 5 to − 10	− 15.8%	− 17.1%	+ 32.9%

Note: Marginal effects were calculated by generating predicted values from the probit model while changing the values of defender's domestic constraints and holding the others at their means or modes. The predicted values were transformed into probabilities that the outcome would fall into each category by summing the area underneath the cumulative normal distribution between the predicted value and each of the category thresholds.

Numerous examples of this pattern exist throughout my data. To begin with, the USSR consistently showed a willingness to return to previous settlements when faced with bullying from the United States or other democracies. The Cienfuegos crisis illustrated this pattern very nicely, as American threats were immediately accepted as highly credible. The United States and Israel, on the other hand, are rather unwilling to return to previous dispute settlements once they have violated them— even when faced with punishment from their opponent. In this regard, the Six-Day War represents the exception that proves this rule. Although Egypt was not democratic, Nasser faced severe domestic constraints that made compliance extremely difficult. Unfortunately, because he lacked the transparency of democratic institutions to communicate these constraints, diplomats like U Thant did not fully understand the constraints under which Nasser was operating.

Thus consistent with other recent research on crisis bargaining, domestic constraints do appear to have a substantial impact on the credibility of crisis bargaining signals (Fearon 1994b; Gelpi and Griesdorf 2001; Gelpi and Grieco 1998; Schultz 1999). But while the credibility of a bullying strategy is one source of the efficacy of dispute settlements, the perceived legitimacy of the settlements themselves is a second piece of this puzzle. First, as expected, regime changes have a negative impact on the efficacy of previous dispute settlements. The coefficient for the number of regime changes is negative and statistically significant ($b = -1.51$, $p < 0.025$). Moreover, table 7C demonstrates that the impact of regime changes is substantively large. For example, if both the challenging and defending regimes in the current dispute are the same regimes that concluded the previous settlement, then the probability that the challenger will comply with the settlement when faced with bullying by the defender is more than 76 percent. If one of the disputants' regimes has changed since the conclusion of the settlement, however, the probability that the challenger will comply drops by a striking 55 percent! If both the challenger and defender are governed by different regimes, the probability that the settlement will be effective in eliciting compliance following punishment of a violation drops by an additional 20 percent. Thus while disputants honor commitments made between them, they do not appear to view commitments made by previous regimes as legitimate.

Second, consistent with hypothesis 5, dispute settlements appear to have a life cycle. That is, the analysis in table 7A indicates that the length of time that a settlement has existed has a curvilinear impact on its effectiveness. The coefficient for the years of existence is positive and statistically significant ($b = 0.59$, $p < 0.05$), while the coefficient for years squared is negative and just barely misses statistical significance ($b = -0.03$, $p < 0.12$). Jointly, these two coefficients are significant at the 0.05 level (chi-squared = 6.10 [2 d.f.]). This pattern of results indicates that at first settlements become more effective over time as they become more firmly established as the status quo. As time continues to pass, however, their effectiveness erodes as they become less salient and less relevant to current issues and problems. Table 7C demonstrates that this curvilinear life cycle for dispute settlements is of considerable substantive consequence. If the challenger violates a settlement during the same year it was concluded, the probability that it will comply with punishment by the defender is only 4 percent. Such settlements never have a chance to be imbued with legitimacy and perhaps the parties never intended to comply. If the settlement lasts for five years, however, the probability that it will comply with the settlement when punished increases by a striking 63 percent! Settlements that last an additional five years are even more likely to be effective, as the probability of challenger compliance increases by another 23 percent.

After a decade or so, however, the effectiveness of dispute settlements begins to decline. The erosion is modest at first. Between the tenth and fifteenth years, the probability that the challenger will comply in response to punishment drops by 13 percent. After the fifteenth year, however, the decline becomes steeper, with a 38 percent drop in the probability of compliance between years fifteen and eighteen.

As I discussed earlier, these results indicate that both arguments about the longevity of settlements are correct, but that each takes precedence at a different time. At first, dispute settlements increase in efficacy as they

TABLE 7C
Marginal Effects of Legitimacy of Settlement

Change in Independent Variable	Change in P(Compliance)	Change in P(Compromise)	Change in P(Intransigence)
Number of Regime Changes			
None to 1	−55.0%	+21.2%	+33.8%
1 to Both	−20.2%	−30.8%	+51.0%
Number of Years Settlement Has Existed			
0 to 5	+63.4%	+6.1%	−69.5%
5 to 10	+23.1%	−18.0%	−5.1%
10 to 15	−13.6%	+11.1%	+2.5%
15 to 18	−37.9%	+20.9%	+17.0
Year Settlement Created			
1937 to 1959	+18.0%	−7.5%	−10.5%
1949 to 1959	+14.3%	−9.0%	−5.3%
1959 to 1969	+11.7%	−8.9%	−2.8%
1969 to 1979	+8.3%	−7.0%	−1.3%

Note: Marginal effects were calculated by generating predicted values from the probit model while changing the values of the selected variables and holding the others at their means or modes. The predicted values were transformed into probabilities that the outcome would fall into each category by summing the area underneath the cumulative normal distribution between the predicted value and each of the category thresholds.

become more strongly established and accepted aspects of the status quo. Eventually, however, their salience seems to fade as they are superceded by other issues and contexts take precedence.

Although the evidence is rather tentative, there also appears to be a general trend toward settlements becoming more effective over the time period covered by my data. The coefficient for the year the settlement was concluded is positive, but just misses achieving statistical significance in a one-tailed test ($b = 0.04$, $p < 0.06$). Although its statistical significance is tentative, table 7C indicates that the substantive impact of this trend is not negligible. In particular, it is interesting to note that this variable has its largest substantive impact in the shift between settlements that were formed before and after World War II. The probability that the challenger will comply with a settlement in response to punishment of a violation in 1937 is only 38 percent. By 1949, however, the probability of challenger compliance has increased by 18 percent. This trend continues throughout the data set, so that by 1979 the probability of challenger compliance has risen to 90 percent.

Although this pattern of results is rather interesting, it should be viewed with some caution. Specifically, the 1930s may not be an appropriate baseline for comparing the effectiveness of dispute settlements. That era is widely recognized as one of the most ruthless in recent diplomatic history, and thus virtually any other decade might look law-bound by comparison. Many of these disputes occurred in the shadow of an impending (and widely anticipated) world war. Thus the shadow of the future that is so important in maintaining the effectiveness of international norms may have been unusually short in the 1930s. Nonetheless, even between 1945 and 1979 I still observe a trend toward more effective settlements. The statistical significance of this coefficient erodes substantially if I drop the crises of the 1930s, but the substantive size of the coefficient remains virtually unchanged.

Perhaps the only really puzzling result in this analysis is the impact of the persistence of the challenger's regime. Recall I had hypothesized— consistent with the literature on regime change and international conflict—that challenging regimes that had been members of the international system for a longer period of time would be more likely to be influenced by previous dispute settlements because these regimes had become invested in the status quo and the legitimacy of the international system. Instead, my analysis indicates that challenging regimes become more *resistant* to the influence of settlements as they become mature members of the international system. The coefficient for the log of the challenger's persistence is -0.63, although it falls somewhat short of statistical significance ($p < 0.15$). Any explanation of this effect is, of course, tentative and post hoc, but several possibilities exist. Perhaps most plausibly, this coefficient is positive because regime persistence is strongly correlated with democracy in my data. Specifically, the correlation between the log of the challenger's persistence and the challenger's democracy score is 0.32. Thus in this case persistence may be picking up on some of the influence of domestic constraints not captured by the relative constraints variable. A second alternative is that persistent regimes are so strongly invested in the legitimacy of dispute settlements that they are extremely unlikely to violate them to begin with. According to this logic, any mature regime that decides to violate a dispute settlement must have some very strong motivation to do so. Consequently, such regimes will be unlikely to respond to punishments once they decide to violate settlements. Either explanation of this anomalous result is plausible, and so a definitive answer must await further research. Moreover, this result reminds us that my analysis represents only the first step toward understanding when dispute settlements and other international norms will be effective.

The final assumption that was critical to building my argument concerning the impact of international norms was that challengers must prefer a return to a legitimate previous settlement over the escalation of a conflict to war. If challengers do not prefer the settlement to war, then the disputants are no longer engaged in a prisoner's dilemma bargaining situation and the logic of reputation and the impact of settlements collapses. Contrary to my expectations, the substantive nature of the previous settlement does not appear to have an impact on its subsequent efficacy. Specifically, the coefficient for a challenger victory in the crisis that produced the previous settlement is actually negative ($b = -0.30$), although it does not approach statistical significance. In at least one sense, however, this result is encouraging for an institutionalist approach to crisis bargaining because it suggests that challengers can become invested in a dispute settlement and begin to view it as legitimate *even* when it represents a defeat for their substantive interests. The Soviet behavior in the Cienfuegos crisis stands as an excellent example of this process. The Kennedy-Khrushchev understanding clearly represented a defeat for Soviet interests in the Cuban missile crisis. Nonetheless, the Soviet leadership clearly came to view this understanding as legitimate and placed importance on maintaining their reputation for upholding this agreement.

Nonetheless, the validity of my assumption that challengers prefer the settlement to an escalation of violence does appear to be critical in generating the efficacy of dispute settlements. The second measure I use to tap into this concept is the demands that the challenger makes of the defender in the current crisis. The severity of the challenger's demands has a strongly negative impact on the efficacy of previous dispute settlements. The impact of this variable is perhaps the largest and most robust of any in the analysis ($b = -1.24$, $p < 0.00$).

The marginal effects of the challenger's demands are displayed in table 7D. When the challenger's demands are very modest, the probability that it will comply with a previous settlement when punished for a violation is very high. In fact, if the challenger is only demanding economic concessions or other minor issues from the defender, then the model estimates its likelihood of compliance at more than 99 percent! An increase in the challenger's demands from economic concessions to issues surrounding the defender's regional influence reduces the probability that the challenger will be willing to comply when punished by a rather modest 2.5 percent. Thus when challengers seek to undermine the regional influence of the defender, they remain highly constrained by the influence of previous dispute settlements. As the challenger's goals increase, however, the efficacy of settlements begins to decline. If the challenger increases its demands to territorial concessions from the defender, the probability it will comply with the previous settlement when punished drops by 21 percent. Still, it is rather striking that my model estimates that challengers will yield on territorial issues more than 76 percent of the time if they are punished for violating a previous settlement. If the challenger increases its demands to include changing the regime in the defending state, the probability it will comply with punishment drops by a very substantial 46 percent. Thus if the challenger seeks to alter the defending regime, the probability that it will comply with the defender's punishment is only 30 percent. It is worth noting, however, that the predicted probability of compromise in this context is 46 percent. Thus even if the challenger wants to alter the defender's regime, the predicted response to the punishment of such a violation is a compromise. Absent the presence of a settlement, the predicted outcome for such an interaction would be intransigence by the challenger. If the defender seeks to inflict grave damage on the defender, the probability that it will comply with the defender's demands drops by an additional 26 percent, and at this point the predicted outcome in the model shifts to intransigence. Finally—and not surprisingly—if the challenger seeks to eliminate the defending state entirely, then it is very likely to remain intransigent when punished. The likelihood of compliance only drops by 4 percent in this context because the likelihood of compliance is already low if the challenger seeks to inflict grave damage. If the challenger seeks to eliminate the defending state, then the probability that it will comply with the defender's punishment is less than 1 percent. Conversely, the probability that it will remain intransigent is nearly 97 percent.

Clearly, the impact of the challenger's demands on the efficacy of settlements is substantial. In particular, there appear to be two steps up this ladder of demands that represent qualitative shifts in the intentions of the challenger. First, challengers that aim to make territorial adjustments or seek to undermine the defender's regional influence appear to be strongly constrained by the presence of a previous settlement. These states are very likely to abandon their claims and comply with the settlement if punished for their violation. Second, challengers who seek to change the regime of the defending state feel less constrained by previous settlements. However, they are not entirely willing to ignore these agreements, since punishment of a violation is more likely to lead to a compromise rather than the intransigence that would result in the absence of a settlement. Finally, challengers that seek to inflict grave damage on the defender or eliminate the state entirely appear to have decided already that they will abandon the settlement regardless of the defender's actions. My discussion of the Six-Day War in the previous chapter provides an excellent illustration of this problem. In that case Nasser's substantial domestic constraints forced him to abandon the UNEF settlement in an ill-fated attempt to demand the elimination of Israel. Under these circumstances compromise becomes extremely difficult.

TABLE 7D
Marginal Effects of Challenger Demands

Change in Challenger Demands	Change in P(Compliance)	Change in P(Compromise)	Change in P(Intransigence)
Low to Regional	−2.5%	−2.4%	+0.1%
Regional to Territory	−21.1%	+18.0%	+3.2%
Territory to Regime	−46.2%	+22.2%	−24.0%
Regional to Grave Damage	−26.2%	−20.2%	+46.4%
Damage to Existence	−3.8%	−19.5%	+23.3%

Note: Marginal effects were calculated by generating predicted values from the probit model while changing the values of the challenger demands variable and holding the others at their means or modes. The predicted values were transformed into probabilities that the outcome would fall into each category by summing the area underneath the cumulative normal distribution between the predicted value and each of the category thresholds.

The impact of the challenger's demands makes a great deal of sense in terms of our current understanding of international deterrence and coercion. As I discussed in chapter 3, rationalist theories of deterrence and coercion focus on four central variables: (1) the value the challenger places on complying with the defender, (2) the value the challenger places on fighting with the defender, (3) the perceived probability that the defender will fight if attacked, and (4) the value that the challenger places on the capitulation of the defender. My argument about the impact of legitimate international agreements and the costs of being punished for a violation address the first three of these variables. It does not, however, address the fourth issue. As is the case with most rationalist theories of deterrence and coercion, the goals of the challenger remain largely beyond the influence of the defender. These preferences are simply a given that must be coped with in the bargaining interaction. Dispute settlements appear capable of influencing the behavior of challengers with moderate and even substantial demands for changes in the status quo. However, they cannot alter the behavior of challengers that seek to eliminate the state with which they have an agreement. Perhaps we should not have expected them to.

CONCLUSIONS

The results discussed in this chapter strongly support my arguments concerning *when* we should expect previous dispute settlements to be effective in constraining challenger behavior. These arguments were drawn from the assumptions that I made in chapter 3 in constructing an institutionalist argument about why dispute settlements and other legitimate international agreements might affect crisis bargaining *at all*. Thus my analysis here of when international norms succeed and fail supports and complements my previous analysis demonstrating that dispute settlements do have an impact on subsequent crisis bargaining.

Despite the relatively small number of cases available for analysis, the results in this chapter clearly demonstrate that dispute settlements are most likely to be effective in altering state behavior when the three central assumptions made by my argument are most likely to be valid. In this sense, the failure of dispute settlements to constrain challengers that seek to eliminate the defending state is a failure of norms that is consistent with and could be anticipated by my original theory.[7] Similarly, the failure of dispute settlements to constrain states that have changed domestic regimes is also something that my argument anticipates. Thus the analyses in this chapter supplement my discussion in the case studies by providing additional evidence that dispute settlements are effective in constraining crisis bargaining *for the reasons* that I discussed in chapter 3. That is, dispute settlements alter subsequent crisis bargaining in two important ways. First, they act as normative referents that alter the interpretation of subsequent crisis-bargaining behavior both by identifying a solution to the dispute that alleviates fears of demands for future concessions, and by defining a set of acts that both sides consider illegitimate. Second, in combination with the response to their violation, dispute settlements inflict reputational costs on states that violate them.

My analysis in chapter 5 demonstrated that legitimate dispute settlements *do* establish standards of behavior that influence subsequent crisis bargaining. Next, the case studies helped to illustrate *how* dispute settlements wield this influence. And finally in this chapter I have sought to understand *when* we should expect dispute settlements to have this normative impact. Together, these three different perspectives on the influence of legitimate dispute settlements help to provide a more complete and nuanced understanding of these important institutions. Significantly, each of the analyses fits closely together in describing a coherent pattern and process for the influence of dispute settlements. The complementary nature of these analyses should increase our confidence in the robustness and the veracity of the arguments I have made.

[7] I would draw an analogy here to the distinction between a failure of deterrence and a failure of deterrence theory (see Huth and Russett 1990). Deterrence theory does not predict that deterrence strategies will always succeed. Similarly, the assumptions necessary to generate my hypotheses about the impact of legitimate dispute settlements anticipate that these settlements will not always be effective. The results in this chapter suggest that my original theory can accurately anticipate the circumstances under which settlements will be effective.

I turn now to a concluding chapter in which I explore the implications of my results for theoretical work on international conflict and crisis bargaining. In addition, I consider what implications this research might have for policy makers interesting in building a world more closely guided by international law, international norms, and international institutions.

CHAPTER 8

Security Norms and Future Research on International Conflict

I began this work by suggesting that the end of the bipolar Cold War system has led to a reevaluation of our theories of international relations. Realist theory, which has dominated the study of international relations and security affairs, was of remarkably little use in explaining the collapse of the USSR and its Eastern European empire. Realism directs scholars to examine relative power and national interests in explaining foreign policy choices. Yet no discernible change in the Soviet geostrategic position preceded their dramatic shift in foreign policy behavior. Instead, it appears that the most plausible explanations of the end of the Cold War center on the changes in beliefs of policy makers both in the USSR and Eastern Europe. In particular, it seems impossible to explain the changes in Soviet behavior during the late 1980s and the dissolution of the USSR in 1991 without reference to elite beliefs concerning the nature of legitimate Soviet security interests, the proper strategy for achieving those interests, and the legitimacy of using force to impose pro-Soviet communist rule.

Since our theories appear to reflect our historical experiences, it should come as little surprise that the role of norms, ideas, and Soviet "new thinking" has led us to review our investigation of the independent role of ideas in international politics. In particular, these events have sparked a renewed interest in the influence of normative concepts—or what might be thought of as "rules of the game"—on foreign policy behavior. In fact, some scholars have even considered the possibility that such norms and rules could fundamentally change the structure of world politics. Such a change might be built through the reinvigoration of an international organization like the United Nations, or it could involve a reconceptualization of who counts as an actor in world politics. These new norms and institutions could complement or even replace the power-oriented concepts of power and structure used in realist theory.

Given the relatively primitive state of the empirical literature on international norms—especially concerning their effect on security affairs—my aim in this work has been somewhat more modest. I have examined the influence of bilaterally constructed norms on dispute-bargaining behavior. Specifically, I have examined the influence of norms and the concept of legitimacy—as embodied in the bilateral settlements of security disputes—on subsequent bargaining over the same disputed issue. Not only is this topic important in its own right, I also believe that we must establish the empirical import of norms on this kind of decentralized level before we begin to speculate about the construction of elaborate global security norms or institutions.

To date the empirical literature on international norms has been plagued with at least two significant problems. The first difficulty, which has been essentially methodological and conceptual, concerns the differentiation between the influence of shared norms and shared interests. As I discussed in chapter 2, there are strong reasons to believe that states that agree to common normative standards of behavior will also share a common interest in cooperative outcomes. Because of the underdeveloped state of our theorizing and measurement of the sources of national interests, it has been difficult to sort out the independent empirical effects of shared interests and shared norms.

A second significant shortcoming in the research on international norms has been its nearly exclusive focus on international economic relations. There are good reasons to believe that shared norms are more likely to affect economic relations rather than security affairs. The reason for this difference concerns the costs of being caught with one's guard down when a norm is violated. In general, the costs resulting from the violation of a security-related norm are likely to be higher than they are for economic norms. The cost of having one's partner cheat on an economic norm is generally something like a temporarily poor balance of trade or an undesirable exchange rate. Cheating on a security norm, however, can result in the total destruction of a state. I do not dispute the logic of this argument, but any resulting difference in the influence of norms on economics and security issues is purely a matter of degree. There is no theoretical reason to believe that the arguments concerning the influence of norms on economics do not also operate in the area of security affairs. Whether or not security norms can be powerful enough to overcome these fears of exploitation, however, is an empirical question which to large extent has gone unanswered.

My research has addressed both of these problems. First, by focusing on the violation of norms, I have been able to separate the independent influence of shared norms from the effects of common interests. I am able to do this because the violation of the previous dispute settlement clearly establishes that some conflict of interest exists concerning the issue at stake. Thus any influence that the explicit construction of a norm has following such a violation cannot be attributed to shared interests. Instead, as I argued in chapter 3, the influence is a result of the impact that the norm has on the beliefs of policy makers in terms of their estimation of the interests and intentions of other actors. In addition to resolving this methodological puzzle, I have also extended the study of international norms into the area of security affairs and militarized dispute bargaining.

My research has built on the insights of previous work in this area by combining an attention to international norms with a recognition that bargaining and coercion remain central aspects of international politics. My findings indicate that international norms can influence security-related behavior. Moreover, I have shown that despite the paucity of formal international security organizations, the institutionalist concern for dispersing information about states' intentions and preferences and developing focal points for cooperation remains important in security relations. Thus my analysis represents both a theoretical and an empirical extension of institutionalism to the analysis of informal security norms.

WHAT HAVE I FOUND?

My central finding is that bilateral security norms as established in dispute settlements help to legitimate coercive responses to a violation of the settlement. Specifically, I contend that settlements help to create normative referents that alter interpretations of international behavior and to generate a reputation for trustworthiness. In doing so, these settlements stabilize cooperation *even* between states that represent substantial security risks to one another. In the absence of normative referents for interpreting international behavior, coercive bargaining strategies are generally viewed by other states as threatening and generate fears of aggressive demands for concessions. Conciliation, on the other hand, can be viewed as a sign of weakness and is often exploited. Thus in an entirely anarchic system, states must perform a difficult balancing act to achieve and maintain cooperative relations. International norms, however, stabilize cooperation by constructing referents for the interpretation of subsequent behavior and by investing state interests in a reputation for trustworthiness. States that violate a norm recognize coercive responses as legitimate punishments for their transgressions and not the precursors to additional demands for concessions. Consequently, they are more likely to respond to coercive strategies by reestablishing their compliance with the norm.

This result was clearly demonstrated in chapter 5 where I found that a bullying response by the defender in a crisis was more than 40 percent more likely to result in compliance or compromise by the challenger if the challenger had violated a dispute settlement. My analysis of the Cienfuegos submarine base crisis in chapter 6 also provides a good illustration of the process by which dispute settlements facilitate compliance by transgressors and help to reestablish cooperation. In discussing that case I noted that the first US-Soviet crisis over Cuba—the Cuban missile crisis—

took the superpowers to the brink of nuclear war. That crisis ended, however, in a negotiated settlement of the Cuban issue. Then, when the Soviets violated this understanding eight years later, the sharp American response brought quick compliance from the USSR and a renewal of progress toward détente. The change in Soviet behavior between 1962 and 1970 demonstrates the influence of international norms.

This stabilizing effect of dispute settlements does come at a price, however. In particular, the parties to dispute settlements must be willing to enforce the stipulations of their agreement, for my analysis showed that responding weakly to the violation of a settlement left the defending states in an even worse position than if there had been no settlement.

Finally, in chapter 7 I took the first steps toward explaining the conditions under which these dispute settlements will be effective in restoring compliance with the agreement. While coercion was not always effective as a punishment for violating a dispute settlement, the reasons why settlements were effective proved largely consistent with the logic and assumptions of my initial argument. Thus all three of my separate analyses converge on the same fundamental conclusions about norms, legitimate dispute settlements, and crisis bargaining. That is, dispute settlements alter subsequent crisis bargaining in two important ways. First, they act as normative referents that alter the interpretation of subsequent crisis-bargaining behavior both by identifying a solution to the dispute that alleviates fears of demands for future concessions, and by defining a set of acts that both sides consider illegitimate. Second, in combination with the response to their violation, dispute settlements inflict reputational costs on states that violate them.

These findings represent a challenge to realist scholars who argue that peace can only be maintained by military force and deterrent threats. Power and threats *do* play an important role in determining behavior in international crises. But this realist view overlooks at least two important aspects of crisis bargaining. First, it neglects the fact that threats can be interpreted in a variety of ways. As a result, policy makers' normative referents—which shape the meaning of coercive strategies—have as important an influence on the outcome of international crises as do relative power and bargaining strategies. Second, in emphasizing the importance of a reputation for toughness, the realist paradigm ignores the value that states place on a reputation for trustworthiness. It is both by altering these referents and by engaging state reputations that international norms have a powerful influence on state responses to coercive behavior. These results represent a particularly strong challenge to the realist approach because my analysis focuses on militarized behavior in security-related disputes. Of all the issues within international politics, this is the kind of behavior that realism is supposed to be best able to explain. Realists are right to emphasize that ideas cannot stand alone in shaping state behavior; but the significant independent role that normative ideas can play in the resolution of security conflicts suggests that, while realism contains some important truths, it too cannot stand alone and must be expanded to incorporate the role of normative referents in international politics.

FUTURE RESEARCH ON NORMS AND CRISIS BARGAINING

First and foremost, my research suggests scholars should continue to explore the independent role of ideas in foreign policy. The core finding of my research indicates that crisis-bargaining behaviors do not have "objective" meanings that can be understood without reference to normative context or the beliefs and perceptions of state leaders. However, this simple—perhaps even banal—result opens up innumerable possibilities for theories that supplement—or even supplant—traditional materialist approaches to international politics. The beliefs and ideas that I have pursued in this research concern the kinds of causal attributions that state leaders attach to coercive bargaining behavior. These ideational effects are important, but they represent only one of myriad ways in which ideas can influence international behavior. The dominance of materialist approaches such as realism has meant that our understanding of the impact of ideas remains relatively rudimentary, but the past decade has seen an explosion of research in this area. I hope that my results provide some further impetus for this avenue of research.

Discussing the role of ideas means more, however, than simply noting that policy makers' ideas about the world are important. Scholars must carefully specify what kind of ideas should affect foreign policy, and they must specify the precise behavioral effects that these ideas should be expected to have. I have tried to accomplish both of these tasks in this work, and I believe that other scholars should do the same while pressing on to examine other issues. For example, future work should begin to expand on my analysis of dispute settlements by examining "easier" issues for security norms to influence—such as arms control negotiations—as well as "harder" issues—such as the enforcement of postwar settlements. By "easier" issues, I mean issues in which the costs of being caught off guard by a state that violates the norm are lower than they are for dispute settlements, while "harder" issues have even higher potential costs of exploitation. In addressing such a range of issues we could begin to develop an empirical map of the influence of international norms.

Over the past decade the literature on "constructivist" approaches to international politics has taken the lead in investigating the impact of ideas on world politics (Wendt 1992, 1999; Legro 1995; Klotz 1995;

Price 1995; Finnemore 1996; Katzenstein 1996; Keck and Sikkink 1998). My own arguments about norms have been limited to what would be termed an "institutionalist" approach to the impact of ideas. That is, I have argued that norms convey information that alters behavior, but I have not considered that norms would alter states' fundamental preferences, their understanding of their own identity, or their understanding of what constitutes an actor in world politics. Recent studies within the constructivist paradigm have made some provocative and interesting claims regarding these broader effects of norms and ideas. Moreover, empirical work in the constructivist vein has produced a number of intriguing "existence proofs" regarding the constitutive impact of ideas (Legro 1995; Klotz 1995; Price 1995; Finnemore 1996; Keck and Sikkink 1998). That is, these studies have produced some interesting examples of norms transforming international politics in nontrivial ways. If this promising research program is to continue to move forward, however, I believe it must move beyond "existence proofs" to a more systematic exploration of the constitutive norms and the mapping of their effects that I mentioned earlier.

Another important question for future research is seeking to understand where legitimate dispute settlements come from. Now that I have demonstrated that these agreements matter, the next obvious question is: how do we get them? A great deal of work in international relations has been done on strategies and policies for resolving militarized disputes short of war. This is obviously an important dimension of international conflict, but it leaves much of the normative and ideational aspects of crisis bargaining unexplored. For example, most studies of crisis bargaining would fail to distinguish between a crisis that ended peacefully because one side capitulated under pressure from a crisis that ended peacefully because the parties negotiated a settlement that resolved the underlying disputed issue. Similarly, most studies would not distinguish between wars that ended in a stalemate from one that ended in a comprehensive settlement. My research indicates that these outcomes should have substantially different implications for the future of conflict between such countries.

Of course, a good deal of research has been done on the conclusion of negotiated settlements to disputes. Unfortunately, most of this work—located primarily in the literature on international mediation—has been ignored by scholars of international politics (Young 1967; Northedge and Donelan 1971; Touval and Zartman 1985; Stullberg 1987; Thakur 1988; Berkovitch, Anagnoson, and Wille 1991; Berkovitch and Rubin 1992; Princen 1992; Berkovitch 1996). Thus my research would suggest that political scientists concerned with crisis bargaining should attempt to reach out to those who classify themselves as students of "conflict resolution." Political scientists may have avoided this literature because it does not always seek to test its findings in a systematic way.[1] I would contend, however, that this situation represents an unusual opportunity for synthesis. The mediation literature has developed a number of hypotheses regarding the conclusion of settlements and has conducted numerous historical studies to explore these hypotheses. It is in precisely this context that one can best begin to construct systematic, generalizable, and theoretically motivated tests of these hypotheses.

Some research has already begun on this systematic examination of the causes of dispute settlements. Unfortunately, many of these studies do not focus on variables that policy makers can generally manipulate in a crisis. For example, William Dixon's (1994) research focuses specifically on dispute settlements as its dependent variable, but Dixon's analysis concerns the impact of democracy on the incidence of settlements. Consistent with normative arguments about the democratic peace, Dixon finds that democracies are more likely to conclude peaceful settlements to international disputes.[2] While Dixon's work is both interesting and informative, it yields few *policy* prescriptions other than a general finding that spreading democracy across the globe will also facilitate the construction of dispute settlements (Dixon 1994). This is an important result, but the spreading of democracy is a slow and uncertain process at best. It would be useful to explore strategies that may yield more immediate benefits in the construction of international norms.

Similarly, the literature on international regimes has considered the conditions under which regimes are likely to develop. In this case, however, the focus has largely been on structural conditions—such as the presence or absence of hegemony—that may facilitate the construction of regimes. Once again, such analyses, while interesting, yield few policy prescriptions (Krasner 1983; Keohane 1984). Thus analyzing bargaining strategies and policies that may facilitate dispute settlements seems to be a natural next place for us to turn our attention.

In addition to understanding where norms and dispute settlements come from, we also need to develop a better understanding of when

---

[1] A good deal of work has been done, for example, on bargaining in business environments and on generic interpersonal bargaining situations. Many of these works speculate about the application of their findings to international relations, but their suggestions are necessarily anecdotal and don't represent rigorous tests of their hypotheses in the international arena. See, for example, Fischer and Ury (1981). Within the mediation literature in international politics, much of the work has focused on detailed historical description rather than systematic generalization. See, for example, Touval (1982) and Princen (1992). Some exceptions are Berkovitch and Rubin (1992) and Berkovitch (1996).

[2] For a fuller description of the so-called normative model of the democratic peace, see Maoz and Russett (1993) and Russett (1993).

these norms will be effective. In chapter 7 I took some early steps toward explaining the conditions under which dispute settlements were effective in restoring compliance with an agreement, but clearly much remains to be done. One significant issue that I have been unable to address in this work is what happens when multiple norms can plausibly be invoked? Which one takes precedence and why? My research design was constructed to focus as carefully as possible on a single relevant standard of legitimacy. Clearly, however, the world is full of norms that often conflict with one another. What happens when multiple norms are relevant to a dispute? How do states decide which one is most appropriate, or do the norms simply cancel one another out and become irrelevant? These important questions are only beginning to be asked.

One final theoretical implication of this work is that it illustrates the need for an integration of our theories of foreign policy. The approach of this work has been largely analytic in the sense that I have dissected and separated realist and institutionalist conceptions of crisis bargaining and then I set them up in competition with one another. This strategy seems appropriate given our fairly primitive understanding of causal processes in international politics. It is important to begin our investigation by sharpening and separating individual arguments and hypotheses about foreign policy, for by doing so we can determine which ideas have sufficient validity to merit further study. But as the results of this work indicate, no single narrow framework or approach provides an entirely satisfactory explanation—even of a single-issue area such as militarized dispute bargaining. As I showed in chapter 5, for example, security norms continue to have a powerful effect on crisis bargaining even when we test this argument against six variants of the domestic politics model. Nonetheless, as my discussion of the Six-Day War and my analysis in chapter 7 show, in some cases constituency pressures overwhelm the influence of international norms. If I find such a patchwork of theoretical explanations just concerning militarized dispute bargaining, imagine how varied the quilt must become for us to build a more general theory of foreign policy.

Progress toward a unified theory of foreign policy can only be achieved by moving beyond analytic approaches such as this one toward a synthetic integration of various theoretical models. Such a synthesis would have to outline the conditional relationships between the variables in each model and foreign policy outcomes. Robert Putnam (1988) has given us a conceptual framework for beginning to think about such a synthesis in his discussion of two-level games as a model of diplomatic interaction. Foreign policy is conducted on more than two levels, however, so perhaps what we need is an N-level game that identifies the multiple constraints and contexts within which international policy makers must act. Such a complex N-level game, much less a general theory of foreign policy, is obviously still well beyond our grasp, but perhaps we could begin moving toward such a theory by beginning to specify the conditions under which each level of the game is likely to be most influential.

This work has already identified several such conditions—like the normative context of the interaction and the existence of domestic constraints. But some other nuanced interactions have emerged from this analysis as well. The presence and enforcement of dispute settlements, for example, generally overwhelmed the influence of realist variables such as the possession of nuclear weapons. Nonetheless, my examination of the cases in which at least one of the parties possessed a nuclear capability suggested that these weapons *were* effective deterrents when used between Great Powers. When their opponents were minor powers, however, nuclear states often refrained from making even oblique nuclear threats. Similarly, my analysis showed that holding an advantage in the military balance of forces did not—as realists hypothesize—make highly coercive behavior more effective. At the same time, however, an advantage in the balance of forces did have a significant effect when a state used lower levels of coercion. The fact that the findings from this study alone do not fit easily within a single theoretical model suggests that our integrative task is a daunting one. Thus perhaps at this stage the most we can say is that research on international conflict would benefit from an analysis of the conditions under which various models of conflict behavior apply. After we have outlined these conditions, perhaps we can begin to integrate our theories more formally, more carefully, and more successfully.

International Norms and International Policy Making

I believe that one should always be cautious in drawing policy implications from social science research. After all, my research has focused on general patterns of behavior—to which there are always exceptions. Policy makers, however, are often only interested in general trends if they can point out the solution to the *particular* situation they are dealing with at that moment. Such "point predictions" still remain beyond the grasp of most social science research, but more general findings can and have had an important effect on American foreign policy.[3] Thus with some trepidation I will offer some possible implications of my work for the conduct of foreign policy.

[3] Perhaps the most prominent examples of international politics research that has had an impact on American foreign policy are the rationalist literature on deterrence and coercion (Schelling 1960, 1966; and Russett 1967) and the recent literature on the democratic peace (Maoz and Russett 1993; Russett 1993; Ray 1995).

To begin with, my research should reassure policy makers that they can have a substantial impact on the outcomes of international crises. That is, crisis outcomes are not structurally determined—if policy makers were ever concerned about such a possibility. Perhaps more important, my research indicates that dispute settlements can have a substantial impact on the future of a conflictual relationship. These agreements are not mere scraps of paper that codify existing interests. Nor are such settlements useless once they have been violated. The act of negotiation and the common understandings that it can construct are critical aspects of conflict bargaining. Policy makers hold it within their power to shape the way in which coercive behavior will be interpreted. Such a capacity cannot be underestimated, for it can often make the difference between a crisis that is settled peacefully—like the Cienfuegos crisis—and one like the Cuban missile crisis that runs a substantial risk of war and destruction.

Although I have not focused specifically on mediation, to the extent that mediations efforts help to produce legitimate dispute settlements, my research should also encourage state leaders to invest their time and resources in mediating international disputes. Not only can such activities strengthen global peace and security, they also can serve to stabilize the security environment of the mediator. Moreover, my results indicate that mediated settlements can continue to have this stabilizing effect even if they are subsequently violated.

My empirical results also give some encouragement to those who wish to build such ideas into a broader international normative framework based on the United Nations or some other global organization. Such a framework may indeed be able to give a new structure to the international system that could reshape the realist, power-oriented international structure. At this time none of the existing security institutions appear remotely capable of providing such a structure for international affairs. Nonetheless, normative and institutional concepts do have an influence on security policy, and there is reason to believe that this influence may become more substantial and systematic over time. The GATT began as a fairly ad hoc and accidental institution that was hamstrung by unwieldy rules and procedures that vitiated its coercive impact. Nonetheless, over time this institution constructed and propagated norms that had a powerful impact on global trade relations. Moreover, as the strength of GATT's norms grew, the institution itself was able to grow stronger and more influential. Thus nearly forty years after it was initially conceived, the GATT was able to transform into the World Trade Organization. Not only did this institutional growth help to entrench the norms of fair trade and market access more deeply, it also improved the dispute resolution procedures so as to avoid many of the pitfalls that had burdened the

GATT dispute resolution process. Perhaps this example of institutional growth can serve as an example for the growth of regional and global security organizations such as NATO (North Atlantic Treaty Organization), the OAS (Organization of American States), the OAU (Organization of African Unity), ASEAN (Association of South East Asia Nations), and the UN.

Finally, perhaps the most important policy implication of my research is that policy makers should be sensitive to the normative context in which they are operating. In particular, my research has demonstrated that the response to coercive behavior depends critically upon the context in which the behavior takes place. It may be tempting for a leader to assume that others understand and interpret his or her behavior in the same manner that it was intended. For example, a leader that is satisfied with the status quo on a particular issue might be tempted to take a very strong coercive stance in defense of that status quo because he or she assumes that the opponent will understand that the leader has no intention of altering the previous status quo. Such common knowledge of intentions cannot be assumed, but it can be constructed. Thus leaders who wish to defend the status quo would do well to codify agreements and understandings that clearly and credibly communicate their intentions to friends and foes alike. By doing so they can be more confident that a firm diplomatic stance will not be misinterpreted as aggression. In the absence of such explicitly constructed and codified norms, however, leaders engaged in crisis bargaining must perform a difficult balancing act between being perceived as irresolute and being feared as belligerent.

Bibliography

Abbott, Kenneth W., Robert O. Keohane, Andrew Moravcsik, Anne-Marie Slaughter, and Duncan Snidal. "The Concept of Legalization." *International Organization* 54, no. 3 (2000).

Achen, Christopher, 1986. *The Statistical Analysis of Quasi-Experiments*. Berkeley: University of California Press.

Allison, Graham T., and William Ury, eds. 1989. *Windows of Opportunity: From Cold War to Peaceful Competition in US-Soviet Relations*. New York: Ballinger Publishing.

Axelrod, Robert. "An Evolutionary Approach to Norms." *American Political Science Review* 80, no. 4 (1986).

———. 1984. *The Evolution of Cooperation*. New York: Basic Books.

———. "The Rational Timing of Surprise." *World Politics* 31 (1979).

Axelrod, Robert, and Robert Keohane. "Achieving Cooperation under Anarchy: Strategies and Institutions." *World Politics* 38, no. 1 (1985).

Bar-Zohar, Michael. 1970. *Embassies in Crisis*. Englewood Cliffs, N.J.: Prentice-Hall.

Bender, Lynne. 1975. *The Politics of Hostility: Castro's Revolution and United States Policy*. Hato Rey, P. R.: Inter-American University Press.

Berkovitch, Jacob, ed. 1996. *Resolving International Conflicts: The Theory and Practice of Mediation*. Boulder, Colo.: Lynne Rienner Publishers.

Berkovitch, Jacob, Ted Anagnoson, and Donnette Wille. "Conceptual Issues and Empirical Trends in the Study of Successful Mediation." *Journal of Peace Research*, 28, no. 1 (1991).

Berkovitch, Jacob, and Jeffrey Z. Rubin. 1992. *Mediation in International Relations: Multiple Approaches to Conflict Management*. New York: St. Martin's Press.

Betts, Richard K. 1987. *Nuclear Blackmail and Nuclear Balance*. Washington, D.C.: Brookings Institution.

Bialer, Seweryn, ed. 1969. *Stalin and His Generals: Soviet Memoirs of World War II*. New York: Pegasus Publishers.

Blechman, Barry M., and Stephanie E. Levinson. "Soviet Submarine Visits to Cuba." *U.S. Naval Institute Proceedings* 101, no. 9 (September 1975).

Brecher, Michael. 1980. *Decisions in Crisis*. Berkeley: University of California Press.

———. 1968. *India and World Politics: Krishna Menon's View of the World*. London: Oxford University Press.

———. 1959. *Nehru: A Political Biography*. London: Oxford University Press.

Brecher, Michael, and Jonathan Wilkenfeld. 1997. *A Study of Crisis*. Ann Arbor: University of Michigan Press.

Brecher, Michael, Jonathan Wilkenfeld, and Sheila Moser. 1988. *Crises in the Twentieth Century*. Vols. 1–3. New York: Pergamon Press.

Bueno de Mesquita, Bruce. "The War Trap Revisited." *American Political Science Review* 79 (1985).

——. 1981. *The War Trap*. New Haven, Conn.: Yale University Press.

Bueno de Mesquita, Bruce, and David Lalman. 1992. *War and Reason: Domestic and International Imperatives*. New Haven, Conn.: Yale University Press.

Bull, Hedley. 1977. *The Anarchical Society: A Study of Order in World Politics*. New York: Columbia University Press.

Carr, E. H. 1946. *The Twenty Years' Crisis, 1919–1939*. New York: Harper and Row.

Checkel, Jeff. "Ideas, Institutions, and the Gorbachev Foreign Policy Revolution." *World Politics* 45, no. 2, (1993).

Dixon, William. "Democracy and the Peaceful Settlement of International Conflict." *American Political Science Review* 88, no. 1 (1994).

Dobrynin, Anatoly. 1995. *In Confidence: Moscow's Ambassador to America's Six Cold War Presidents (1962–1986)*. New York: Random House.

Downs, George W. 1995. *Optimal Imperfection? Domestic Uncertainty and Institutions in International Relations*. Princeton, N.J.: Princeton University Press.

Draper, Theodore. 1968. *Israel and World Politics: Roots of the Third Arab-Israeli War*. New York: Viking Press.

Duffield, John, "International Regimes and Alliance Behavior: Explaining NATO Conventional Force Levels." *International Organization* 46, no. 4 (1992).

Dyan, Moshe. 1976. *Moshe Dyan: The Story of My Life*. New York: William Morrow.

Eckstein, Harry. 1961. *A Theory of Stable Democracy*. Research Monograph #10. Princeton, N.J.: Woodrow Wilson School of International and Public Affairs.

Ellsberg, Daniel. 1968. "The Theory and Practice of Blackmail." Rand Paper 3883.

Enterline, Andrew. "Driving While Democratizing (DWD)." *International Security* 20, no. 4 (1996).

Evangelista, Matthew. "Transnational Relations and Security Policy." *International Organization* 49, no. 1 (spring 1995).

Falk, Richard A., Robert C. Johansen, and Samuel S. Kim, eds. 1993. *The Constitutional Foundations of World Peace*. Albany, N.Y.: State University of New York.

Farber, Henry, and Joanne Gowa. "Polities and Peace." *International Security* 20, no. 2 (1995).

Fearon, James. "Signaling versus the Balance of Power and Interests: An Empirical Test of a Crisis Bargaining Model." *Journal of Conflict Resolution* 38, no. 2 (1994a).

——. "Domestic Political Audiences and the Escalation of International Disputes." *American Political Science Review* 88, no. 3 (1994b).

Finnemore, Martha. 1996. *National Interests and International Society*. Ithaca, N.Y.: Cornell University Press.

Fischer, Roger, and William Ury. 1981. *Getting to Yes: Negotiating Agreement Without Giving In*. Boston: Houghton Mifflin.

Franck, Thomas M. 1995. *Fairness in International Law and Institutions*. Oxford: Clarendon Press.

——. 1990. *The Power of Legitimacy among Nations*. Oxford: Oxford University Press.

Fursenko, Aleksandr, and Timoth Naftali. 1997. *One Hell of a Gamble: Khrushchev, Castro, and Kennedy, 1958–1964.* New York: Norton Publishers.

Garthoff, Raymond, "Cuban Missile Crisis: The Soviet Story." *Foreign Policy* 72 (1988).

———. 1985. *Detente and Confrontation.* Washington, D.C.: Brookings Institution.

———. "Handling the Cienfuegos Crisis." *International Security* 8, no. 3 (1983).

———. "American Reaction to Soviet Aircraft in Cuba, 1962 and 1978." *Political Science Quarterly* 95, no. 3 (1980).

Gartner, Scott Sigmund, and Randolph Siverson. "War Expansion and War Outcomes." *Journal of Conflict Resolution* 40, no. 1 (1996).

Gelpi, Christopher. 1999. "Alliances as Instruments of Intra-Allied Control." in *Imperfect Unions,* ed. Helga Haftendorn, Robert Keohane, and Celeste Wallander. New York: Oxford University Press.

———. "Crime and Punishment: The Role of Norms in Crisis Bargaining." *American Political Science Review* 91, no. 2 (1997).

Gelpi, Christopher, and Joseph Grieco. 1999. "Democracy, Crisis Bargaining, and the Survival of Political Leaders." Unpublished manuscript.

———. "Democracy, Crisis Escalation, and the Survival of Political Leaders, 1918–1994." Paper prepared for the 1998 APSA annual meeting, Boston, Mass., September 1–4, 1998.

Gelpi, Christopher, and Michael Griesdorf. "Winners or Losers? Democracies in International Crisis, 1918–1994." *American Political Science Review* 95, no. 3 (September 2001).

George, Alexander, and Richard Smoke. 1974. *Deterrence in American Foreign Policy.* New York: 1Columbia University Press.

Glaser, Charles. "Political Consequences of Military Strategy: Expanding and Refining the Spiral and Deterrence Models." *World Politics* 44, no. 2 (1992).

———. 1990. *Analyzing the Strategic Nuclear Debate: Theories, Alternative Worlds, and Choices in MAD.* Princeton, N.J.: Princeton University Press.

Gochman, Charles, and Zeev Maoz. "Militarized Interstate Disputes." *Journal of Conflict Resolution* 28, no. 4 (1984).

Goemans, H. E. 2000. *Domestic Politics and the Causes of War Termination: The Fate of Leaders and the First World War.* Ithaca, N.Y.: Cornell University Press.

Goertz, Gary, and Paul Diehl. "Toward a Theory of International Norms: Some Conceptual and Measurement Issues." *Journal of Conflict Resolution* 36, no. 4 (1992).

Goldschmidt, Bertrand. 1982. *The Atomic Complex: A Worldwide History of Nuclear Energy.* La Grange Park, Ill.: American Nuclear Society.

Goldstein, Joshua S. "Reciprocity in Superpower Relations: An Empirical Analysis." *International Studies Quarterly* 35, no. 2 (1991).

Goldstein, Joshua S., and John R. Freeman. 1990. *Three-Way Street: Strategy and Reciprocity in World Politics.* Chicago: University of Chicago Press.

Goldstein, Judith, Miles Kahler, Robert O. Keohane, and Anne-Marie Slaughter, "Introduction: Legalization and World Politics." *International Organization* 54, no. 3 (2000).

Goldstein, Judith, and Robert O. Keohane, eds. 1993. *Ideas and Foreign Policy:*

Beliefs, Institutions, and Political Change. Ithaca, N.Y.: Cornell University Press.

Grieco, Joseph M. 1990. *Cooperation Among Nations.* Ithaca, N.Y.: Cornell University Press.

———. "Anarchy and the Limits of Cooperation: A Realist Critique of the Newest Liberal Institutionalism." *International Organization* 40, no. 3 (summer 1988).

Gromyko, Anatoly, and Martin Hellman, eds. 1988. *Breakthrough: Emerging New Thinking.* New York: Walker and Company.

Gurr, Ted Robert, ed. 1980. *Handbook of Political Conflict.* New York: Free Press Publishers.

———. "Persistence and Change in Political Systems." *American Political Science Review* 68, no. 4 (1974).

Gurr, Ted Robert, and Keith Jaggers. 1995. *Polity III Dataset.* Available at website http://ezinfo.ucs.indiana.edu/~rmtucker.data.html.

Haftendorn, Helga, Robert O. Keohane, and Celeste Wallander. 1999. *Imperfect Unions: Security Institutions over Time and Space.* New York: Oxford University Press.

Haig, Alexander. 1991. *Inner Circles: How America Changed the World.* New York: Warner Books.

Hanushek, Eric, and John Jackson. 1977. *Statistical Methods for the Social Sciences.* New York: Academic Press.

Hart, Herbert Lionel Adolphus. 1961. *The Concept of Law.* Oxford: Clarendon Press.

Hensel, Paul. "One Thing Leads to Another: Recurrent Militarized Disputes in Latin America, 1816–1986." *Journal of Peace Research* 31, no. 3 (1994).

Herzog, Don. 1989. *Happy Slaves: A Critique of Consent Theory.* Chicago: University of Chicago Press.

Hopf, Ted. "Managing Soviet Disintegration: A Demand for Behavioral Regimes." *International Security* 17, no. 1 (1992).

House Armed Services Committee. 1967. *The Changing Strategic Military Balance: USA vs. USSR.* Study prepared by the National Strategy Committee of the American Security Council. Washington, D.C.

Howell, Llewellyn D. "A Comparative Study of the WEIS and COPDAB Data Sets." *International Studies Quarterly* 27, no. 2 (1983).

Hurd, Ian. "Legitimacy and Authority in International Politics." *International Organization* 53, no. 2 (1999).

Huth, Paul. "The Extended Deterrent Value of Nuclear Weapons." *Journal of Conflict Resolution* 34, no. 2 (1990).

Huth, Paul K. 1988. *Extended Deterrence and the Prevention of War.* New Haven, Conn.: Yale University Press.

Huth, Paul, D. Scott Bennett, and Christopher Gelpi. "System Uncertainty, Risk Propensity, and International Conflict." *Journal of Conflict Resolution* 36, no. 3 (1992).

Huth, Paul, Christopher Gelpi, and D. Scott Bennett "The Escalation of Great Power Militarized Disputes: Testing Rational Deterrence Theory and Structural Realism." *American Political Science Review* 87, no. 3 (1993).

Huth, Paul, and Bruce Russett. "General Deterrence between Enduring Rivals: Testing Three Competing Models." *American Political Science Review* 87, no. 1 (March 1993).

———. "Testing Deterrence Theory: Rigor Makes a Difference" *World Politics* 42 no. 4 (1990).

Institute for Strategic Studies. 1970. *The Military Balance 1970–1971*. London.

Jervis, Robert. "Realism, Game Theory, and Cooperation." *World Politics* 40 (1988).

———. 1984. *The Illogic of American Nuclear Strategy*. Ithaca, N.Y.: Cornell University Press.

———. "Cooperation under the Security Dilemma." *World Politics* 30, no. 2 (January 1978).

———. 1976. *Perception and Misperception in International Politics*. Princeton, N.J.: Princeton University Press.

———. 1970. *The Logic of Images in International Relations*. Princeton, N.J.: Princeton University Press.

Johnston, Iain. "Thinking about Strategic Culture." *International Security* 19, no. 4 (spring 1995).

Katzenstein, Peter, ed. 1996. *The Culture of National Security: Norms and Identity in World Politics*. New York: Columbia University Press.

Keck, Margaret, and Kathryn Sikkink. 1998. *Activists beyond Borders: Advocacy Networks in International Politics*. Ithaca, N.Y.: Cornell University Press.

Keesing's Contemporary Archives. 1931–c. 1986. London: Keesing's Limited.

Keesing's Research Report. 1968. *The Arab Israeli Conflict: The 1967 Campaign*. New York: Charles Scribner's Sons.

Kegley, Charles W. "The Neoidealist Moment in International Studies? Realist Myths and the New International Realities." *International Studies Quarterly* 37, no. 2 (1993).

Kegley, Charles W., and Gregory Raymond. 1990. *When Trust Breaks Down: Alliance Norms and World Politics*. Columbia: University of South Carolina Press.

Kennedy, Robert F. 1968. *Thirteen Days: A Memoir of the Cuban Missile Crisis*. New York: W. W. Norton.

Keohane, Robert O., ed. 1986. *Neorealism and its Critics* New York: Columbia University Press.

———. 1984. *After Hegemony: Cooperation and Discord in the World Political Economy*. Princeton, N.J.: Princeton University Press.

Keohane, Robert O., and Lisa Martin. "The Promise of Institutionalist Theory." *International Security* 20, no. 1 (summer 1995).

Keohane, Robert O., Andrew Moravcsik, and Anne-Marie Slaughter. "Legalized Dispute Resolution: Interstate and Transnational." *International Organization* 54, no. 3 (2000).

Keohane, Robert O., and Joseph Nye. 1989. *Power and Interdependence*. 2d ed. Glenview, Ill.: Scott Foresman.

King, Gary. 1989. *Unifying Political Methodology: The Likelihood Theory of Statistical Inference*. New York: Cambridge University Press.

King, Gary, Robert O. Keohane, and Sidney Verba. 1994. *Designing Social Inquiry*. Princeton, N.J.: Princeton University Press.

Kissinger, Henry. 1982. *Years of Upheaval*. Boston: Little, Brown.

Klotz, Audie. 1995. *Norms in International Relations: The Struggle against Apartheid*. Ithaca, N.Y.: Cornell University Press.

Kocs, Stephen A. "Explaining the Strategic Behavior of States: International Law as System Structure." *International Studies Quarterly* 38, no. 4 (1994).

Koenker, Diane P., and Ronald Bachman, eds. 1997. *Revelations from the Russian Archives: Documents in English Translation*. Washington, D.C.: Library of Congress Press.

Kozlowski, Rey, and Friedrich Kratochwil. "Understanding Change in International Politics: The Soviet Empire's Demise and the International System." *International Organization* 48, no. 2 (1994).

Krasner, Stephen. 1995. "Compromising Westphalia." *International Security* 20, no. 3 (winter 1995): 115–52.

———. , ed. 1983. *International Regimes*. Ithaca, N.Y.: Cornell University Press.

Kratochwil, Friedrich. 1989. *Rules, Norms, and Decisions: On the Conditions of Practical and Legal Reasoning in International Relations*. Cambridge: Cambridge University Press.

Kupchan, Charles A., and Clifford A. Kupchan. "Concerts, Collective Security, and the Future of Europe." *International Security* 16, no. 1 (1991).

Lacoutre, Jean. 1973. *Nasser: A Biography*. New York: Alfred A. Knopf.

Larson, Deborah Welch. "Credibility, Promises, and Reputation: From Conflict to Cooperation in US-Soviet Relations." Paper presented at the thirty-third annual meeting of the International Studies Association, Atlanta Ga., 1992.

Lebow, Richard Ned. "The Long Peace, the End of the Cold War, and the Failure of Realism." *International Organization* 48, no. 2 (1994).

———. 1981. *Between Peace and War*. Baltimore, Md.: Johns Hopkins University Press.

Legro, Jeffrey. 1995. *Cooperation under Fire: Anglo-German Restraint during World War II*. Ithaca, N.Y.: Cornell University Press.

Legro, Jeffrey, and Andrew Moravcsik. "Is Anybody Still a Realist?" *International Security* 24, no. 2 (1999).

Leng, Russell. 1993. *Interstate Crisis Behavior, 1816–1980*. New York: Cambridge University Press.

———. 1989. *Behavioral Correlates of War Data Codebook*. 2d ed. Ann Arbor, Mich.: Inter-University Consortium for Political and Social Research [distributor].

———. "When Will They Ever Learn?" *Journal of Conflict Resolution* 27, no. 3 (1983).

Leng, Russell, and Hugh Wheeler. "Influence Strategies, Success, and War." *Journal of Conflict Resolution* 23, no. 4 (1979).

Levy, Jack S. "Domestic Politics and War." *Journal of Interdisciplinary History* 18 (1988).

———. 1983. *War in the Modern Great Power System, 1495–1975*. Lexington: University of Kentucky Press.

Linz, Juan J., and Seymour Martin Lipsett, eds. 1990. *Politics in Developing Countries: Comparing Experiences with Democracy*. Boulder, Colo.: Lynne Rienner Publishers.

Mansfield, Edward D., and Jack Snyder. "Democratization and the Danger of War." *International Security* 20, no. 1 (1995).

Maoz, Zeev. "Joining the Club of Nations: Political Development and International Conflict, 1816–1976." *International Studies Quarterly* 33, no. 2 (1989).

Maoz, Zeev, and Bruce M. Russett. "Normative and Structural Causes of Democratic Peace." *American Political Science Review* 87, no. 3 (1993).

Mearsheimer, John. 2001. *The Tragedy of Great Power Politics*. New York: W. W. Norton.

———. "The False Promise of International Institutions." *International Security* 19, no. 3 (winter 1994/1995).

———. "Back to the Future: Instability in Europe after the Cold War." *International Security* 15, no. 1 (1990).

———. 1983. *Conventional Deterrence*. Ithaca, N.Y.: Cornell University Press.

Mendelson, Sarah. "Internal Battles and External Wars: Politics, Learning, and the Soviet Withdrawal from Afghanistan." *World Politics* 45, no. 2 (1993).

Meyer, Stephen. "The Sources and Prospects of Gorbachev's New Thinking on Security." *International Security* 14, no. 2 (1988).

Mezerik, A. G., ed. 1969. *The Suez Canal: 1956 Crisis—1967 War*. New York: International Review Service.

Midlarsky, Manus I., ed. 1989. *Handbook of War Studies*. Boston: Unwin Hyman Publishers.

Morgenthau, Hans J. 1985. *Politics among Nations*. 6th ed., New York: Alfred A. Knopf.

Morrow, James. "Modeling the Forms of International Cooperation." *International Organization* 48, no. 3 (1994).

Nalebuff, Barry. "Rational Deterrence in an Imperfect World." *World Politics* 43, no. 3 (1991).

New York Times and Index. New York: New York Times Co., 1857–2002.

Nixon, Richard M. 1978. *The Memoirs of Richard Nixon*. New York: Grosset and Dunlap.

Northedge, Fred, and Michael Donelan. 1971. *International Disputes: The Political Aspects*. London: Europa Press.

Nowak, Martin, and Karl Sigmund. "A Strategy of Win-Stay, Lose-Shift that Outperforms Tit-For-Tat in the Prisoner's Dilemma Game." *Nature* 364 (July 1, 1993).

———. "Tit-For-Tat in Heterogeneous Populations." *Nature* 355 (January 16, 1992).

Nutting, Anthony. 1967. *No End of a Lesson: The Story of Suez*. London: Constable and Co.

Organski, A.F.K., and Jacek Kugler. 1980. *The War Ledger*. Chicago: University of Chicago Press.

Ostrom, Charles, and Brian Job. "The President and the Political Use of Force." *American Political Science Review* 80, no. 2 (1985).

Oye, Kenneth A., ed. 1986. *Cooperation under Anarchy*. Princeton, N.J.: Princeton University Press.

Pape, Robert. 1996. *Bombing to Win*. Ithaca: Cornell University Press.

Parker, Richard B. 1993. *The Politics of Miscalculation in the Middle East*. Bloomington: Indiana University Press.

Paul, T. V. "The Nuclear Taboo and War Initiation in Regional Conflicts." *Journal of Conflict Resolution* 39, no. 4 (December 1995).

Porter, Bruce D. 1984. *The USSR in Third World Conflicts: Soviet Arms and Diplomacy in Local Wars, 1945–1980.* New York: Cambridge University Press.

Powell, Robert. "Absolute and Relative Gains in International Relations Theory." *American Political Science Review* 85, no. 4 (1991).

———. 1990. *Nuclear Deterrence Theory.* New York: Cambridge University Press.

Price, Richard. "A Genealogy of the Chemical Weapons Taboo." *International Organization* 49, no. 1 (spring 1995).

Price, Richard, and Nina Tannenwald. 1996. "The Non-Use of Nuclear and Chemical Weapons." in *Norms and National Security*, ed. Peter Katzenstein. Ithaca, N.Y.: Cornell University Press.

Princen, Thomans. 1992. *Intermediaries in International Conflict.* Princeton, N.J.: Princeton University Press.

Putnam, Robert D. "Diplomacy and Domestic Politics: The Logic of Two Level Games." *International Organization* 42, no. 3 (1988).

Quester, George. "Missiles in Cuba." *Foreign Affairs* 49, no. 3 (1971).

Rasmussen, Eric. 1989. *Games and Information.* Cambridge: Cambridge University Press.

Ray, James Lee. 1995. *Democracy and International Conflict: An Evaluation of the Democratic Peace Proposition.* Columbia: University of South Carolina Press.

Rhode, David. "Studying Congressional Norms: Concepts and Evidence." *Congress and the Presidency* 15, no. 2 (fall 1988).

Risse-Kapen, Thomas. "Ideas Do Not Float Freely." *International Organization* 48, no. 2 (1994).

Rochester, J. Martin. 1993. *Waiting for the Millennium: The United Nations and the Future of the World Order.* Columbia: University of South Carolina Press.

Rosenau, James, ed. 1992. *Governance Without Government.* Cambridge: Cambridge University Press.

Ruggie, John G., ed. 1993. *Multilateralism Matters: The Theory and Praxis of Institutional Form.* New York: Columbia University Press.

Rusk, Dean. 1990. *As I Saw It.* New York: W. W. Norton.

Russett, Bruce. 1993. *Grasping the Democratic Peace: Principles for a Post–Cold War World.* Princeton, N.J.: Princeton University Press.

———. 1987. *Economic Decline, Electoral Pressure, and the Initiation of International Conflict.* New Haven, Conn.: Yale University Press.

———. "Pearl Harbor: Deterrence Theory and Decision Theory." *Journal of Peace Research* 4, no. 2 (1967).

Schelling, Thomas. 1966. *Arms and Influence.* New Haven, Conn.: Yale University Press.

———. 1960. *The Strategy of Conflict.* Cambridge: Harvard University Press.

Schultz, Kenneth A. "Do Democratic Institutions Constrain or Inform? Contrasting Two Institutional Perspectives on Democracy and War." *International Organization* 53, no. 2 (1999).

Signorino, Curtis S. "Simulating International Cooperation under Uncertainty:

The Effects of Symmetric and Asymmetric Noise." *Journal of Conflict Resolution* 40, no. 1 (1996).

Simmons, Beth A. "International Law and State Behavior: Commitment and Compliance in International Monetary Affairs." *American Political Science Review* 94, no. 4 (1999).

Siverson, Randolph, and Harvey Starr. "Regime Change and the Restructuring of Alliances." *American Journal of Political Science* 38, no. 1 (February 1994).

Slaughter, Anne-Marie, Andrew Tumello, and Stepan Wood. "International Law and International Relations Theory: A New Generation of Interdisciplinary Scholarship." *American Journal of International Law* 92, no. 3 (1998).

Slaughter-Burley, Anne-Marie. "International Law and International Relations Theory: A Dual Agenda." *American Journal of International Law* 87, no. 2 (1993).

Snidal, Duncan. "International Cooperation among Relative Gains Maximizers." *International Studies Quarterly* 35, no. 4 (December 1991).

———. "Relative Gains and the Pattern of International Cooperation." *American Political Science Review* 85, no. 3 (September 1991).

Snyder, Glenn, and Paul Diesing. 1977. *Conflict among Nations: Bargaining, Decisionmaking, and System Structure in International Crises.* Princeton, N.J.: Princeton University Press.

Snyder, Jack. 1991. *Myths of Empire: Domestic Politics and International Ambition.* Ithaca, N.Y.: Cornell University Press.

———. "The Gorbachev Revolution: A Waning of Soviet Expansionism?" *International Security* 13, no. 4 (1987).

Sorenson, Theodore. 1965. *Kennedy.* New York: Harper and Row.

Stein, Janice Gross. "Political Learning By Doing: Gorbachev as an Uncommitted Thinker and Motivated Learner." *International Organization* 48, no. 2 (1994).

Stephens, Robert. 1971. *Nasser: A Political Biography.* London: Allen Lane.

Stinchcombe, Arthur. 1987. *Constructing Social Theories.* Chicago: University of Chicago Press.

Stullberg, Joseph B. 1987. *Taking Charge/Managing Conflict.* Lexington, Mass.: Lexington Books.

Tannenwald, Nina. "The Nuclear Taboo: The United States and the Normative Basis of Nuclear Non-Use." *International Organization* 53, no. 3 (1999).

Tetlock, Philip E., Jo L. Husbands, Robert Jervis, Paul C. Stern, and Charles Tilly, eds. 1989. *Behavior, Society, and Nuclear War. Vol. 1.* New York: Oxford University Press.

Thakur, Ramesh. 1988. *International Conflict Resolution.* Boulder, Colo.: Westview Press.

Touval, Saadia. 1982. *Peace Brokers: Mediators in the Arab-Israeli Conflict, 1948–1979.* Princeton, N.J.: Princeton University Press.

Touval, Saadia, and I. William Zartman. 1985. *International Mediation in Theory and Practice.* Boulder, Colo.: Westview Press.

Wallander, Celeste. 1999. *Mortal Friends: German-Russian Cooperation after the Cold War.* Ithaca, N.Y.: Cornell University Press.

Walt, Stephen. 1996. *Revolution and War.* Ithaca, N.Y.: Cornell University Press.

Waltz, Kenneth N. 1979. *Theory of International Politics.* Reading, Mass.: Addison-Wesley.

Walzer, Michael. 1977. *Just and Unjust Wars.* New York: Basic Books.

Ward, M. D. "Cooperation and Conflict in Foreign Policy Behavior." *International Studies Quarterly* 26, no. 1 (1982).

Washington Post. Washington: Washington Post Co., 1877–2002.

Weiss, Thomas G., ed. 1993. *Collective Security in a Changing World.* Boulder, Colo.: Lynne Rienner Publishers.

Welch, David A. 1993. *Justice and the Genesis of War.* Cambridge: Cambridge University Press.

Wendt, Alexander. 1999. *Social Theory of International Politics.* New York: Cambridge University Press.

———. "Anarchy Is What States Make of It: The Social Construction of Power Politics." *International Organization* 46, no. 2 (1992).

Wilkenfeld, Jonathan, ed. 1973. *Conflict Behavior and Linkage Politics.* New York: D. McKay.

Young, Oran. 1967. *The Intermediaries: Third Parties in International Crises.* Princeton, N.J.: Princeton University Press.

Zagare, Frank. 1987. *The Dynamics of Deterrence.* Chicago: University of Chicago Press.

Zimmerman, William, ed. 1992. *Beyond the Soviet Threat: Rethinking American Security Policy in a New Era.* Ann Arbor: University of Michigan Press.

Index

"Action Program" by Czech leadership, 83–84
actors: and identification, crisis, 56–61; norm-influencing preferences of, 32–33; relations between two, 48–49; transnational, 19. *See also* rational choice approach, rational coercion theory
adverse selection, 35
agreements. *See* dispute settlements
Alexeev, Alexander, 106
Algeria, 130, 142
alliance norms, 20
Allison, Graham, 30
anarchy, international, 5n.10, 38
Angola, 124
appeasement, 66, 67, 82, 93n.15; in circumstances of previous settlements, 43, 44, 79, 80; in Czech-Soviet crisis of 1968, 85; and intransigence, 84; and Munich crisis of 1938, 86; in opening stages of Six-Day War, 150; and previous settlement, 41, 79
Aqaba, Gulf of. *See* Straits of Tiran
Argentina, 86
arms control negotiations, regarding nuclear weapons, 54–55, 183
Aswan Dam, 129
audience costs, 39
Axelford, Robert, 27, 28

bargaining behavior, 50; previous history of, 72; of third parties, 150–51. *See also* crisis bargaining
bargaining strategies, 32
Beagle Channel dispute, 86
Behavioral Correlates of War (BCOW), 66n.8
Belize, 90n.11
Bender, Lynne, 111, 112
Berlin, 123n.34, 123
Betts, Richard, 118–19, 123n.34, 123, 124–25
bilaterism in establishment of norms for security-related disputes, 6, 179
blackmail, 48–49

Brecher, Michael, 56, 57, 71, 72
Brezhnev, Leonid, 119, 120, 123
Bueno de Mesquita, Bruce, 70n.14, 70
Bull, Hedley, 9–10
bullying strategy by defender, 66, 67, 82–83; in Cuba, 97–98, 118; and credibility of resolve, 157, 168–71; and effectiveness of international norms, 156n.1, 156; and effects of dispute settlements, 86–87; and Israel in Six-Day War, 146; lesser effectiveness of, compared to firm-but-flexible approach, 83–84; measure for and military capabilities, 70; with no previous agreement, 41–42, 79, 94, 128–9; and previous settlement and normative referents, 42–43, 44, 79; and previous settlement and reputational effects, 43–44, 79; and punishment for violation, 80; and response of challenger depending on prior agreement or not, 155–56; and settlements, 93–94, 181; and USSR violation of Tripartite Treaty of Alliance and Iran, 86–87
Bunche, Ralph, 139
Bundy, McGeorge, 110

capitulation, 88
case study research, 74–75
Castro, Fidel, 16, 35; IL-28 bombers and, 106–8, 120–21; and refusal of direct UN inspection, 109, 111
causal model (of interests), 22
challenger state: definition of, 58; measure of demands of, 167, 174–76; persistence and effectiveness in dispute agreements, 162–63, 173; and responses of to defender's coercive behavior, 56, 61, 66; and strategy of defender state with or without agreement, 81–83, 155
Chile, 86
Church, Frank, 114
Cienfuegos crisis, 112–18; and balance of conventional forces, 123–24; basing of nuclear weapons in Cuba and, 93; construction activity in Cienfuegos harbor,

Nasser, 141, 142, 155, 170; and UNEF, 138–40
tit-for-tat (TFT), 27
toughness as strategy, 34, 39, 72, 128, 182
trial-and-error bargaining strategy, 66–67, 150
Tripartite Treaty, 86–87
Truman, Harry, 85
trustworthiness, 17, 34–35, 39, 181
Turkey, 103, 104–5, 109, 118n.33

UNEF. *See* United Nations Emergency Force
Union of Soviet Socialist Republics. *See* USSR
United Kingdom: and reaction to Israeli attack on Egypt in 1956, 130–31; and nationalization of Suez Canal, 129–30; and support of Israel in 1967, 143, 148, 151; withdrawal of aid for Aswan Dam, 129
United Nations (UN): and appeasement of Egypt in early Six-Day War buildup, 150, 151; and Cuban missile crisis, 103, 108, 109; its establishment of Suez settlement and UNEF, 149–50; reinvigoration of and changing norms in world politics, 3, 179, 188; and UNEF, 132, 133–34, 135; and West Irian, 85. *See also* Hammarskjöld, Dag; Thant, U; United Nations Emergency Force
United Nations Emergency Force (UNEF), 129: and credible enforcement of Suez settlement, 133–35, 149–51; and Egyptian unwillingness to have on its territory, 131, 141, 155, 175; formation of, 131; and 1967 Israeli demand for reinstatement, 146; Nasser's request for partial redeployment of, 137–38, 150, 152
United Nations Truce Supervision Organization (UNTSO), 136
United States (US): and anticommunist activity in Latin America, 162n.4; and conflicts involving nuclear weapons, 90; and decision to assume global leadership, 161–62; domestic constraints and, 170; hypothesis regarding action of in Cuba, 97–100; invasion of North Korea and, 85; and Iranian crisis with USSR in 1944, 86–87; its role in helping Israel to confirm Suez agreement, 134; support of Israel in 1967, 143, 148, 150; and West

Irian, 85; and withdrawal of support for Aswan Dam, 129. *See also* Cienfuegos crisis; Cuban missile crisis; Kennedy-Khrushchev understanding
USSR: leaders' changing understanding national of interests, 3, 179; and conflicts and nuclear weapons, 90; and Czechoslovakia in 1968, 84–85; disintegration of, 3; its false report of Israeli attack delivered to Egypt, 136–37, 151; and response to US coercion regarding Cuba, 97–100; and Iran, 86–87, 128; military projection of its capabilities, 124; and possible involvement in Six-Day War, 149n.73, 149; and the US, 93. *See also* Cienfuegos crisis; Cuban missile crisis; Kennedy-Khrushchev understanding

Versailles, treaty of, 54
Vietnam War, 60, 90
Violations of legitimate settlements. 67–8; and bullying strategy, 128; identification of, 60–61; method of study in responses to, 24, 33; and legitimacy norms, 55n.1, 55–56, and Six-Day War, 146; *See also* punishment of violations
violence, 72
Vorontsov, Yuri, 112, 116

Wallander, Celeste, 11, 12, 26
Waltz, Kenneth, 12
War: exclusion of total war crises from study, 57–58; laws of during World War II, 20; and normative doctrines, 12; termination of, 34; vs. previously agreed settlement, 163, 173–76
War of Attrition (1970}, 58, 124
Washington Special Actions Group (WSAG), 113
Wendt, Alexander, 4, 5n.10, 11, 14
West Irian, 85
Wheeler, Hugh, 61
Wilhelm, Kaiser, 15
Wilkenfeld, Jonathan, 56, 57, 71
Wilson, Woodrow, 3–4, 10
World Bank, 129, 162
World Trade Organization (WTO), 29, 161, 188–89

Yemen, civil war in, 124
Yom Kippur War of 1973, 59–60